covenant
history

THE

NEW INTERNATIONAL READER'S VERSION

BOOKS OF THE BIBLE

for kids

ZONDER**kidz**

Library of Congress Catalog Card Number 2017941833

You will be pleased to know that a portion of the purchase price of your new NIrV Bible has been provided to Biblica, Inc.® to help spread the gospel of Jesus Christ around the world!

Contents

introduction to Covenant History

Every nation or other large group of related people have a story of how they came to be. Some of the stories from nations a long time ago, such as Assyria and Babylon, are still around today. We can read them and learn about what these people thought about "gods" and people.

The Hebrew people were called Israel as they formed into a nation. This book contains their story of the Creator God and his creation. It tells how the first people decided to live the way they wanted to instead of obeying God and living the way he told them to. Then God chose Abraham and his children and grandchildren to show the world the right way to live.

This book tells the story of Israel all the way from the Creator and the first people to the last king of Israel in their homeland.

GENESIS, PART I

introduction to Genesis, part I

The Creator God made his world. He wanted it to be his temple, the house where he lived. See the beauty of the creation and how much God loved it. And notice how important people are. Other nations saw people as the slaves of the "gods," but God saw people as ruling with him over the creation. Instead of taking God's offer to rule with him, the first people chose their own way. And this made the whole story go wrong.

In the beginning, God created the heavens and the earth. The earth didn't have any shape. And it was empty. There was darkness over the surface of the waves. At that time, the Spirit of God was hovering over the waters.

God said, "Let there be light." And there was light. God saw that the light was good. He separated the light from the darkness. God called the light "day." He called the darkness "night." There was evening, and there was morning. It was day one.

God said, "Let there be a huge space between the waters. Let it separate water from water." And that's exactly what happened. God made the huge space between the waters. He separated the water under the space from the water above it. God called the huge space "sky." There was evening, and there was morning. It was day two.

God said, "Let the water under the sky be gathered into one place. Let dry ground appear." And that's exactly what happened.

God called the dry ground "land." He called all the water that was gathered together "seas." And God saw that it was good.

Then God said, "Let the land produce plants. Let them produce their own seeds. And let there be trees on the land that grow fruit with seeds in it. Let each kind of plant or tree have its own kind of seeds." And that's exactly what happened. So the land produced plants. Each kind of plant had its own kind of seeds. And the land produced trees that grew fruit with seeds in it. Each kind of tree had its own kind of seeds. God saw that it was good. There was evening, and there was morning. It was day three.

God said, "Let there be lights in the huge space of the sky. Let them separate the day from the night. Let the lights set the times for the holy celebrations and the days and the years. Let them be lights in the huge space of the sky to give light on the earth." And that's exactly what happened. God made two great lights. He made the larger light to rule over the day and the smaller light to rule over the night. He also made the stars. God put the lights in the huge space of the sky to give light on the earth. He put them there to rule over the day and the night. He put them there to separate light from darkness. God saw that it was good. There was evening, and there was morning. It was day four.

God said, "Let the seas be filled with living things. Let birds fly above the earth across the huge space of the sky." So God created the great sea creatures. He created every kind of living thing that fills the seas and moves about in them. He created every kind of bird that flies. And God saw that it was good. God blessed them. He said, "Have little ones so that there will be many of you. Fill the water in the seas. Let there be more and more birds on the earth." There was evening, and there was morning. It was day five.

God said, "Let the land produce every kind of living creature. Let there be livestock, and creatures that move along the ground, and wild animals." And that's exactly what happened. God made every kind of wild animal. He made every kind of livestock. He made every kind of creature that moves along the ground. And God saw that it was good.

Then God said, "Let us make human beings so that they are like us. Let them rule over the fish in the seas and the birds in the sky. Let them rule over the livestock and all the wild animals. And let them rule over all the creatures that move along the ground."

So God created human beings in his own likeness.
He created them to be like himself.
He created them as male and female.

God blessed them. He said to them, "Have children so that there will be many of you. Fill the earth and bring it under your control. Rule over the fish in the seas and the birds in the sky. Rule over every living creature that moves along the ground."

Then God said, "I am giving you every plant on the face of the whole earth that produces its own seeds. I am giving you every tree that has fruit with seeds in it. All of them will be given to you for food. I am giving every green plant as food for all the land animals and for all the birds in the sky. I am also giving the plants to all the creatures that move along the ground. I am giving them to every living thing that breathes." And that's exactly what happened.

God saw everything he had made. And it was very good. There was evening, and there was morning. It was day six.

So the heavens and the earth and everything in them were completed.

By the seventh day God had finished the work he had been doing. So on that day he rested from all his work. God blessed the seventh day and made it holy. He blessed it because on that day he rested from all the work he had done.

〰️

Here is the story of the heavens and the earth when they were created. The Lord God made the earth and the heavens.

At that time, bushes had not yet appeared on the earth. Plants had not started to grow. The Lord God had not sent rain on the earth. And there was no one to farm the land. But streams came from the earth. They watered the entire surface of the ground. Then the Lord God formed a man. He made him out of the dust of the ground. God breathed the breath of life into him. And the man became a living person.

The Lord God had planted a garden in the east in Eden. He put in the garden the man he had formed. The Lord God made every kind of tree grow out of the ground. The trees were pleasing to look at. Their fruit was good to eat. There were two trees in the middle of the garden. One of them had fruit that let people live forever. The other had fruit that let people tell the difference between good and evil.

The Lord God put the man in the Garden of Eden. He put him there to farm its land and take care of it. The Lord God gave the man a command. He said, "You may eat fruit from any tree in the garden. But you must not eat the fruit from the tree of the knowledge of good and evil. If you do, you will certainly die."

The Lord God said, "It is not good for the man to be alone. I will make a helper who is just right for him."

The Lord God had formed all the wild animals and all the birds in the sky. He had made all of them out of the ground. He brought them to the man to see what names he would give them. And the name the man gave each living creature became its name. So the man gave names to all the livestock, all the birds in the sky, and all the wild animals.

But Adam didn't find a helper that was just right for him. So the Lord God caused him to fall into a deep sleep. While the man was sleeping, the Lord God took out one of the man's ribs. Then the Lord God closed the opening in the man's side. Then the Lord God made a woman. He made her from the rib he had taken out of the man. And the Lord God brought her to the man.

The man said,

"Her bones have come from my bones.
    Her body has come from my body.
She will be named 'woman,'
    because she was taken out of a man."

That's why a man leaves his father and mother and is joined to his wife. The two of them become one.

Adam and his wife were both naked. They didn't feel any shame.

The serpent was more clever than any of the wild animals the Lord God had made. The serpent said to the woman, "Did God really say, 'You must not eat fruit from any tree in the garden'?"

The woman said to the serpent, "We may eat fruit from the trees in the garden. But God did say, 'You must not eat the fruit from the tree in the middle of the garden. Do not even touch it. If you do, you will die.'"

"You will certainly not die," the serpent said to the woman. "God knows that when you eat fruit from that tree, you will know things you have never known before. Like God, you will be able to tell the difference between good and evil."

The woman saw that the tree's fruit was good to eat and pleasing to look at. She also saw that it would make a person wise. So she took some of the fruit and ate it. She also gave some to her husband, who was with her. And he ate it. Then both of them knew things they had never known before. They realized they were naked. So they sewed together fig leaves and made clothes for themselves.

Then the man and his wife heard the Lord God walking in the garden. It was during the coolest time of the day. They hid from the Lord God among the trees of the garden. But the Lord God called out to the man. "Where are you?" he asked.

"I heard you in the garden," the man answered. "I was afraid, because I was naked. So I hid."

The Lord God said, "Who told you that you were naked? Have you eaten fruit from the tree I commanded you not to eat from?"

The man said, "It's the fault of the woman you put here with me. She gave me some fruit from the tree. And I ate it."

Then the Lord God said to the woman, "What have you done?"

The woman said, "The serpent tricked me. That's why I ate the fruit."

God spoke to the serpent, the woman and Adam. Each one would have a more difficult life because they disobeyed God.

Adam named his wife Eve. She would become the mother of every living person.

The Lord God made clothes out of animal skins for Adam and his wife to wear. The Lord God said, "Just like one of us, the man can now tell the difference between good and evil. He must not be allowed to reach out and pick fruit from the tree of life and eat it. If he does, he will live forever." So the Lord God drove the man out of the Garden of Eden. He sent the man to farm the ground he had been made from. The Lord God drove him out and then placed angels on the east side of the garden. He also placed there a flaming sword that flashed back and forth. The angels and the sword guarded the way to the tree of life.

Adam loved his wife Eve. She became pregnant and gave birth to Cain. She said, "With the Lord's help I have had a baby boy." Later she gave birth to his brother Abel.

remember what you read

1. What is something you noticed for the first time?

_____

_____

_____

_____

2. What questions did you have?

_____

_____

_____

_____

3. Was there anything that bothered you?

_____

_____

_____

_____

4. What did you learn about loving God?

_____

_____

_____

_____

5. What did you learn about loving others?

_____

_____

_____

_____

GENESIS, PART 2

introduction to Genesis, part 2

Adam and Eve's choice in the garden began a series of sad stories of how people looked out only for their own interests and did terrible things to each other.

Abel took care of sheep. Cain farmed the land. After some time, Cain gathered some things he had grown. He brought them as an offering to the LORD. And Abel also brought an offering. He brought the fattest parts of some animals from his flock. They were the first animals born to their mothers. The LORD was pleased with Abel and his offering. But he wasn't pleased with Cain and his offering. So Cain became very angry, and his face was sad.

Then the LORD said to Cain, "Why are you angry? Why are you looking so sad? Do what is right and then you will be accepted. If you don't do what is right, sin is waiting at your door to grab you. It desires to control you. But you must rule over it."

Cain said to his brother Abel, "Let's go out to the field." So they went out. There Cain attacked his brother Abel and killed him.

Then the LORD said to Cain, "Where is your brother Abel?"

"I don't know," Cain replied. "Am I supposed to take care of my brother?"

The LORD said, "What have you done? Listen! Your brother's blood is crying out to me from the ground. So I am putting a curse on you. I am driving you away from this ground. It has opened its mouth to receive your brother's blood from your hand. When you farm the land, it will not produce its crops for you anymore. You will be a restless person who wanders around on the earth."

Cain said to the LORD, "You are punishing me more than I can take. Today you are driving me away from the land. I will be hidden from you. I'll be a restless person who wanders around on the earth. Anyone who finds me will kill me."

But the LORD said to him, "No. Anyone who kills you will be paid back seven times." The LORD put a mark on Cain. Then anyone who found him wouldn't kill him. So Cain went away from the LORD. He lived in the land of Nod. It was east of Eden.

Adam and Eve had another son named Seth. He was the father of a long family line, too, including a man named Noah.

The LORD saw how bad the sins of everyone on earth had become. They only thought about evil things. The LORD was very sad that he had made human beings on the earth. His heart was filled with pain. So the LORD said, "I created human beings, but I will wipe them out. I will also destroy the animals, the birds in the sky, and the creatures that move along the ground. I am very sad that I have made human beings." But the LORD was very pleased with Noah.

Here is the story of Noah's family line.

Noah was a godly man. He was without blame among the people of his time. He walked faithfully with God. Noah had three sons. Their names were Shem, Ham and Japheth.

The earth was very sinful in God's eyes. It was full of people who did mean and harmful things. God saw how sinful the earth had become. All its people were living very sinful lives. So God said to Noah, "I am going to put an end to everyone. They have filled the earth with their harmful acts. I am certainly going to destroy them and the earth. So make yourself an ark out of cypress wood. Make rooms in it. Cover it with tar inside and out. Here is how I want you to build it. The ark has to be 450 feet long. It has to be 75 feet wide and 45 feet high. Make a roof for it. Leave below the roof an opening all the way around that is a foot and a half high. Put a door in one side of the ark. Make lower, middle and upper decks. I am going to bring a flood on the earth. It will destroy all life under the sky. It will destroy every living creature that breathes. Everything on earth will die. But I will make my covenant with you. You will go into the ark. Your sons and your wife and your sons' wives will enter it with you. Bring a male and a female of every living thing into the ark. They will be kept alive with you. Two of every kind of bird will come to you. Two of every kind of animal will also come to you. And so will two of every kind of creature that moves along the ground. All of them will be kept alive with you. Take every kind of food that you will need. Store it away as food for you and them."

Noah did everything just as God commanded him.

Then the Lord said to Noah, "Go into the ark with your whole family. I know that you are a godly man among the people of today. Take seven pairs of every kind of 'clean' animal with you. Take a male and a female of each kind. Take one pair of every kind of animal that is not 'clean.' Take a male and a female of each kind. Also take seven pairs of every kind of bird. Take a male and a female of each kind. Then every kind will be kept alive. They can spread out again over the whole earth. Seven days from now I will send rain on the earth. It will rain for 40 days and 40 nights. I will destroy from the face of the earth every living creature I have made."

Noah did everything the Lord commanded him to do.

For 40 days the flood kept coming on the earth. As the waters rose higher, they lifted the ark high above the earth. The waters rose higher and higher on the earth. And the ark floated on the water. The waters rose on the earth until all the high mountains under the entire sky were covered. The waters continued to rise until they covered the mountains by more than 20 feet. Every living thing that moved on land died. The birds, the livestock and the wild animals died. All of the creatures that fill the earth also died. And so did every human being. Every breathing thing on dry land died. Every living thing on earth was wiped out. People and animals were destroyed. The creatures that move along the ground and the birds in the sky were wiped out. Everything on earth was destroyed. Only Noah and those with him in the ark were left.

The waters flooded the earth for 150 days.

But God showed concern for Noah. He also showed concern for all the wild animals and livestock that were with Noah in the ark. So God sent a wind to sweep over the earth. And the waters began to go down. The springs at the bottom of the oceans had been closed. The windows of the sky had also been closed. And the rain had stopped falling from the sky. The water on the earth continued to go down. At the end of the 150 days the water had gone down. On the 17th day of the seventh month, the ark came to rest on the mountains of Ararat. The waters continued to go down until the tenth month. On the first day of that month, the tops of the mountains could be seen.

After 40 days Noah opened a window he had made in the ark. He sent out a raven. It kept flying back and forth until the water on the earth had dried up. Then Noah sent out a dove. He wanted to see if the water on the surface of the ground had gone down. But the dove couldn't find any place to rest. Water still covered the whole surface of the earth. So the dove returned to Noah in the ark. Noah reached out his hand and took the dove in. He brought it back to himself in the ark. He waited seven more days. Then he sent out the dove again from the ark. In the evening the dove returned to him. There in its beak was a freshly picked olive leaf! So Noah knew that the water on the earth had gone down. He waited seven more days. Then he sent out the dove again. But this time it didn't return to him.

It was the first day of the first month of Noah's 601st year. The water on the earth had dried up. Then Noah removed the covering from the ark. He saw that the surface of the ground was dry. By the 27th day of the second month the earth was completely dry.

Then God said to Noah, "Come out of the ark. Bring your wife and your sons and their wives with you. Bring out every kind of living thing that is with you. Bring the birds, the animals, and all the creatures that move along the ground. Then they can multiply on the earth. They can have little ones and the number of them can increase."

So Noah came out of the ark. His sons and his wife and his sons' wives were with him. All the animals came out of the ark. The creatures that move along the ground also came out. So did all the birds. Everything that moves on land came out of the ark, one kind after another.

Then Noah built an altar to honor the LORD. He took some of the "clean" animals and birds. He sacrificed them on the altar as burnt offerings. The smell of the offerings pleased the LORD. He said to himself, "I will never put a curse on the ground again because of human beings. I will not do it even though their hearts are always directed toward evil. Their thoughts are evil from the time they are young. I will never destroy all living things again, as I have just done.

"As long as the earth lasts,
    there will always be a time to plant
    and a time to gather the crops.
As long as the earth lasts,
    there will always be cold and heat.
There will always be summer and winter,
    day and night."

Then God blessed Noah and his sons. He said to them, "Have children so that there are many of you. Fill the earth. All the land animals will be afraid of you. All the birds in the sky will be afraid of you. Every creature that moves along the ground will be afraid of you. So will every fish in the seas. Every living thing is put under your control. Everything that lives and moves about will be food for you. I have already given you the green plants for food. Now I am giving you everything.

Then God spoke to Noah and to his sons who were with him. He said, "I am now making my covenant with you and with all your children who will be born after you. I am making it also with every living creature that was with you in the ark. I am making my covenant with the birds, the livestock and all the wild animals. I am making it with all the creatures that came out of the ark with you. In fact, I am making it with every living thing on earth. Here is my covenant I am making with you. The waters of a flood will never again destroy all life. A flood will never again destroy the earth."

So God said to Noah, "The rainbow is the sign of my covenant. I have made my covenant between me and all life on earth."

The sons of Noah who came out of the ark were Shem, Ham and Japheth. Ham was the father of Canaan. The people who were scattered over the earth came from Noah's three sons.

remember what you read

1. What is something you noticed for the first time?

_____

_____

_____

_____

2. What questions did you have?

_____

_____

_____

_____

3. Was there anything that bothered you?

_____

_____

_____

_____

4. What did you learn about loving God?

_____

_____

_____

_____

5. What did you learn about loving others?

_____

_____

_____

_____

GENESIS, PART 3

introduction to Genesis, parts 3-10

Noah's family had children and began to fill the earth like God wanted.
Some people tried to stop God's plan by staying together and building
a city. Then God called one man, Abram (later renamed Abraham)
and his family to bring God's blessing to the entire world.

∽∿∿∿∼

The whole world had only one language, and everyone spoke it. They moved to the east and found a broad valley in Babylon. There they made their home.

They said to one another, "Come on! Let's make bricks and bake them well." They used bricks instead of stones. They used tar to hold the bricks together. Then they said, "Come on! Let's build a city for ourselves. Let's build a tower that reaches to the sky. We'll make a name for ourselves. Then we won't be scattered over the whole earth."

But the LORD came down to see the city and the tower the people were building. He said, "All these people are united and speak the same language. That is why they can do all this. Now they will be able to do anything they plan. Come on! Let us go down and mix up their language. Then they will not be able to understand one another."

So the LORD scattered them from there over the whole earth. And they stopped building the city. There the LORD mixed up the language of the whole world. That's why the city was called Babel. From there the LORD scattered them over the whole earth.

The family lines of Noah's sons Shem, Ham and Japheth grew into the nations that spread out over the earth after the flood. Shem's line included a man named Abram.

The Lord had said to Abram, "Go from your country, your people and your father's family. Go to the land I will show you.

"I will make you into a great nation.
    And I will bless you.
I will make your name great.
    You will be a blessing to others.
I will bless those who bless you.
    I will put a curse on anyone who puts a curse on you.
All nations on earth
    will be blessed because of you."

So Abram went, just as the Lord had told him. Lot went with him. Abram was 75 years old when he left Harran. He took his wife Sarai and his nephew Lot. They took all the people and possessions they had acquired in Harran. They started out for the land of Canaan. And they arrived there.

Abram traveled through the land. He went as far as the large tree of Moreh at Shechem. At that time the Canaanites were living in the land. The Lord appeared to Abram at Shechem. He said, "I will give this land to your family who comes after you." So Abram built an altar there to honor the Lord, who had appeared to him.

From there, Abram went on toward the hills east of Bethel. He set up his tent there. Bethel was to the west, and Ai was to the east. Abram built an altar there and called on the name of the Lord.

God blessed both Abram and Lot so much that they couldn't stay together. They had too many animals and people. So they separated. Lot went to a city called Sodom.

So Abram went to live near the large trees of Mamre at Hebron. There he pitched his tents and built an altar to honor the Lord.

Some kings joined together and invaded the land. They took all the things that belonged to Sodom and Gomorrah. They carried away

Abram's nephew Lot and the things he owned. Abram called out his 318 men who were trained as soldiers. They attacked the kings and rescued Lot. On his way home, Melchizedek, the king of Jerusalem, met him.

He brought out bread and wine. He was the priest of the Most High God. He gave a blessing to Abram. He said,

"May the Most High God bless Abram.
   May the Creator of heaven and earth bless him.
Give praise to the Most High God.
   He gave your enemies into your hand."

Then Abram gave Melchizedek a tenth of everything.

Some time later, Abram had a vision. The LORD said to him,

"Abram, do not be afraid.
   I am like a shield to you.
   I am your very great reward."

But Abram said, "LORD and King, what can you give me? I still don't have any children. My servant Eliezer comes from Damascus. When I die, he will get everything I own." Abram continued, "You haven't given me any children. So this servant of mine will get everything I own."

Then a message from the LORD came to Abram. The LORD said, "When you die, what you have will not go to this man. You will have a son of your own. He will get everything you have." The LORD took Abram outside and said, "Look up at the sky. Count the stars, if you can." Then he said to him, "That's how many children will be born into your family."

Abram believed the LORD. The LORD was pleased with Abram because he believed. So Abram's faith made him right with the LORD.

He also said to Abram, "I am the LORD. I brought you out of Ur in the land of Babylon. I will give you this land to have as your very own."

God made a very serious agreement with Abram so Abram could be sure that God would keep his promises.

Abram's wife Sarai had never had any children by him. But she had a female slave from Egypt named Hagar. So she said to Abram, "The LORD has kept me from having children. Maybe I can have a family through my slave."

Abram agreed to what Sarai had said. His wife Sarai gave him her slave Hagar to be his wife. That was after he had been living in Canaan for ten years. Then Hagar became pregnant.

When Hagar knew she was pregnant, she began to look down on the woman who owned her. Then Sarai said to Abram, "It's your fault that I'm suffering like this. I put my slave in your arms. Now that she knows she's pregnant, she looks down on me. May the LORD judge between you and me. May he decide which of us is right."

"Your slave belongs to you," Abram said. "Do with her what you think is best." Then Sarai treated Hagar badly. So Hagar ran away from her.

God saw Hagar and told her to go back to Sarah. He promised to bless her son.

So Hagar had a son by Abram and Abram gave him the name Ishmael. Abram was 86 years old when Hagar had Ishmael by him.

When Abram was 99 years old, the LORD appeared to him. He said, "I am the Mighty God. Walk faithfully with me. Live in a way that pleases me. I will now act on my covenant between me and you. I will greatly increase the number of your children after you."

Then God said to Abraham, "You must keep my covenant. You and your family after you must keep it for all time to come. Here is my covenant that you and your family after you must keep. You and every male among you must be circumcised. That will be the sign of the covenant between me and you. It must be done for all time to come. Every male among you who is eight days old must be circumcised. That includes those who are born into your own family or outside it. It also includes those bought with money from a stranger. So any male born into your family or bought with your money must be circumcised. My covenant will last forever. Your body will have the mark of my covenant on it. Any male who has not been circumcised will be separated from his people. He has broken my covenant."

God also said to Abraham, "Do not continue to call your wife by the name Sarai. Her name will be Sarah. I will give her my blessing. You can be sure that I will give you a son by her. I will bless her so that she will be the mother of nations. Kings of nations will come from her."

Abraham fell with his face to the ground. He laughed and said to himself, "Can a 100-year-old man have a son? Can Sarah have a child at the age of 90?" Abraham said to God, "I really wish Ishmael could receive your blessing!"

Then God said, "Yes, I will bless Ishmael. But your wife Sarah will have a son by you. And you will name him Isaac. I will establish my covenant with him. That covenant will last forever. It will be for Isaac and his family after him. I have heard what you said about Ishmael. I will surely bless him. I will make his family very large. He will be the father of 12 rulers. And I will make him into a great nation. But I will establish my covenant with Isaac. By this time next year, Sarah will have a son by you." When God had finished speaking with Abraham, God left him.

On that same day Abraham circumcised his son Ishmael. He also circumcised every male who was born into his family or bought with his money. He did exactly as God had told him. Abraham was 99 years old when he was circumcised. His son Ishmael was 13. Abraham and his son Ishmael were both circumcised on that same day. And every male in Abraham's household was circumcised along with him. That included those born into his family or bought from a stranger.

Then God visited Abraham. Abraham had Sarah prepare a meal. God promised that in one year Sarah would have a son. But Sarah laughed because this sounded impossible to her.

The LORD was gracious to Sarah, just as he had said he would be. The LORD did for Sarah what he had promised to do. Sarah became pregnant. She had a son by Abraham when he was old. The child was born at the exact time God had promised. Abraham gave the name Isaac to the son Sarah had by him. When his son Isaac was eight days old, Abraham circumcised him. He did it exactly as God had commanded him. Abraham was 100 years old when his son Isaac was born to him.

Sarah said, "God has given laughter to me. Everyone who hears about this will laugh with me." She also said, "Who would have said to Abraham that Sarah would breast-feed children? But I've had a son by him when he is old."

Isaac grew. The time came for his mother to stop breast-feeding him. On that day Abraham prepared a big celebration. But Sarah saw Ishmael making fun of Isaac. Ishmael was the son Hagar had by Abraham. Hagar was Sarah's Egyptian slave. Sarah said to Abraham, "Get rid of that slave woman! Get rid of her son! That woman's son will never have a share of the family's property. All of it belongs to my son Isaac."

What Sarah said upset Abraham very much. After all, Ishmael was his son. But God said to Abraham, "Do not be so upset about the boy and your slave Hagar. Listen to what Sarah tells you, because your family line will continue through Isaac. I will also make the son of your slave into a nation. I will do it because he is your child."

Abraham sent Ishmael and Hagar away. They almost died in the desert, but God heard them crying for help. He saved them and provided for them.

Sarah lived to be 127 years old. She died at Kiriath Arba. Kiriath Arba is also called Hebron. It's in the land of Canaan. Sarah's death made Abraham very sad. He went to the place where her body was lying. There he wept over her.

Abraham bought a cave from Ephron the Hittite so he could bury his wife Sarah. He bought it so his family would be sure they owned that land.

By that time Abraham was very old. The Lord had blessed Abraham in every way. The best servant in his house was in charge of everything Abraham had. Abraham said to him, "Put your hand under my thigh. The LORD is the God of heaven and the God of earth. I want you to make a promise to me in his name. I'm living among the people of Canaan. But I want you to promise me that you won't get a wife for my son from their daughters. Instead, promise me that you will go to my country and to my own relatives. Get a wife for my son Isaac from there."

The servant traveled to Abraham's homeland. He prayed for God to help him find a wife for Isaac.

Before he had finished praying, Rebekah came out. She was carrying a jar on her shoulder. She was the daughter of Milkah's son Bethuel. Milkah was the wife of Abraham's brother Nahor. The young woman was very beautiful. She went down to the spring. She filled her jar and came up again.

The servant hurried to meet her. He said, "Please give me a little water from your jar."

"Have a drink, sir," she said. She quickly lowered the jar to her hands and gave him a drink.

remember what you read

1. What is something you noticed for the first time?

_____

_____

_____

_____

2. What questions did you have?

_____

_____

_____

_____

3. Was there anything that bothered you?

_____

_____

_____

_____

4. What did you learn about loving God?

_____

_____

_____

_____

5. What did you learn about loving others?

_____

_____

_____

_____

After she had given him a drink, she said, "I'll get water for your camels too. I'll keep doing it until they have had enough to drink." So she quickly emptied her jar into the stone tub. Then she ran back to the well to get more water. She got enough for all his camels. The man didn't say a word. He watched her closely. He wanted to learn whether the Lord had given him success on the journey he had made.

The camels finished drinking. Then the man took out a gold nose ring. It weighed about a fifth of an ounce. He also took out two gold bracelets. They weighed about four ounces. Then he asked, "Whose daughter are you? And please tell me something else. Is there room in your father's house for us? Can we spend the night there?"

She answered, "I'm the daughter of Bethuel. He's the son Milkah had by Nahor." She continued, "We have plenty of straw and feed for your camels. We also have room for you to spend the night."

Then the man bowed down and worshiped the Lord. He said, "I praise the Lord, the God of my master Abraham. The Lord hasn't stopped being kind and faithful to my master. The Lord has led me on this journey. He has brought me to the house of my master's relatives."

The young woman ran home. She told her mother's family what had happened. Rebekah had a brother named Laban. He hurried out to the spring to meet the man. Laban had seen the nose ring. He had seen the bracelets on his sister's arms. And he had heard Rebekah tell what the man had said to her. So Laban went out to the man. He found him standing by the camels near the spring.

"The LORD has given you his blessing," he said. "So come with me. Why are you standing out here? I've prepared my house for you. I also have a place for the camels."

So the man went to the house. The camels were unloaded. Straw and feed were brought for the camels. And water was brought for him and his men to wash their feet. Then food was placed in front of him. But he said, "I won't eat until I've told you what I have to say."

"Then tell us," Laban said.

Abraham's servant told his whole story. Then he asked the family to send Rebekah back with him to be Isaac's wife.

Laban and Bethuel answered, "The LORD has done all of this. We can't say anything to you one way or the other. Here is Rebekah. Take her and go. Let her become the wife of your master's son, just as the LORD has said."

Abraham's servant heard what they said. So he bowed down to the LORD with his face to the ground. He brought out gold and silver jewelry and articles of clothing. He gave all of them to Rebekah. He also gave expensive gifts to her brother and her mother. Then Abraham's servant and the men who were with him ate and drank. They spent the night there.

When they got up the next morning, Abraham's servant said, "Send me back to my master."

But her brother and her mother replied, "Let the young woman stay with us ten days or so. Then you can go."

But he said to them, "Don't make me wait. The LORD has given me success on my journey. Send me on my way so I can go to my master."

Then they said, "Let's get Rebekah and ask her about it." So they sent for her and asked, "Will you go with this man?"

"Yes, I'll go," she said.

So they sent their sister Rebekah on her way with Abraham's servant and his men. They also sent Rebekah's servant with her. And they gave Rebekah their blessing. They said to her,

"Dear sister, may your family grow
   by thousands and thousands.
May they take over
   the cities of their enemies."

Then Rebekah and her female servants got ready. They got on their camels to go back with the man. So Abraham's servant took Rebekah and left.

By that time Isaac had come from Beer Lahai Roi. He was living in the Negev Desert. One evening he went out to the field. He wanted to spend some time thinking. When he looked up, he saw camels approaching. Rebekah also looked up and saw Isaac. She got down from her camel. She asked the servant, "Who is that man in the field coming to meet us?"

"He's my master," the servant answered. So she covered her face with her veil.

Then the servant told Isaac everything he had done. Isaac brought Rebekah into the tent that had belonged to his mother Sarah. And he married Rebekah. She became his wife, and he loved her. So Isaac was comforted after his mother died.

Abraham lived a total of 175 years. He took his last breath and died when he was very old. He had lived a very long time. Then he joined the members of his family who had already died. Abraham's sons Isaac and Ishmael buried him. They put his body in the cave of Machpelah near Mamre. It was in the field of Ephron, the son of Zohar the Hittite. Abraham had bought the field from the Hittites. He was buried there with his wife Sarah. After Abraham died, God blessed his son Isaac. At that time Isaac was living near Beer Lahai Roi.

Rebekah couldn't have children. So Isaac prayed to the LORD for her. And the LORD answered his prayer. His wife Rebekah became pregnant. The babies struggled with each other inside her. She said, "Why is this happening to me?" So she went to ask the LORD what she should do.

The Lord said to her,

"Two nations are in your body.
　Two tribes that are now inside you will be separated.
One nation will be stronger than the other.
　The older son will serve the younger one."

The time came for Rebekah to have her babies. There were twin boys in her body. The first one to come out was red. His whole body was covered with hair. So they named him Esau. Then his brother came out. His hand was holding onto Esau's heel. So he was named Jacob. Isaac was 60 years old when Rebekah had them.

The boys grew up. Esau became a skillful hunter. He liked the open country. But Jacob was content to stay at home among the tents. Isaac liked the meat of wild animals. So Esau was his favorite son. But Rebekah's favorite was Jacob.

One day Jacob was cooking some stew. Esau came in from the open country. He was very hungry. He said to Jacob, "Quick! I'm very hungry! Let me have some of that red stew!" That's why he was also named Edom.

Jacob replied, "First sell me the rights that belong to you as the oldest son in the family."

"Look, I'm dying of hunger," Esau said. "What good are those rights to me?"

But Jacob said, "First promise to sell me your rights." So Esau promised to do it. He sold Jacob all the rights that belonged to him as the oldest son.

Then Jacob gave Esau some bread and some lentil stew. Esau ate and drank. Then he got up and left.

So Esau didn't value the rights that belonged to him as the oldest son.

Isaac planted crops in that land. That same year he gathered 100 times more than he planted. That was because the Lord blessed him. Isaac became rich. His wealth continued to grow until he became very rich. He had many flocks and herds and servants. Isaac had so much that the Philistines became jealous of him. So they stopped up all the wells the servants of his father Abraham had dug. They filled them with dirt.

Then Abimelek said to Isaac, "Move away from us. You have become too powerful for us."

Isaac went up to Beersheba. That night the LORD appeared to him. He said, "I am the God of your father Abraham. Do not be afraid. I am with you. I will bless you. I will increase the number of your children because of my servant Abraham."

Isaac built an altar there and worshiped the LORD. There he set up his tent. And there his servants dug a well. They told him about it. They said, "We've found water!" So he named it Shibah. To this day the name of the town has been Beersheba.

Isaac had become old. His eyes were so weak he couldn't see anymore. One day he called for his older son Esau. He said to him, "My son."

"Here I am," he answered.

Isaac said, "I'm an old man now. And I don't know when I'll die. Now then, get your weapons. Get your bow and arrows. Go out to the open country. Hunt some wild animals for me. Prepare for me the kind of tasty food I like. Bring it to me to eat. Then I'll give you my blessing before I die."

Rebekah was listening when Isaac spoke to his son Esau. Esau left for the open country. He went to hunt for a wild animal and bring it back. Then Rebekah said to her son Jacob, "Look, I heard your father speaking to your brother Esau. He said, 'Bring me a wild animal. Prepare some tasty food for me to eat. Then I'll give you my blessing before I die. The LORD will be my witness.'" Rebekah continued, "My son, listen carefully. Do what I tell you. Go out to the flock. Bring me two of the finest young goats. I will prepare tasty food for your father. I'll make it just the way he likes it. I want you to take it to your father to eat. Then he'll give you his blessing before he dies."

Jacob said to his mother Rebekah, "My brother Esau's body is covered with hair. But my skin is smooth. What if my father touches me? He would know I was trying to trick him. He would curse me instead of giving me a blessing."

His mother said to him, "My son, let the curse be on me. Just do what I say. Go and get the goats for me."

So he went and got the goats. He brought them to his mother. And she prepared some tasty food. She made it just the way his father liked it. The clothes of her older son Esau were in her house. She took Esau's best clothes and put them on her younger son Jacob. She covered his hands with the skins of the goats. She also covered the smooth part of his neck with them. Then she handed to her son Jacob the tasty food and the bread she had made.

He went to his father and said, "My father."

"Yes, my son," Isaac answered. "Who is it?"

Jacob said to his father, "I'm your oldest son Esau. I've done as you told me. Please sit up. Eat some of my wild meat. Then give me your blessing."

Isaac asked his son, "How did you find it so quickly, my son?"

"The Lord your God gave me success," he replied.

Then Isaac said to Jacob, "Come near so I can touch you, my son. I want to know whether you really are my son Esau."

Jacob went close to his father. Isaac touched him and said, "The voice is the voice of Jacob. But the hands are the hands of Esau." Isaac didn't recognize Jacob. Jacob's hands were covered with hair like those of his brother Esau. So Isaac blessed him. "Are you really my son Esau?" he asked.

"I am," Jacob replied.

remember what you read

1. What is something you noticed for the first time?

_____

_____

_____

_____

2. What questions did you have?

_____

_____

_____

_____

3. Was there anything that bothered you?

_____

_____

_____

_____

4. What did you learn about loving God?

_____

_____

_____

_____

5. What did you learn about loving others?

_____

_____

_____

_____

Isaac said, "My son, bring me some of your wild meat to eat. Then I'll give you my blessing."

Jacob brought it to him. So Isaac ate. Jacob also brought some wine. And Isaac drank. Then Jacob's father Isaac said to him, "Come here, my son. Kiss me."

So Jacob went to him and kissed him. When Isaac smelled the clothes, he gave Jacob his blessing. He said,

"It really is the smell of my son.
  It's like the smell of a field
  that the LORD has blessed.
May God give you dew from heaven.
  May he give you the richness of the earth.
  May he give you plenty of grain and fresh wine.
May nations serve you.
  May they bow down to you.
Rule over your brothers.
  May the sons of your mother bow down to you.
May those who curse you be cursed.
  And may those who bless you be blessed."

When Isaac finished blessing him, Jacob left his father. Just then his brother Esau came in from hunting. He too prepared some tasty food. He brought it to his father. Then Esau said to him, "My father, please sit up. Eat some of my wild meat. Then give me your blessing."

His father Isaac asked him, "Who are you?"

"I'm your son," he answered. "I'm Esau, your oldest son."

Isaac began to shake all over. He said, "Then who hunted a wild animal and brought it to me? I ate it just before you came. I gave him my blessing. And he will certainly be blessed!"

Esau heard his father's words. Then he yelled loudly and bitterly. He said to his father, "Bless me! Bless me too, my father!"

But Isaac said, "Your brother came and tricked me. He took your blessing."

Esau said, "Isn't Jacob just the right name for him? This is the second time he has taken advantage of me. First, he took my rights as the oldest son. And now he's taken my blessing!" Then Esau asked, "Haven't you saved any blessing for me?"

Isaac answered Esau, "I've made him ruler over you. I've made all his relatives serve him. And I've provided him with grain and fresh wine. So what can I possibly do for you, my son?"

Esau said to his father, "Do you have only one blessing, my father? Bless me too, my father!" Then Esau wept loudly.

His father Isaac answered him,

"You will live far away from the fruit of the earth.
    You will live far away from the dew of heaven above.
You will live by using the sword.
    And you will serve your brother.
But you will grow restless.
    Then you will throw off the heavy load
    he has caused you to carry."

Esau was angry with Jacob. He was angry because of the blessing his father had given to Jacob. He said to himself, "The days of sorrow over my father's death are near. Then I'll kill my brother Jacob."

Rebekah was told what her older son Esau had said. So she sent for her younger son Jacob. She said to him, "Your brother Esau is planning to get back at you by killing you. Now then, my son, do what I say. Run away at once to my brother Laban in Harran. Stay with him until your brother's anger calms down. When he forgets what you did to him, I'll let you know. Then you can come back from there. Why should I lose both of you in one day?"

Then Rebekah spoke to Isaac. She said, "I'm sick of living because of Esau's Hittite wives. Suppose Jacob also marries a Hittite woman. If he does, my life won't be worth living."

So Isaac called for Jacob and blessed him. Then he commanded him, "Don't get married to a Canaanite woman. Go at once to Paddan Aram. Go to the house of your mother's father Bethuel. Find a wife for yourself there. Take her from among the daughters of your mother's brother Laban. May the Mighty God bless you. May he give you children. May he make your family larger until you become a community of nations. May he give you and your children after you the blessing he gave to Abraham. Then you can take over the land where you now live as an outsider. It's the land God gave to Abraham." Isaac sent Jacob on his way. Jacob went to Paddan Aram. He went to Laban, the son of Bethuel the Aramean. Laban was Rebekah's brother. And Rebekah was the mother of Jacob and Esau.

Jacob left Beersheba and started out for Harran. He reached a certain place and stopped for the night. The sun had already set. He took one of the stones there and placed it under his head. Then he lay down to sleep. In a dream he saw a stairway standing on the earth. Its top reached to heaven. The angels of God were going up and coming down on it. The LORD stood beside the stairway. He said, "I am the LORD. I am the God of your grandfather Abraham and the God of Isaac. I will give you and your children after you the land you are lying on. They will be like the dust of the earth that can't be counted. They will spread out to the west and to the east. They will spread out to the north and to the south. All nations on earth will be blessed because of you and your children after you. I am with you. I will watch over you everywhere you go. And I will bring you back to this land. I will not leave you until I have done what I have promised you."

Jacob woke up from his sleep. Then he thought, "The LORD is surely in this place. And I didn't even know it." Jacob was afraid. He said, "How holy this place is! This must be the house of God. This is the gate of heaven."

Early the next morning Jacob took the stone he had placed under his head. He set it up as a sacred stone. And he poured olive oil on top of it. He named that place Bethel. But the city used to be called Luz.

Then Jacob made a promise. He said, "May God be with me. May he watch over me on this journey I'm taking. May he give me food to eat and clothes to wear. May he do as he has promised so that I can return safely to my father's home. Then you, LORD, will be my God. This stone I've set up as a sacred stone will be God's house. And I'll give you a tenth of everything you give me."

Then Jacob continued on his journey. He came to the land where the eastern tribes lived. There he saw a well in the open country. Three flocks of sheep were lying near it. The flocks were given water from the well. The stone over the opening of the well was large. All the flocks would gather there. The shepherds would roll the stone away from the well's opening. They would give water to the sheep. Then they would put the stone back in its place over the opening of the well.

Jacob asked the shepherds, "My friends, where are you from?"

"We're from Harran," they replied.

He said to them, "Do you know Nahor's grandson Laban?"

"Yes, we know him," they answered.

Then Jacob asked them, "How is he?"

"He's fine," they said. "Here comes his daughter Rachel with the sheep."

He was still talking with them when Rachel came with her father's sheep. It was her job to take care of the flock. Rachel was the daughter of Laban, Jacob's uncle. When Jacob saw Rachel with Laban's sheep, he went over to the well. He rolled the stone away from the opening. He gave water to his uncle's sheep. Jacob kissed Rachel. Then he began to cry because he was so happy. He had told Rachel he was a relative of her father. He had also said he was Rebekah's son. Rachel ran and told her father what Jacob had said.

As soon as Laban heard the news about his sister's son Jacob, he hurried to meet him. Laban hugged Jacob and kissed him. Then Laban brought him to his home. There Jacob told him everything. Then Laban said to him, "You are my own flesh and blood."

Jacob stayed with Laban for a whole month. Then Laban said to him, "You are one of my relatives. But is that any reason for you to work for me for nothing? Tell me what your pay should be."

Laban had two daughters. The name of the older one was Leah. And the name of the younger one was Rachel. Leah was plain, but Rachel was beautiful. She had a nice figure. Jacob was in love with Rachel. He said to Laban, "I'll work for you for seven years so I can marry your younger daughter Rachel."

Laban said, "It's better for me to give her to you than to some other man. Stay here with me." So Jacob worked for seven years so he could marry Rachel. But they seemed like only a few days to him because he loved her so much.

Then Jacob said to Laban, "Give me my wife. I've completed my time."

So Laban brought all the people of the place together and had a feast prepared. But when evening came, he gave his daughter Leah to Jacob. Laban gave his female servant Zilpah to his daughter as her servant.

When Jacob woke up the next morning, there was Leah next to him! So he said to Laban, "What have you done to me? I worked for you so I could marry Rachel, didn't I? Why did you trick me?"

Laban replied, "It isn't our practice here to give the younger daughter to be married before the older one. Complete this daughter's wedding week. Then we'll give you the younger one also. But you will have to work for another seven years."

So Jacob completed the week with Leah. Then Laban gave him his daughter Rachel to be his wife. Laban gave his female servant Bilhah to his daughter Rachel as her servant. He loved Rachel more than he loved Leah. And he worked for Laban for another seven years.

During those years Jacob had many children. Leah had six sons, named Reuben, Simeon, Levi, Judah, Issachar, and Zebulun, and a daughter named Dinah. Rachel had a son named Joseph. Jacob also married Bilhah, Rachel's servant, and she had sons named Dan and Naphtali. And he married Zilpah, Leah's servant, and she had sons named Gad and Asher.

After Rachel had Joseph, Jacob spoke to Laban. He said, "Send me on my way. I want to go back to my own home and country. Give me my wives and children. I worked for you to get them. So I'll be on my way. You know how much work I've done for you."

But Laban said to him, "If you are pleased with me, stay here. I've discovered that the LORD has blessed me because of you." He continued, "Name your pay. I'll give it to you."

Jacob said to him, "You know how hard I've worked for you. You know that your livestock has done better under my care. You had only a little before I came. But that little has become a lot. The LORD has blessed you everywhere I've been. But when can I do something for my own family?"

"What should I give you?" Laban asked.

"Don't give me anything," Jacob replied. "Just do one thing for me. Then I'll go on taking care of your flocks and watching over them. Let me go through all your flocks today. Let me remove every speckled or spotted sheep. Let me remove every dark-colored lamb. Let me remove every speckled or spotted goat. They will be my pay. My honesty will be a witness about me in days to come. It will be a witness every time you check on what you have paid me. Suppose I have a goat that doesn't have speckles or spots. Or suppose I have a lamb that isn't dark colored. Then it will be considered stolen."

Jacob took care of the flocks in a way that all the babies were spotted or streaked. Laban's sons became angry and accused Jacob of stealing from their father.

remember what you read

1. What is something you noticed for the first time?

_____

_____

_____

_____

2. What questions did you have?

_____

_____

_____

_____

3. Was there anything that bothered you?

_____

_____

_____

_____

4. What did you learn about loving God?

_____

_____

_____

_____

5. What did you learn about loving others?

_____

_____

_____

_____

GENESIS, PART 6

Then the LORD spoke to Jacob. He said, "Go back to your father's land and to your relatives. I will be with you."

Then Jacob put his children and wives on camels. He drove all his livestock ahead of him. He also took with him everything he had acquired in Paddan Aram. He left to go to his father Isaac in the land of Canaan.

Laban had gone to clip the wool from his sheep. While he was gone, Rachel stole the statues of the family gods that belonged to her father. And that's not all. Jacob tricked Laban, the Aramean. He didn't tell him he was running away. So Jacob ran off with everything he had. He crossed the Euphrates River. And he headed for the hill country of Gilead.

On the third day Laban was told that Jacob had run away. He took his relatives with him and went after Jacob. Seven days later he caught up with him in the hill country of Gilead. Then God came to Laban, the Aramean, in a dream at night. He said to him, "Be careful. Do not say anything to Jacob, whether it is good or bad."

Laban was angry with Jacob for running away and stealing the family gods, but they made a peace agreement.

So Jacob set up a stone as a way to remember. He said to his relatives, "Get some stones." So they took stones and put them in a pile. And they ate there by it. Laban named the pile of stones Jegar Sahadutha. Jacob named it Galeed.

Laban said, "This pile of stones is a witness between you and me today." That's why it was named Galeed. It was also called Mizpah.

That's because Laban said, "May the LORD keep watch between you and me when we are away from each other. Don't treat my daughters badly. Don't get married to any women besides my daughters. There isn't anyone here to see what we're doing. But remember that God is a witness between you and me."

Early the next morning Laban kissed his grandchildren and his daughters. He gave them his blessing. Then he left and returned home.

Jacob also went on his way. The angels of God met him. Jacob saw them. He said, "This is the army of God!" So he named that place Mahanaim.

Jacob sent messengers ahead of him to his brother Esau. Esau lived in the land of Seir. It was also called the country of Edom. Jacob told the messengers what to do. He said, "Here's what you must tell my master Esau. 'Your servant Jacob says, "I've been staying with Laban. I've remained there until now. I have cattle and donkeys and sheep and goats. I also have male and female servants. Now I'm sending this message to you. I hope I can please you."'"

The messengers came back to Jacob. They said, "We went to your brother Esau. He's coming now to meet you. He has 400 men with him."

Jacob was very worried and afraid. So he separated the people with him into two groups. He also separated the flocks and herds and camels. He thought, "Esau might come and attack one group. If he does, the group that's left can escape."

Then Jacob prayed, "You are the God of my grandfather Abraham. You are the God of my father Isaac. LORD, you are the one who said to me, 'Go back to your country and your relatives. Then I will give you success.' You have been very kind and faithful to me. But I'm not worthy of any of this. When I crossed this Jordan River, all I had was my walking stick. But now I've become two camps. Please save me from the hand of my brother Esau. I'm afraid he'll come and attack me and the mothers with their children. But you have said, 'I will surely give you success. I will make your children as many as the grains of sand on the seashore. People will not be able to count them.'"

Jacob spent the night there. He chose a gift for his brother Esau from what he had with him. He chose 200 female goats and 20 male goats. He chose 200 female sheep and 20 male sheep. He chose 30 female camels with their little ones. He chose 40 cows and ten bulls. And he chose 20 female donkeys and ten male donkeys. He put each herd by itself. Then he put his servants in charge of them. He said to his servants, "Go on ahead of me. Keep some space between the herds."

Jacob spoke to his servant who was leading the way. He said, "My brother Esau will meet you. He'll ask, 'Who is your master? Where are you going? And who owns all these animals in front of you?' Then say to Esau, 'They belong to your servant Jacob. They are a gift to you from him. And Jacob is coming behind us.' "

He also spoke to the second and third servants. He told them and all the others who followed the herds what to do. He said, "Say the same thing to Esau when you meet him. Make sure you say, 'Your servant Jacob is coming behind us.' " Jacob was thinking, "I'll make peace with him with these gifts I'm sending on ahead. When I see him later, maybe he'll welcome me." So Jacob's gifts went on ahead of him. But he himself spent the night in the camp.

That night Jacob got up. He took his two wives, his two female servants and his 11 sons and sent them across the Jabbok River. After they had crossed the stream, he sent over everything he owned. So Jacob was left alone. A man wrestled with him until morning. The man saw that he couldn't win. So he touched the inside of Jacob's hip. As Jacob wrestled with the man, Jacob's hip was twisted. Then the man said, "Let me go. It is morning."

But Jacob replied, "I won't let you go unless you bless me."

The man asked him, "What is your name?"

"Jacob," he answered.

Then the man said, "Your name will not be Jacob anymore. Instead, it will be Israel. You have wrestled with God and with people. And you have won."

Jacob said, "Please tell me your name."

But he replied, "Why do you want to know my name?" Then he blessed Jacob there.

So Jacob named the place Peniel. He said, "I saw God face to face. But I'm still alive!"

The sun rose above Jacob as he passed by Peniel.

Jacob looked and saw Esau coming with his 400 men! So Jacob separated the children. He put them with Leah, Rachel and the two female servants. He put the servants and their children in front. He put Leah and her children next. And he put Rachel and Joseph last. He himself went on ahead. As he came near his brother, he bowed down to the ground seven times.

But Esau ran to meet Jacob. He hugged him and threw his arms around his neck. He kissed him, and they cried for joy. Then Esau looked around and saw the women and children. "Who are these people with you?" he asked.

Jacob answered, "They are the children God has so kindly given to me."

Then the female servants and their children came near and bowed down. Next, Leah and her children came and bowed down. Last of all came Joseph and Rachel. They bowed down too.

Esau asked, "Why did you send all those herds I saw?"

"I hoped I could do something to please you," Jacob replied.

But Esau said, "I already have plenty, my brother. Keep what you have for yourself."

"No, please!" said Jacob. "If I've pleased you, accept this gift from me. Seeing your face is like seeing the face of God. You have welcomed me so kindly. Please accept the present that was brought to you. God has given me so much. I have everything I need." Jacob wouldn't give in. So Esau accepted it.

So that day Esau started on his way back to Seir. But Jacob went to Sukkoth. There he built a place for himself. He also made shelters for his livestock. That's why the place is named Sukkoth.

After Jacob came from Paddan Aram, he arrived safely at the city of Shechem in Canaan. He camped where he could see the city. For 100 pieces of silver he bought a piece of land. He got it from Hamor's sons. Hamor was the father of Shechem. Jacob set up his tent on that piece of land. He also set up an altar there. He named it El Elohe Israel.

Then God said to Jacob, "Go up to Bethel and live there. Build an altar there to honor me. That's where I appeared to you when you were running away from your brother Esau."

So Jacob spoke to his family and to everyone with him. He said, "Get rid of the statues of false gods you have with you. Make yourselves pure by washing and changing your clothes. Come, let's go up to Bethel. There I'll build an altar to honor God. He answered me when I was in trouble. He's been with me everywhere I've gone." So they gave Jacob all the statues of false gods they had. They also gave him their earrings. Jacob buried those things under the oak tree at Shechem. Then Jacob and everyone with him started out. The terror of God fell on the towns all around them. So no one chased them.

After Jacob returned from Paddan Aram, God appeared to him again. And God blessed him. God said to him, "Your name is Jacob. But you will not be called Jacob anymore. Your name will be Israel." So he named him Israel.

God said to him, "I am the Mighty God. Have children so that there will be many of you. You will become the father of a nation and a community of nations. Your later family will include kings. I am giving you the land I gave to Abraham and Isaac. I will also give it to your children after you." Then God left him at the place where he had talked with him.

Jacob set up a sacred stone at the place where God had talked with him. He poured out a drink offering on it. He also poured olive oil on it. Jacob named the place Bethel. That's where God had talked with him.

They moved on from Bethel. Ephrath wasn't very far away when Rachel began to have a baby. She was having a very hard time of it. The woman who helped her saw that she was having problems. So she said to Rachel, "Don't be afraid. You have another son." But Rachel was dying. As she took her last breath, she named her son Ben-Oni. But his father named him Benjamin.

So Rachel died. She was buried beside the road to Ephrath. Ephrath was also called Bethlehem. Jacob set up a stone marker over her tomb. To this day, the stone marks the place where Rachel was buried.

Jacob came home to his father Isaac in Mamre. Mamre is near Kiriath Arba, where Abraham and Isaac had stayed. The place is also called Hebron. Isaac lived 180 years. Then he took his last breath and died. He was very old when he joined the members of his family who had already died. His sons Esau and Jacob buried him.

remember what you read

1. What is something you noticed for the first time?

_____

_____

_____

_____

2. What questions did you have?

_____

_____

_____

_____

3. Was there anything that bothered you?

_____

_____

_____

_____

4. What did you learn about loving God?

_____

_____

_____

_____

5. What did you learn about loving others?

_____

_____

_____

_____

Here is the story of the family line of Jacob.

Joseph was a young man. He was 17 years old. He was taking care of the flocks with some of his brothers. They were the sons of Bilhah and the sons of Zilpah, the wives of his father Jacob. Joseph brought their father a bad report about his brothers.

Israel loved Joseph more than any of his other sons. That's because Joseph had been born to him when he was old. Israel made him a beautiful robe. Joseph's brothers saw that their father loved him more than any of them. So they hated Joseph. They couldn't even speak one kind word to him.

Joseph had a dream. When he told it to his brothers, they hated him even more. He said to them, "Listen to the dream I had. We were tying up bundles of grain out in the field. Suddenly my bundle stood up straight. Your bundles gathered around my bundle and bowed down to it."

His brothers said to him, "Do you plan to be king over us? Will you really rule over us?" So they hated him even more because of his dream. They didn't like what he had said.

Then Joseph had another dream. He told it to his brothers. "Listen," he said. "I had another dream. This time the sun and moon and 11 stars were bowing down to me."

He told his father as well as his brothers. Then his father rebuked him. He said, "What about this dream you had? Will your mother and I and your brothers really do that? Will we really come and bow down to the ground in front of you?" His brothers were jealous of him. But his father kept the dreams in mind.

Joseph's brothers had gone to take care of their father's flocks near Shechem. Israel said to Joseph, "As you know, your brothers are taking care of the flocks near Shechem. Come. I'm going to send you to them."

"All right," Joseph replied.

So Israel said to him, "Go to your brothers. See how they are doing. Also see how the flocks are doing. Then come back and tell me." So he sent him away from the Hebron Valley.

Joseph met his brothers. They wanted to kill him. But Judah convinced them to sell Joseph to some traders.

Then they got Joseph's beautiful robe. They killed a goat and dipped the robe in the blood. They took the robe back to their father. They said, "We found this. Take a look at it. See if it's your son's robe."

Jacob recognized it. He said, "It's my son's robe! A wild animal has eaten him up. Joseph must have been torn to pieces."

Jacob tore his clothes. He put on the rough clothing people wear when they're sad. Then he mourned for his son many days. All Jacob's other sons and daughters came to comfort him. But they weren't able to. He said, "I will continue to mourn until I go down into the grave to be with my son." So Joseph's father mourned for him.

But the traders from Midian sold Joseph to Potiphar in Egypt. Potiphar was one of Pharaoh's officials. He was the captain of the palace guard.

The Lord was with Joseph. He gave him great success. Joseph lived in Potiphar's house. Joseph's master saw that the Lord was with him. He saw that the Lord made Joseph successful in everything he did. So Potiphar was pleased with Joseph and made him his attendant. He put Joseph in charge of his house. He trusted Joseph to take care of everything he owned. From that time on, the Lord blessed Potiphar's family and servants because of Joseph. He blessed everything Potiphar had in his house and field. So Joseph took good care of everything Potiphar owned. With Joseph in charge, Potiphar didn't have to worry about anything except the food he ate.

Joseph was strong and handsome. After a while, his master's wife noticed Joseph. She said to him, "Come to bed with me!"

But he refused. "My master has put me in charge," he told her. "Now he doesn't have to worry about anything in the house. He trusts me to take care of everything he owns. No one in this house is in a higher position than I am. My master hasn't held anything back from me, except you. You are his wife. So how could I do an evil thing like that? How could I sin against God?" She spoke to Joseph day after day. But he told her he wouldn't go to bed with her. He didn't even want to be with her.

One day Joseph went into the house to take care of his duties. None of the family servants was inside. Potiphar's wife grabbed him by his coat. "Come to bed with me!" she said. But he left his coat in her hand. And he ran out of the house.

She saw that he had left his coat in her hand and had run out of the house. So she called her servants. "Look," she said to them, "this Hebrew slave has been brought here to make fun of us! He came in here to force me to do something that isn't right. But I screamed for help. He heard my scream. So he left his coat beside me and ran out of the house."

She kept Joseph's coat with her until Potiphar came home. Then she told him her story. She said, "That Hebrew slave you brought us came to me to rape me. But I screamed for help. So he left his coat beside me and ran out of the house."

Potiphar's wife told him, "That's how your slave treated me." When Joseph's master heard her story, he became very angry. So he put Joseph in prison. It was the place where the king's prisoners were kept.

While Joseph was there in the prison, the Lord was with him. He was kind to him. So the man running the prison was pleased with Joseph. He put Joseph in charge of all the prisoners. He made him responsible for everything done there. The man who ran the prison didn't pay attention to anything in Joseph's care. That's because the Lord was with Joseph. He gave Joseph success in everything he did.

Some time later, the Egyptian king's baker and wine taster did something their master didn't like. So Pharaoh became angry with his two officials, the chief wine taster and the chief baker. He put them in prison in the house of the captain of the palace guard. It was the same prison where Joseph was kept. The captain put Joseph in charge of those men. So Joseph took care of them.

Some time passed while they were in prison. Then each of the two men had a dream. The men were the Egyptian king's baker and wine taster. They were being held in prison. Both of them had dreams the same night. Each of their dreams had its own meaning.

Joseph came to them the next morning. He saw that they were sad. They were Pharaoh's officials, and they were in prison with Joseph in his master's house. So he asked them, "Why do you look so sad today?"

"We both had dreams," they answered. "But no one can tell us what they mean."

Then Joseph said to them, "Only God knows what dreams mean. Tell me your dreams."

They shared their dreams. Joseph gave them the meanings: in three days the wine taster would be given his job back. At the same time, Pharaoh would kill the baker.

The third day was Pharaoh's birthday. He had a feast prepared for all his officials. He brought the chief wine taster and the chief baker out of prison. He did it in front of his officials. He gave the chief wine taster's job back to him. Once again the wine taster put the cup into Pharaoh's hand. But Pharaoh had a pole stuck through the chief baker's body. Then he had the pole set up. Everything happened just as Joseph had told them when he explained their dreams.

But the chief wine taster didn't remember Joseph. In fact, he forgot all about him.

When two full years had passed, Pharaoh had a dream. In his dream, he was standing by the Nile River. Seven cows came up out of the river. They looked healthy and fat. They were eating some of the tall grass growing along the river. After them, seven other cows came up out of the Nile. They looked ugly and skinny. They were standing beside the other cows on the riverbank. The ugly, skinny cows ate up the seven cows that looked healthy and fat. Then Pharaoh woke up.

He fell asleep again and had a second dream. In that dream, seven heads of grain were growing on one stem. They were healthy and good. After them, seven other heads of grain came up. They were thin and dried up by the east wind. The thin heads of grain swallowed up the seven healthy, full heads. Then Pharaoh woke up. It had been a dream.

In the morning he was worried. So he sent for all the magicians and wise men of Egypt. Pharaoh told them his dreams. But no one could tell him what they meant.

Then the chief wine taster spoke up. He said to Pharaoh, "Now I remember that I've done something wrong. Pharaoh was once angry with his servants. He put me and the chief baker in prison. We were in the house of the captain of the palace guard. Each of us had a dream the same night. Each dream had its own meaning. A young Hebrew servant was there with us. He was a servant of the captain of the guard. We told him our dreams. And he explained them to us. He told each of us the meaning of our dreams. Things turned out exactly as he said they would. I was given back my job. The other man had a pole stuck through his body."

So Pharaoh sent for Joseph. He was quickly brought out of the prison. Joseph shaved and changed his clothes. Then he came to Pharaoh.

Pharaoh said to Joseph, "I had a dream. No one can tell me what it means. But I've heard that when you hear a dream you can explain it."

"I can't do it," Joseph replied to Pharaoh. "But God will give Pharaoh the answer he wants."

Then Pharaoh told Joseph what he had dreamed. He said, "I was standing on the bank of the Nile River. Seven cows came up out of the river. They were fat and looked healthy. They were eating the tall grass growing along the river. After them, seven other cows came up. They were bony and very ugly and thin. I had never seen such ugly cows in the whole land of Egypt. The thin, ugly cows ate up the seven fat cows that came up first. But no one could tell that the thin cows had eaten the fat cows. That's because the thin cows looked just as ugly as they had before. Then I woke up.

"In my dream I also saw seven heads of grain. They were full and good. They were all growing on one stem. After them, seven other heads of grain came up. They were weak and thin and dried up by the east wind. The thin heads of grain swallowed up the seven good heads. I told my dream to the magicians. But none of them could explain it to me."

remember what you read

1. What is something you noticed for the first time?

_____

_____

_____

_____

2. What questions did you have?

_____

_____

_____

_____

3. Was there anything that bothered you?

_____

_____

_____

_____

4. What did you learn about loving God?

_____

_____

_____

_____

5. What did you learn about loving others?

_____

_____

_____

_____

GENESIS, PART 8

Then Joseph said to Pharaoh, "Both of Pharaoh's dreams have the same meaning. God has shown Pharaoh what he is about to do. The seven good cows are seven years. And the seven good heads of grain are seven years. Both dreams mean the same thing. The seven thin, ugly cows that came up later are seven years. So are the seven worthless heads of grain dried up by the east wind. They are seven years when there won't be enough food.

"It's just as I said to Pharaoh. God has shown Pharaoh what he's about to do. Seven years with plenty of food are coming to the whole land of Egypt. But seven years when there won't be enough food will follow them. Then everyone will forget about all the food Egypt had. Terrible hunger will destroy the land. There won't be anything left to remind people of the years when there was plenty of food in the land. That's how bad the hunger that follows will be. God gave the dream to Pharaoh in two forms. That's because the matter has been firmly decided by God. And it's because God will do it soon.

"So Pharaoh should look for a wise and understanding man. He should put him in charge of the land of Egypt. Pharaoh should appoint officials to be in charge of the land. They should take a fifth of the harvest in Egypt during the seven years when there's plenty of food. They should collect all the extra food of the good years that are coming. Pharaoh should give them authority to store up the grain. They should keep it in the cities for food. The grain should be stored up for the country to use later. It will be needed during the seven years when there isn't enough food in Egypt. Then the country won't be destroyed just because it doesn't have enough food."

The plan seemed good to Pharaoh and all his officials. So Pharaoh said to them, "The spirit of God is in this man. We can't find anyone else like him, can we?"

Pharaoh told Joseph to use the wisdom God gave him to take care of all of Egypt. He told him to prepare for the years when there wouldn't be enough food. Joseph got married and had two sons, Manasseh and Ephraim.

The seven years when there was plenty of food in Egypt came to an end. Then the seven years when there wasn't enough food began. It happened just as Joseph had said it would. There wasn't enough food in any of the other lands. But in the whole land of Egypt there was food. When all the people of Egypt began to get hungry, they cried out to Pharaoh for food. He told all the Egyptians, "Go to Joseph. Do what he tells you."

Jacob found out that there was grain in Egypt. So he said to his sons, "Why do you just keep looking at one another?" He continued, "I've heard there's grain in Egypt. Go down there. Buy some for us. Then we'll live and not die."

So ten of Joseph's brothers went down to Egypt to buy grain there. But Jacob didn't send Joseph's brother Benjamin with them. He was afraid Benjamin might be harmed. Israel's sons were among the people who went to buy grain. There wasn't enough food in the land of Canaan.

Joseph was the governor of the land. He was the one who sold grain to all its people. When Joseph's brothers arrived, they bowed down to him with their faces to the ground. As soon as Joseph saw his brothers, he recognized them. But he pretended to be a stranger. He spoke to them in a mean way. "Where do you come from?" he asked.

"From the land of Canaan," they replied. "We've come to buy food."

Joseph recognized his brothers, but they didn't recognize him. Then Joseph remembered his dreams about them. So he said to them, "You are spies! You have come to see the places where our land isn't guarded very well."

"No, sir," they answered. "We've come to buy food. All of us are the sons of one man. We're honest men. We aren't spies."

"No!" he said to them. "You have come to see the places where our land isn't guarded very well."

But they replied, "We were 12 brothers. All of us were the sons of one man. He lives in the land of Canaan. Our youngest brother is now with our father. And one brother is gone."

Joseph said to them, "I still say you are spies! So I'm going to test you. And here's the test. You can be sure that you won't leave this place unless your youngest brother comes here. You can be just as sure of this as you are sure that Pharaoh lives. I give you my word that you won't leave here unless your brother comes. Send one of you back to get your brother. The rest of you will be kept in prison. I'll test your words. Then we'll find out whether you are telling the truth. You can be sure that Pharaoh lives. And you can be just as sure that if you aren't telling the truth, we'll know that you are spies!" So Joseph kept all of them under guard for three days.

On the third day, Joseph spoke to them again. He said, "Do what I say. Then you will live, because I have respect for God. If you are honest men, let one of your brothers stay here in prison. The rest of you may go and take grain back to your hungry families. But you must bring your youngest brother to me. That will prove that your words are true. Then you won't die." So they did what he said.

They said to one another, "God is surely punishing us because of our brother. We saw how upset he was when he begged us to let him live. But we wouldn't listen. That's why all this trouble has come to us."

Reuben replied, "Didn't I tell you not to sin against the boy? But you wouldn't listen! Now we're being paid back for killing him." They didn't realize that Joseph could understand what they were saying. He was using someone else to explain their words to him in the Egyptian language.

Joseph turned away from his brothers and began to weep. Then he came back and spoke to them again. He had Simeon taken and tied up right there in front of them.

Joseph gave orders to have their bags filled with grain. He had each man's money put back into his sack. He also made sure they were given food for their journey. Then the brothers loaded their grain on their donkeys and left.

When night came, they stopped. One of them opened his sack to get feed for his donkey. He saw his money in the top of his sack. "My money has been given back," he said to his brothers. "Here it is in my sack."

They had a sinking feeling in their hearts. They began to tremble. They turned to one another and said, "What has God done to us?"

They came to their father Jacob in the land of Canaan. They told him everything that had happened to them. They said, "The man who is the governor of the land spoke to us in a mean way. He treated us as if we were spying on the land. But we said to him, 'We're honest men. We aren't spies. We were 12 brothers. All of us were the sons of one father. But now one brother is gone. And our youngest brother is with our father in Canaan.'

"Then the man who is the governor of the land spoke to us. He said, 'Here's how I will know whether you are honest men. Leave one of your brothers here with me. Take food for your hungry families and go. But bring your youngest brother to me. Then I'll know that you are honest men and not spies. I'll give your brother back to you. And you will be free to trade in the land.'"

They began emptying their sacks. There in each man's sack was his bag of money! When they and their father saw the money bags, they were scared to death. Their father Jacob said to them, "You have taken my children away from me. Joseph is gone. Simeon is gone. Now you want to take Benjamin. Everything is going against me!"

Then Reuben spoke to his father. He said, "You can put both of my sons to death if I don't bring Benjamin back to you. Trust me to take care of him. I'll bring him back."

But Jacob said, "My son will not go down there with you. His brother is dead. He's the only one left here with me. Suppose he's harmed on the journey you are taking. Then I would die as a sad old man."

There still wasn't enough food anywhere in the land. After a while Jacob's family had eaten all the grain the brothers had brought from Egypt. So their father said to them, "Go back. Buy us a little more food."

But Judah said to him, "The man gave us a strong warning. He said, 'You won't see my face again unless your brother Benjamin is with you.' So send our brother along with us. Then we'll go down and buy food for you. If you won't send him, we won't go down. The man said to us, 'You won't see my face again unless your brother is with you.' "

Israel asked, "Why did you bring this trouble to me? Why did you tell the man you had another brother?"

They replied, "The man questioned us closely about ourselves and our family. He asked us, 'Is your father still living? Do you have another brother?' We just answered his questions. How could we possibly know he would say, 'Bring your brother down here'?"

Judah spoke to Israel his father. "Send the boy along with me," he said. "We'll go right away. Then we and you and our children will live and not die. I myself promise to keep Benjamin safe. You can blame me if I don't bring him back to you. I'll set him right here in front of you. If I don't, you can put the blame on me for the rest of my life. As it is, we've already waited too long. We could have made the trip to Egypt and back twice by now."

Then their father Israel spoke to them. He said, "If that's the way it has to be, then do what I tell you. Put some of the best things from our land in your bags. Take them down to the man as a gift. Take some lotion and a little honey. Take some spices and myrrh. Take some pistachio nuts and almonds. Take twice the amount of money with you. You have to give back the money that was put in your sacks. Maybe it was a mistake. Also take your brother. Go back to the man at once. May the Mighty God cause him to show you mercy. May the man let your other brother and Benjamin come back with you. And if I lose my sons, I lose them."

So the men took the gifts. They took twice the amount of money. They also took Benjamin. They hurried down to Egypt and went to Joseph. When Joseph saw Benjamin with them, he spoke to the manager of his house. "Take these men to my house," he said. "Kill an animal and prepare a meal. I want them to eat with me at noon."

remember what you read

1. What is something you noticed for the first time?

_____

_____

_____

_____

2. What questions did you have?

_____

_____

_____

_____

3. Was there anything that bothered you?

_____

_____

_____

_____

4. What did you learn about loving God?

_____

_____

_____

_____

5. What did you learn about loving others?

_____

_____

_____

_____

The manager did what Joseph told him to do. He took the men to Joseph's house. They were frightened when they were taken to Joseph's house. They thought, "We were brought here because of the money that was put back in our sacks the first time. He wants to attack us and overpower us. Then he can hold us as slaves and take our donkeys."

So they went up to Joseph's manager. They spoke to him at the entrance to the house. "Please, sir," they said. "We came down here the first time to buy food. We opened our sacks at the place where we stopped for the night. Each of us found in our sacks the exact amount of the money we had paid. So we've brought it back with us. We've also brought more money with us to buy food. We don't know who put our money in our sacks."

"It's all right," the manager said. "Don't be afraid. Your God, the God of your father, has given you riches in your sacks. I received your money." Then he brought Simeon out to them.

The manager took the men into Joseph's house. He gave them water to wash their feet. He provided feed for their donkeys. The brothers prepared their gifts for Joseph. He was planning to arrive at noon. They had heard that they were going to eat there.

When Joseph came home, they gave him the gifts they had brought into the house. They bowed down low in front of him. He asked them how they were. Then he said, "How is your old father you told me about? Is he still living?"

They replied, "Your servant our father is still alive and well." And they bowed down to show him honor.

Joseph looked around. Then he saw his brother Benjamin, his own mother's son. He asked, "Is this your youngest brother? Is he the one you told me about?" He continued, "May God be gracious to you, my son." It moved him deeply to see his brother. So Joseph hurried out and looked for a place to cry. He went into his own room and cried there.

Then he washed his face and came out. He calmed down and said, "Serve the food."

They served Joseph by himself. They served the brothers by themselves. They also served the Egyptians who ate with Joseph by themselves. Because of their beliefs, Egyptians couldn't eat with Hebrews. The brothers had been given places in front of Joseph. They had been seated in the order of their ages, from the oldest to the youngest. That made them look at each other in great surprise. While they were eating, some food was brought to them from Joseph's table. Benjamin was given five times as much as anyone else. So all Joseph's brothers ate and drank a lot with him.

Joseph told the manager of his house what to do. "Fill the men's sacks with as much food as they can carry," he said. "Put each man's money in his sack. Then put my silver cup in the youngest one's sack. Put it there along with the money he paid for his grain." So the manager did what Joseph told him to do.

When morning came, the men were sent on their way with their donkeys. They hadn't gone very far from the city when Joseph spoke to his manager. "Go after those men right away," he said. "Catch up with them. Say to them, 'My master was good to you. Why have you paid him back by doing evil? Isn't this the cup my master drinks from? Doesn't he also use it to find things out? You have done an evil thing.'"

When the manager caught up with them, he told them what Joseph had said. But they said to him, "Why do you say these things? We would never do anything like that! We even brought back to you from Canaan the money we found in our sacks. So why would we steal silver or gold from your master's house? If you find out that any of us has the cup, he will die. And the rest of us will become your slaves."

Each of them quickly put his sack down on the ground and opened it. Then the manager started to search. He began with the oldest and ended with the youngest. The cup was found in

Benjamin's sack. When that happened, they were so upset they tore their clothes. Then all of them loaded their donkeys and went back to the city.

Joseph was still in the house when Judah and his brothers came in. They threw themselves down on the ground in front of him. Joseph said to them, "What have you done? Don't you know that a man like me has ways to find things out?"

"What can we say to you?" Judah replied. "What can we say? How can we prove we haven't done anything wrong? God has shown you that we are guilty. We are now your slaves. All of us are, including the one found to have the cup."

But Joseph said, "I would never do anything like that! Only the man found to have the cup will become my slave. The rest of you may go back to your father in peace."

Then Judah went up to him. He said, "Please, sir. Let me speak a word to you. Don't be angry with me, even though you are equal to Pharaoh himself. You asked us, 'Do you have a father or a brother?' We answered, 'We have an old father. A young son was born to him when he was old. His brother is dead. He's the only one of his mother's sons left. And his father loves him.'

"Then you said to us, 'Bring him down to me. I want to see him for myself.' We said to you, 'The boy can't leave his father. If he does, his father will die.' But you told us, 'Your youngest brother must come down here with you. If he doesn't, you won't see my face again.' So we went back to my father. We told him what you had said.

"Then our father said, 'Go back. Buy a little more food.' But we said, 'We can't go down. We'll only go if our youngest brother goes there with us. We can't even see the man's face unless our youngest brother goes with us.'

"Your servant my father said to us, 'You know that my wife had two sons by me. One of them went away from me. And I said, "He must have been torn to pieces." I haven't seen him since. What if you take this one from me too and he is harmed? Then you would cause me to die as a sad old man. I would go down into the grave full of pain and suffering.'

"So now, what will happen if the boy isn't with us when I go back to my father? His life depends on the boy's life. When he sees that the boy isn't with us, he'll die. Because of us, he'll go down into the grave as a sad old man. I promised my father I would keep the boy safe. I said, 'Father, I'll bring him back to you. If I don't, you can put the blame on me for the rest of my life.'

"Now then, please let me stay here. Let me be your slave in place of the boy. Let the boy return with his brothers. How can I go back to my father if the boy isn't with me? No! Don't let me see the pain and suffering that would come to my father."

Joseph couldn't control himself anymore in front of all his attendants. He cried out, "Have everyone leave me!" So there wasn't anyone with Joseph when he told his brothers who he was. He wept so loudly that the Egyptians heard him. Everyone in Pharaoh's house heard about it.

Joseph said to his brothers, "I am Joseph! Is my father still alive?" But his brothers weren't able to answer him. They were too afraid of him.

Joseph said to his brothers, "Come close to me." So they did. Then he said, "I am your brother Joseph. I'm the one you sold into Egypt. But don't be upset. And don't be angry with yourselves because you sold me here. God sent me ahead of you to save many lives. For two years now, there hasn't been enough food in the land. And for the next five years, people won't be plowing or gathering crops. But God sent me ahead of you to keep some of you alive on earth. He sent me here to save your lives by an act of mighty power.

"So then, it wasn't you who sent me here. It was God. He made me like a father to Pharaoh. He made me master of Pharaoh's entire house. God made me ruler of the whole land of Egypt. Now hurry back to my father. Say to him, 'Your son Joseph says, "God has made me master of the whole land of Egypt. Come down to me. Don't waste any time. You will live in the area of Goshen. You, your children and grandchildren, your flocks and herds, and everything you have will be near me. There I will provide everything you need. There are still five years to come when there won't be enough food. If you don't come down here, you and your family and everyone who belongs to you will lose everything." '

"My brothers, I am Joseph. You can see for yourselves that I am the one speaking to you. My brother Benjamin can see it too. Tell my father about all the honor given to me in Egypt. Tell him about everything you have seen. And bring my father down here quickly."

Then Joseph threw his arms around his brother Benjamin and wept. Benjamin also hugged him and wept. Joseph kissed all his brothers and wept over them. After that, his brothers talked with him.

The news reached Pharaoh's palace that Joseph's brothers had come. Pharaoh and all his officials were pleased. Pharaoh said to Joseph, "Here's what I want you to tell your brothers. Say to them, 'Load your animals. Return to the land of Canaan. Bring your father and your families back to me. I'll give you the best land in Egypt. You can enjoy all the good things in the land.'

"And here's something else I want you to tell them. Say to them, 'Take some carts from Egypt. Your children and your wives can use them. Get your father and come back. Don't worry about the things you have back there. The best of everything in Egypt will belong to you.'"

Then the sons of Israel did so. Joseph gave them carts, as Pharaoh had commanded. He also gave them supplies for their journey. He gave new clothes to each of them. But he gave Benjamin more than seven pounds of silver. He also gave him five sets of clothes. He sent his father ten male donkeys loaded with the best things from Egypt. He also sent ten female donkeys loaded with grain and bread and other supplies for his journey. Then Joseph sent his brothers away. As they were leaving he said to them, "Don't argue on the way!"

So they went up out of Egypt. They came to their father Jacob in the land of Canaan. They told him, "Joseph is still alive! In fact, he is ruler of the whole land of Egypt." Jacob was shocked. He didn't believe them. So they told him everything Joseph had said to them. Jacob saw the carts Joseph had sent to carry him back. That gave new life to their father Jacob. Israel said, "I believe it now! My son Joseph is still alive. I'll go and see him before I die."

remember what you read

1. What is something you noticed for the first time?

_____

_____

_____

_____

2. What questions did you have?

_____

_____

_____

_____

3. Was there anything that bothered you?

_____

_____

_____

_____

4. What did you learn about loving God?

_____

_____

_____

_____

5. What did you learn about loving others?

_____

_____

_____

_____

So Israel started out with everything that belonged to him. When he reached Beersheba, he offered sacrifices to the God of his father Isaac.

God spoke to Israel in a vision at night. "Jacob! Jacob!" he said.

"Here I am," Jacob replied.

"I am God. I am the God of your father," he said. "Do not be afraid to go down to Egypt. There I will make you into a great nation. I will go down to Egypt with you. I will surely bring you back again. And when you die, Joseph will close your eyes with his own hand."

Then Jacob left Beersheba. Israel's sons put their father Jacob and their families in the carts that Pharaoh had sent to carry him. So Jacob and his whole family went to Egypt. They took their livestock with them. And they took everything they had acquired in Canaan. Jacob brought his sons and grandsons with him to Egypt. He also brought his daughters and granddaughters. He brought his whole family with him.

Jacob sent Judah ahead of him to Joseph. He sent him to get directions to Goshen. And so they arrived in the area of Goshen. Then Joseph had his servants get his chariot ready. He went to Goshen to meet his father Israel. As soon as he came to his father, Joseph threw his arms around him. Then Joseph wept for a long time.

Israel said to Joseph, "I have seen for myself that you are still alive. Now I'm ready to die."

Joseph went to Pharaoh. He told him, "My father and brothers have come from the land of Canaan. They've brought along their flocks and herds and everything they own. They are now in Goshen." Joseph had chosen five of his brothers to meet with Pharaoh.

Pharaoh asked the brothers, "What do you do for a living?"

"We're shepherds," they replied to Pharaoh. "And that's what our fathers were." They also said to him, "We've come to live in Egypt for a while. There isn't enough food anywhere in Canaan. There isn't any grass for our flocks. So please let us live in Goshen."

Pharaoh said to Joseph, "Your father and your brothers have come to you. The land of Egypt is open to you. Let your father and brothers live in the best part of the land. Let them live in Goshen. Do any of them have special skills? If they do, put them in charge of my own livestock."

Then Joseph brought his father Jacob in to meet Pharaoh. Jacob gave Pharaoh his blessing. Then Pharaoh asked him, "How old are you?"

Jacob said to Pharaoh, "The years of my journey through life are 130. My years have been few and hard. They aren't as many as the years of my father and grandfather before me." Jacob gave Pharaoh his blessing. Then he left him.

So Joseph helped his father and his brothers make their homes in Egypt. He gave them property in the best part of the land, just as Pharaoh had directed him to do. That part was known as the territory of Rameses. Joseph also provided food for his father and brothers. He provided for them and the rest of his father's family. He gave them enough for all their children.

The people of Israel lived in Egypt in the area of Goshen. They received property there. They had children and so became many.

Jacob lived 17 years in Egypt. He lived a total of 147 years. The time came near for Israel to die. So he sent for his son Joseph. He said to him, "If you are pleased with me, put your hand under my thigh. Promise me that you will be kind and faithful to me. Don't bury me in Egypt. When I join the members of my family who have already died, carry me out of Egypt. Bury me where they are buried."

"I'll do exactly as you say," Joseph said.

"Give me your word that you will do it," Jacob said. So Joseph gave him his word. And Israel worshiped God as he leaned on the top of his walking stick.

Some time later Joseph was told, "Your father is sick." So he took his two sons Manasseh and Ephraim along with him. Jacob was told, "Your son Joseph has come to you." So Israel became stronger and sat up in bed.

Jacob said to Joseph, "The Mighty God appeared to me at Luz in the land of Canaan. He blessed me there. He said to me, 'I am going to give you children. I will make your family very large. I will make you a community of nations. And I will give this land to your children after you. It will belong to them forever.'

"Now then, two sons were born to you in Egypt. It happened before I came to you here. They will be counted as my own sons. Ephraim and Manasseh will belong to me, in the same way that Reuben and Simeon belong to me. Any children born to you after them will belong to you. Any territory they receive will come from the land that will be given to Ephraim and Manasseh. As I was returning from Paddan, Rachel died. It made me very sad. She died in the land of Canaan while we were still on the way. We weren't very far away from Ephrath. So I buried her body there beside the road to Ephrath." Ephrath was also called Bethlehem.

Israel saw Joseph's sons. He asked, "Who are they?"

"They are the sons God has given me here," Joseph said to his father.

Then Israel said, "Bring them to me. I want to give them my blessing."

Israel's eyes were weak because he was old. He couldn't see very well. So Joseph brought his sons close to him. His father kissed them and hugged them.

Israel said to Joseph, "I never thought I'd see your face again. But now God has let me see your children too."

Then Jacob sent for his sons.

He gave each one the blessing that was just right for him.

Then Jacob gave directions to his sons. He said, "I'm about to join the members of my family who have already died. Bury me with them in the cave in the field of Ephron, the Hittite. The cave is in the field of Machpelah near Mamre in Canaan. Abraham had bought it as a place where he could bury his wife's body. He had bought the cave and the field from Ephron, the Hittite.

The bodies of Abraham and his wife Sarah were buried there. So were the bodies of Isaac and his wife Rebekah. I also buried Leah's body there. Abraham bought the field and the cave from the Hittites."

When Jacob had finished telling his sons what to do, he pulled his feet up into his bed. Then he took his last breath and died. He joined the members of his family who had already died.

Joseph threw himself on his father's body. He wept over him and kissed him. Then Joseph talked to the doctors who served him. He told them to prepare the body of his father Israel to be buried. So the doctors prepared it. They took 40 days to do it. They needed that much time to prepare a body in the right way. The Egyptians mourned for Jacob 70 days.

Jacob's family took his body back to Canaan. They buried him in the cave that Abraham bought to bury his wife Sarah.

Now that their father was dead, Joseph's brothers were worried. They said, "Remember all the bad things we did to Joseph? What if he decides to hold those things against us? What if he pays us back for them?" So they sent a message to Joseph. They said, "Your father gave us directions before he died. He said, 'Here's what you must say to Joseph. Tell him, "I'm asking you to forgive your brothers. Forgive the terrible things they did to you. Forgive them for treating you so badly." ' Now then, please forgive our sins. We serve the God of your father." When their message came to Joseph, he wept.

Then his brothers came and threw themselves down in front of him. "We are your slaves," they said.

But Joseph said to them, "Don't be afraid. Do you think I'm God? You planned to harm me. But God planned it for good. He planned to do what is now being done. He wanted to save many lives. So then, don't be afraid. I'll provide for you and your children." He calmed their fears. And he spoke in a kind way to them.

Joseph stayed in Egypt, along with all his father's family. He lived 110 years. He lived long enough to see Ephraim's children and grandchildren. When the children of Makir were born, they were placed on Joseph's knees and counted as his own children. Makir was the son of Manasseh.

Joseph said to his brothers, "I'm about to die. But God will surely come to help you. He'll take you up out of this land. He'll bring you to the land he promised to give to Abraham, Isaac and Jacob." Joseph made the Israelites promise him. He said, "God will surely come to help you. Then you must carry my bones up from this place."

So Joseph died at the age of 110. They prepared his body to be buried. Then he was placed in a casket in Egypt.

Introduction to Exodus, part 1

As we begin reading the book of Exodus, we see the story take a dark turn.

∽∾∾

Here are the names of Israel's children who went to Egypt with Jacob. Each one went with his family. Jacob's sons were

Reuben, Simeon, Levi, Judah,
Issachar, Zebulun, Benjamin,
Dan, Naphtali,
Gad and Asher.

The total number of Jacob's children and grandchildren was 70. Joseph was already in Egypt.

Joseph and all his brothers died. So did all their children. The people of Israel had many children. The number of them greatly increased. There were so many of them that they filled the land.

Then a new king came to power in Egypt. Joseph didn't mean anything to him. "Look," he said to his people. "The Israelites are far too many for us. Come. We must deal with them carefully. If we don't, there will be even more of them. Then if war breaks out, they'll join our enemies. They'll fight against us and leave the country."

So the Egyptians put slave drivers over the people of Israel. The slave drivers treated them badly and made them work hard. The Israelites built the cities of Pithom and Rameses so Pharaoh could store things there. But the worse the slave drivers treated the Israelites, the more Israelites there were. So the Egyptians became afraid of them. They made them work hard. They didn't show them any pity. The people suffered because of their hard labor. The slave drivers forced them to work with bricks and mud. And they made them do all kinds of work in the fields. The Egyptians didn't show them any pity at all. They made them work very hard.

There were two Hebrew women named Shiphrah and Puah. They helped other women having babies. The king of Egypt spoke to them. He said, "You are the ones who help the other Hebrew women. Watch them when they get into a sitting position to have their babies. Kill the boys. Let the girls live." But Shiphrah and Puah had respect for God. They didn't do what the king of Egypt had told them to do. They let the boys live. Then the king of Egypt sent for the women. He asked them, "Why have you done this? Why have you let the boys live?"

The women answered Pharaoh, "Hebrew women are not like the women of Egypt. They are strong. They have their babies before we get there."

So God was kind to Shiphrah and Puah. And the number of Israelites became even greater. Shiphrah and Puah had respect for God. So he gave them families of their own.

remember what you read

1. What is something you noticed for the first time?

_____

_____

_____

_____

2. What questions did you have?

_____

_____

_____

_____

3. Was there anything that bothered you?

_____

_____

_____

_____

4. What did you learn about loving God?

_____

_____

_____

_____

5. What did you learn about loving others?

_____

_____

_____

_____

introduction to Exodus, parts 2-4

In this section, we meet Moses. He had an amazing meeting and got a special new job. Over the next few sections, we will see how God uses Moses to turn the story of his people around.

Then Pharaoh gave an order to all his people. He said, "You must throw every Hebrew baby boy into the Nile River. But let every Hebrew baby girl live."

A man and a woman from the tribe of Levi got married. She became pregnant and had a son by her husband. She saw that her baby was a fine child. And she hid him for three months. After that, she couldn't hide him any longer. So she got a basket made out of the stems of tall grass. She coated the basket with tar. She placed the child in the basket. Then she put it in the tall grass that grew along the bank of the Nile River. The child's sister wasn't very far away. She wanted to see what would happen to him.

Pharaoh's daughter went down to the Nile River to take a bath. Her attendants were walking along the river bank. She saw the basket in the tall grass. So she sent her female slave to get it. When she opened it, Pharaoh's daughter saw the baby. He was crying. She felt sorry for him. "This is one of the Hebrew babies," she said.

Then his sister spoke to Pharaoh's daughter. She asked, "Do you want me to go and get one of the Hebrew women? She could breast-feed the baby for you."

"Yes. Go," she answered. So the girl went and got the baby's mother. Pharaoh's daughter said to her, "Take this baby and feed him for me. I'll pay you." So the woman took the baby and fed him. When the child grew older, she took him to Pharaoh's daughter. And he became her son. She named him Moses. She said, "I pulled him out of the water."

Moses grew up. One day, he went out to where his own people were. He watched them while they were hard at work. He saw an Egyptian hitting a Hebrew man. The man was one of Moses' own people. Moses looked around and didn't see anyone. So he killed the Egyptian. Then he hid his body in the sand. The next day Moses went out again. He saw two Hebrew men fighting. He asked the one who had started the fight a question. He said, "Why are you hitting another Hebrew man?"

The man said, "Who made you ruler and judge over us? Are you thinking about killing me as you killed the Egyptian?" Then Moses became afraid. He thought, "People must have heard about what I did."

When Pharaoh heard about what had happened, he tried to kill Moses. But Moses escaped from Pharaoh and went to live in Midian. There he sat down by a well. A priest of Midian had seven daughters. They came to fill the stone tubs with water. They wanted to give water to their father's flock. Some shepherds came along and chased the girls away. But Moses got up and helped them. Then he gave water to their flock.

The girls returned to their father Reuel. He asked them, "Why have you returned so early today?"

They answered, "An Egyptian saved us from the shepherds. He even got water for us and gave it to the flock."

"Where is he?" Reuel asked his daughters. "Why did you leave him? Invite him to have something to eat."

Moses agreed to stay with the man. And the man gave his daughter Zipporah to Moses to be his wife. Zipporah had a son by him. Moses named him Gershom. That's because Moses said, "I'm an outsider in a strange land."

After a long time, the king of Egypt died. The people of Israel groaned because they were slaves. They also cried out to God.

Their cry for help went up to him. God heard their groans. He remembered his covenant with Abraham, Isaac and Jacob. So God looked on the Israelites with concern for them.

⁋

Moses was taking care of the flock of his father-in-law Jethro. Jethro was the priest of Midian. Moses led the flock to the western side of the desert. He came to Horeb. It was the mountain of God. There the angel of the LORD appeared to him from inside a burning bush. Moses saw that the bush was on fire. But it didn't burn up. So Moses thought, "I'll go over and see this strange sight. Why doesn't the bush burn up?"

The LORD saw that Moses had gone over to look. So God spoke to him from inside the bush. He called out, "Moses! Moses!"

"Here I am," Moses said.

"Do not come any closer," God said. "Take off your sandals. The place you are standing on is holy ground." He continued, "I am the God of your father. I am the God of Abraham. I am the God of Isaac. And I am the God of Jacob." When Moses heard that, he turned his face away. He was afraid to look at God.

The LORD said, "I have seen how my people are suffering in Egypt. I have heard them cry out because of their slave drivers. I am concerned about their suffering. So I have come down to save them from the Egyptians. I will bring them up out of that land. I will bring them into a good land. It has a lot of room. It is a land that has plenty of milk and honey. The Canaanites, Hittites, Amorites, Perizzites, Hivites and Jebusites live there. And now Israel's cry for help has reached me. I have seen how badly the Egyptians are treating them. So now, go. I am sending you to Pharaoh. I want you to bring the Israelites out of Egypt. They are my people."

But Moses spoke to God. "Who am I that I should go to Pharaoh?" he said. "Who am I that I should bring the Israelites out of Egypt?"

God said, "I will be with you. I will give you a sign. It will prove that I have sent you. When you have brought the people out of Egypt, all of you will worship me on this mountain."

Moses said to God, "Suppose I go to the people of Israel. Suppose I say to them, 'The God of your fathers has sent me to you.' And suppose they ask me, 'What is his name?' Then what should I tell them?"

God said to Moses, "I AM WHO I AM. Here is what you must say to the Israelites. Tell them, 'I AM has sent me to you.'"

God also said to Moses, "Say to the Israelites, 'The LORD is the God of your fathers. He has sent me to you. He is the God of Abraham. He is the God of Isaac. And he is the God of Jacob.' My name will always be The LORD. Call me this name for all time to come.

"Go. Gather the elders of Israel together. Say to them, 'The LORD, the God of your fathers, appeared to me. He is the God of Abraham, Isaac and Jacob. God said, "I have watched over you. I have seen what the Egyptians have done to you. I have promised to bring you up out of Egypt where you are suffering. I will bring you into the land of the Canaanites, Hittites, Amorites, Perizzites, Hivites and Jebusites. It is a land that has plenty of milk and honey."'

"The elders of Israel will listen to you. Then you and the elders must go to the king of Egypt. You must say to him, 'The LORD has met with us. He is the God of the Hebrews. Let us take a journey that lasts about three days. We want to go into the desert to offer sacrifices to the LORD our God.' But I know that the king of Egypt will not let you and your people go. Only a mighty hand could make him do that. So I will reach out my hand. I will strike the Egyptians with all the amazing things I will do. After that, their king will let you go.

"I will cause the Egyptians to treat you in a kind way. Then when you leave, you will not go with your hands empty. Every woman should ask her neighbor and any woman living in her house for things made out of silver and gold. Ask them for clothes too. Put them on your children. In that way, you will take the wealth of Egypt along with you."

Moses answered, "What if the elders of Israel won't believe me? What if they won't listen to me? Suppose they say, 'The LORD didn't appear to you.' Then what should I do?"

The LORD said to him, "What do you have in your hand?"

"A walking stick," he said.

The Lord said, "Throw it on the ground."

So Moses threw it on the ground. It turned into a snake. He ran away from it. Then the Lord said to Moses, "Reach your hand out. Take the snake by the tail." So he reached out and grabbed the snake. It turned back into a walking stick in his hand. The Lord said, "When they see this sign, they will believe that I appeared to you. I am the Lord, the God of their fathers. I am the God of Abraham. I am the God of Isaac. And I am the God of Jacob."

Then the Lord said, "Put your hand inside your coat." So Moses put his hand inside his coat. When he took it out, the skin had become as white as snow. His hand was covered with a skin disease.

"Now put it back into your coat," the Lord said. So Moses put his hand back into his coat. When he took it out, the skin was healthy again. His hand was like the rest of his skin.

Then the Lord said, "Suppose they do not believe you or pay attention to the first sign. Then maybe they will believe the second one. But suppose they do not believe either sign. Suppose they will not listen to you. Then get some water from the Nile River. Pour it on the dry ground. The water you take from the river will turn into blood on the ground."

Moses spoke to the Lord. He said, "Lord, I've never been a good speaker. And I haven't gotten any better since you spoke to me. I don't speak very well at all."

The Lord said to him, "Who makes human beings able to talk? Who makes them unable to hear or speak? Who makes them able to see? Who makes them blind? It is I, the Lord. Now go. I will help you speak. I will teach you what to say."

But Moses said, "Lord, please send someone else to do it."

Then the Lord became very angry with Moses. He said, "What about your brother, Aaron the Levite? I know he can speak well. He is already on his way to meet you. He will be glad to see you. Speak to him. Tell him what to say. I will help both of you speak. I will teach you what to do. He will speak to the people for you. He will be like your mouth. And you will be like God to him. But take this walking stick in your hand. You will be able to do signs with it."

Then Moses went back to his father-in-law Jethro. He said to him, "Let me return to my own people in Egypt. I want to see if any of them are still alive."

Jethro said, "Go. I hope everything goes well with you."

remember what you read

1. What is something you noticed for the first time?

_____

_____

_____

_____

2. What questions did you have?

_____

_____

_____

_____

3. Was there anything that bothered you?

_____

_____

_____

_____

4. What did you learn about loving God?

_____

_____

_____

_____

5. What did you learn about loving others?

_____

_____

_____

_____

The LORD spoke to Moses. He said, "When you return to Egypt, do all the amazing things I have given you the power to do. Do them in the sight of Pharaoh. But I will make him stubborn. He will not let the people go. Then say to Pharaoh, 'The LORD says, "Israel is like an oldest son to me. I told you, 'Let my son go. Then he will be able to worship me.' But you refused to let him go. So I will kill your oldest son."'"

The LORD said to Aaron, "Go into the desert to see Moses." So Aaron greeted Moses at the mountain of God and kissed him. Then Moses told Aaron everything the LORD had sent him to say. Moses also told him about all the signs the LORD had commanded him to do.

Moses and Aaron gathered all the elders of Israel together. Aaron told them everything the LORD had said to Moses. He also performed the signs in the sight of the people. And they believed. They heard that the LORD was concerned about them. He had seen their suffering. So they bowed down and worshiped him.

Later on, Moses and Aaron went to Pharaoh. They said, "The LORD is the God of Israel. He says, 'Let my people go. Then they will be able to hold a feast to honor me in the desert.'"

Pharaoh said, "Who is the LORD? Why should I obey him? Why should I let Israel go? I don't even know the LORD. And I won't let Israel go."

Then Moses and Aaron said, "The God of the Hebrews has met with us. Now let us take a journey that lasts about three days. We want to go into the desert to offer sacrifices to the LORD our God.

If we don't, he might strike us with plagues. Or he might let us be killed by swords."

But the king of Egypt said, "Moses and Aaron, why are you taking the people away from their work? Get back to work!" Pharaoh continued, "There are large numbers of your people in the land. But you are stopping them from working."

That same day Pharaoh gave orders to the slave drivers and the overseers in charge of the people. He said, "Don't give the people any more straw to make bricks. Let them go and get their own straw. But require them to make the same number of bricks as before. Don't lower the number they have to make. They are lazy. That's why they are crying out, 'Let us go. We want to offer sacrifices to our God.' Make them work harder. Then they will be too busy to pay attention to lies."

The Israelite overseers realized they were in trouble. They knew it when they were told, "Don't reduce the number of bricks you are required to make each day." When they left Pharaoh, they found Moses and Aaron waiting to meet them. They said to Moses and Aaron, "We want the LORD to look at what you have done! We want him to judge you for it! We are like a very bad smell to Pharaoh and his officials. You have given them an excuse to kill us with their swords."

Moses returned to talk to the LORD. He said to him, "Why, Lord? Why have you brought trouble on these people? Is this why you sent me? I went to Pharaoh to speak to him in your name. Ever since then, he has brought nothing but trouble on these people. And you haven't saved your people at all."

Then the LORD said to Moses, "Now you will see what I will do to Pharaoh. Because of my powerful hand, he will let the people of Israel go. Because of my mighty hand, he will drive them out of his country."

God continued, "I am the LORD. I appeared to Abraham, Isaac and Jacob as the Mighty God. But I did not show them the full meaning of my name, The LORD. I also made my covenant with them. I promised to give them the land of Canaan. That is where they lived as outsiders. Also, I have heard the groans of the Israelites. The Egyptians are keeping them as slaves. But I have remembered my covenant."

Then the LORD said to Moses, "I have made you like God to Pharaoh. And your brother Aaron will be like a prophet to you. You must say everything I command you to say. Then your brother Aaron must tell Pharaoh to let the people of Israel leave his country. But I will make Pharaoh stubborn. I will multiply the signs and amazing things I will do in Egypt. In spite of that, he will not listen to you. So I will use my powerful hand against Egypt. When I judge them with mighty acts, I will bring my people Israel out like an army on the march. Then the Egyptians will know that I am the LORD. I will reach out my powerful hand against them. I will bring the people of Israel out of Egypt."

Moses and Aaron did exactly as the LORD had commanded them. Moses was 80 years old and Aaron was 83 when they spoke to Pharaoh.

The LORD spoke to Moses and Aaron. He said, "Pharaoh will say to you, 'Do a miracle.' When he does, speak to Aaron. Tell him, 'Take your walking stick and throw it down in front of Pharaoh.' It will turn into a snake."

So Moses and Aaron went to Pharaoh. They did exactly as the LORD had commanded them. Aaron threw the stick down in front of Pharaoh and his officials. It turned into a snake. Then Pharaoh sent for wise men and people who do evil magic. By doing their magic tricks, the Egyptian magicians did the same things Aaron had done. Each one threw down his walking stick. Each stick turned into a snake. But Aaron's walking stick swallowed theirs up. In spite of that, Pharaoh became stubborn. He wouldn't listen to them, just as the LORD had said.

Then the LORD said to Moses, "Pharaoh is very stubborn. He refuses to let the people go. In the morning Pharaoh will go down to the Nile River. Go and meet him on the bank of the river. Take in your hand the walking stick that turned into a snake. Say to Pharaoh, 'The LORD, the God of the Hebrews, has sent me to you. He says, "Let my people go. Then they will be able to worship me in the desert. But up to now you have not listened." The LORD says, "Here is how you will know that I am the LORD. I will strike the water of the Nile River with the walking stick that is in my hand. The river will turn into blood. The fish in the river will die.

The river will stink. The Egyptians will not be able to drink its water." ' "

The LORD said to Moses, "Tell Aaron, 'Get your walking stick. Reach your hand out over the waters of Egypt. The streams, canals, ponds and all the lakes will turn into blood. There will be blood everywhere in Egypt. It will even be in the wooden buckets and stone jars.' "

Moses and Aaron did exactly as the LORD had commanded them. Aaron held out his staff in front of Pharaoh and his officials. He struck the water of the Nile River. And all the water turned into blood. The fish in the Nile died. The river smelled so bad the Egyptians couldn't drink its water. There was blood everywhere in Egypt.

Pharaoh became stubborn. He did not let the Israelites go worship God. After the blood, Moses called several more plagues on Egypt. These included frogs, flies, darkness, and a hailstorm. Each terrible plague showed God's power over one of Egypt's gods. Pharaoh kept refusing to let the Israelites travel to the wilderness to worship God.

The LORD had spoken to Moses. He had said, "I will bring one more plague on Pharaoh and on Egypt. After that, he will let you and your people go. When he does, he will drive every one of you away. Tell the men and women alike to ask their neighbors for things made out of silver and gold." The LORD caused the Egyptians to treat the Israelites in a kind way. Pharaoh's officials and the people had great respect for Moses.

Moses told Pharaoh, "The LORD says, 'About midnight I will go through every part of Egypt. Every oldest son in Egypt will die. The oldest son of Pharaoh, who sits on the throne, will die. The oldest son of every female slave, who works at her hand mill, will die. All the male animals born first to their mothers among the cattle will also die. There will be loud crying all over Egypt. It will be worse than it's ever been before. And nothing like it will ever be heard again. But among the Israelites not even one dog will bark at any person or animal.' Then you will know that the LORD treats Egypt differently from us. All your officials will come and bow down to me. They will say, 'Go, you and all the people who follow you!' After that, I will leave." Moses was very angry when he left Pharaoh.

The LORD spoke to Moses and Aaron in Egypt. He said, "From now on, this month will be your first month. Each of your years will begin with it. Speak to the whole community of Israel. Tell them that on the tenth day of this month each man must get a lamb from his flock. A lamb should be chosen for each family and home. Suppose there are not enough people in your family to eat a whole lamb. Then you must share some of it with your nearest neighbor. You must add up the total number of people there are. You must decide how much lamb is needed for each person. The animals you choose must be males that are a year old. They must not have any flaws. You may choose either sheep or goats. Take care of them until the 14th day of the month. Then the whole community of Israel must kill them when the sun goes down. Take some of the blood. Put it on the sides and tops of the doorframes of the houses where you eat the lambs. That same night eat the meat cooked over a fire. Also eat bitter plants. And eat bread made without yeast. Do not eat the meat when it is raw. Don't boil it in water. Instead, cook it over a fire. Cook the head, legs and inside parts. Do not leave any of it until morning. If some is left over until morning, burn it up. Eat the meat while your coat is tucked into your belt. Put your sandals on your feet. Take your walking stick in your hand. Eat the food quickly. It is the LORD's Passover.

"That same night I will pass through Egypt. I will strike down all those born first among the people and animals. And I will judge all the gods of Egypt. I am the LORD. The blood on your houses will be a sign for you. When I see the blood, I will pass over you. No deadly plague will touch you when I strike Egypt."

At midnight the LORD struck down every oldest son in Egypt. He killed the oldest son of Pharaoh, who sat on the throne. He killed all the oldest sons of prisoners. He also killed all the male animals born first to their mothers among the livestock. Pharaoh and all his officials got up during the night. So did all the Egyptians. There was loud crying in Egypt because someone had died in every home.

During the night, Pharaoh sent for Moses and Aaron. He said to them, "Get out of here! You and the Israelites, leave my people! Go. Worship the LORD, just as you have asked. Go. Take your flocks and herds, just as you have said. And also give me your blessing."

remember what you read

1. What is something you noticed for the first time?

_____

_____

_____

_____

2. What questions did you have?

_____

_____

_____

_____

3. Was there anything that bothered you?

_____

_____

_____

_____

4. What did you learn about loving God?

_____

_____

_____

_____

5. What did you learn about loving others?

_____

_____

_____

_____

The Egyptians begged the people of Israel to hurry up and leave the country. "If you don't," they said, "we'll all die!" So the people took their dough before the yeast was added to it. They carried it on their shoulders in bowls for kneading bread. The bowls were wrapped in clothes. They did just as Moses had directed them. They asked the Egyptians for things made out of silver and gold. They also asked them for clothes. The LORD had caused the Egyptians to treat the Israelites in a kind way. So the Egyptians gave them what they asked for. The Israelites took many expensive things that belonged to the Egyptians.

The Israelites traveled from Rameses to Sukkoth. There were about 600,000 men old enough to go into battle. The women and children went with them. So did many other people. The Israelites also took large flocks and herds with them. The Israelites brought dough from Egypt. With it they baked loaves of bread without yeast. The dough didn't have any yeast in it. That's because the people had been driven out of Egypt before they had time to prepare their food.

The Israelites lived in Egypt for 430 years. Then all the LORD's people marched out of Egypt like an army. That happened at the end of the 430 years, to the exact day. The LORD kept watch that night to bring them out of Egypt. So on that same night every year all the Israelites must keep watch. They must do it to honor the LORD for all time to come.

The LORD said to Moses and Aaron, "Here are the rules for the Passover meal.

"No one from another country is allowed to eat it. Any slave you have bought is allowed to eat it after you have circumcised him.

But a hired worker or someone who lives with you for a short time is not allowed to eat it.

"It must be eaten inside the house. Do not take any of the meat outside. Do not break any of the bones. The whole community of Israel must celebrate the Passover.

"Suppose an outsider living among you wants to celebrate the Lord's Passover. Then all the males in that home must be circumcised. After that, the person can take part, just like an Israelite. Only circumcised males may eat it. The same law applies to Israelites and to outsiders living among you."

All the people of Israel did just what the Lord had commanded Moses and Aaron. On that day the Lord brought the Israelites out of Egypt like an army on the march.

The Lord said to Moses, "Set apart for me the first boy born in every family. The oldest son of every Israelite mother belongs to me. Every male animal born first to its mother also belongs to me."

Then Moses said to the people, "Remember this day. It's the day you came out of Egypt. That's the land where you were slaves. The Lord used his mighty hand to bring you out of Egypt. Don't eat anything with yeast in it. You are leaving today. It's the month of Aviv. The Lord will bring you into the land of the Canaanites, Hittites, Amorites, Hivites and Jebusites. He promised your people of long ago that he would give that land to you. It's a land that has plenty of milk and honey. When you get there, celebrate this holy day in this month. For seven days eat bread made without yeast. On the seventh day hold a feast to honor the Lord. Eat bread made without yeast during those seven days. Nothing with yeast in it should be found among you. No yeast should be seen anywhere inside your borders. On that day talk to your child. Say, 'I'm doing this because of what the Lord did for me when I came out of Egypt.' When you celebrate this holy day, it will be like a mark on your hand. It will be like a reminder on your forehead. This law of the Lord must be on your lips. The Lord used his mighty hand to bring you out of Egypt. Obey this law at the appointed time year after year.

"In days to come, your child will ask you, 'What does this mean?'

Say to them, 'The Lord used his mighty hand to bring us out of Egypt. That's the land where we were slaves. Pharaoh was stubborn. He refused to let us go. So the Lord killed every oldest son in Egypt. He also killed all those born first among the people and animals. That's why I sacrifice to the Lord every male animal born first. And that's why I buy back each of my oldest sons for the Lord.' This holy day will be like a mark on your hand. It will be like a sign on your forehead. It will remind you that the Lord used his mighty hand to bring us out of Egypt."

Pharaoh let the people go. The shortest road from Goshen to Canaan went through the Philistine country. But God didn't lead them that way. God said, "If they have to go into battle, they might change their minds. They might return to Egypt." So God led the people toward the Red Sea by taking them on a road through the desert. The Israelites were ready for battle when they went up out of Egypt.

Moses took the bones of Joseph along with him. Joseph had made the Israelites give their word to do this. He had said, "God will surely come to help you. When he does, you must carry my bones up from this place with you."

The people left Sukkoth. They camped at Etham on the edge of the desert. By day the Lord went ahead of them in a pillar of cloud. It guided them on their way. At night he led them with a pillar of fire. It gave them light. So they could travel by day or at night. The pillar of cloud didn't leave its place in front of the people during the day. And the pillar of fire didn't leave its place at night.

Then the Lord spoke to Moses. He said, "Tell the people of Israel to turn back. Have them camp near Pi Hahiroth between Migdol and the Red Sea. They must camp by the sea, right across from Baal Zephon. Pharaoh will think, 'The Israelites are wandering around the land. They don't know which way to go. The desert is all around them.' I will make Pharaoh stubborn. He will chase them. But I will gain glory for myself because of what will happen to Pharaoh and his whole army. And the Egyptians will know that I am the Lord." So the Israelites camped by the Red Sea.

The king of Egypt was told that the people had escaped. Then Pharaoh and his officials changed their minds about them. They said, "What have we done? We've let the people of Israel go! We've lost our slaves and all the work they used to do for us!" So he had his chariot made ready. He took his army with him. He took 600 of the best chariots in Egypt. He also took along all the other chariots. Officers were in charge of all of them. The LORD made Pharaoh, the king of Egypt, stubborn. So he chased the Israelites as they were marching out boldly. The Egyptians went after the Israelites. All Pharaoh's horses and chariots and horsemen and troops chased them. They caught up with the Israelites as they camped by the sea. The Israelites were near Pi Hahiroth, across from Baal Zephon.

As Pharaoh approached, the Israelites looked back. There were the Egyptians marching after them! The Israelites were terrified. They cried out to the LORD. They said to Moses, "Why did you bring us to the desert to die? Weren't there any graves in Egypt? What have you done to us by bringing us out of Egypt? We told you in Egypt, 'Leave us alone. Let us serve the Egyptians.' It would have been better for us to serve the Egyptians than to die here in the desert!"

Moses answered the people. He said, "Don't be afraid. Stand firm. You will see how the LORD will save you today. Do you see those Egyptians? You will never see them again. The LORD will fight for you. Just be still."

Then the LORD spoke to Moses. He said, "Why are you crying out to me? Tell the people of Israel to move on. Hold out your walking stick. Reach out your hand over the Red Sea to divide the water. Then the people can go through the sea on dry ground. I will make the Egyptians stubborn. They will go in after the Israelites. I will gain glory for myself because of what will happen to Pharaoh, his army, chariots and horsemen. The Egyptians will know that I am the LORD. I will gain glory because of what will happen to Pharaoh, his chariots and his horsemen."

The angel of God had been traveling in front of Israel's army. Now he moved back and went behind them. The pillar of cloud also moved away from in front of them. Now it stood behind them. It came between the armies of Egypt and Israel. All through the night the cloud brought darkness to one side and light to the other. Neither army went near the other all night long.

Then Moses reached out his hand over the Red Sea. All that night the LORD pushed the sea back with a strong east wind. He turned the sea into dry land. The waters were divided. The people of Israel went through the sea on dry ground. There was a wall of water on their right side and on their left.

The Egyptians chased them. All Pharaoh's horses and chariots and horsemen followed them into the sea. Near the end of the night the LORD looked down from the pillar of fire and cloud. He saw the Egyptian army and threw it into a panic. He jammed the wheels of their chariots. That made the chariots hard to drive. The Egyptians said, "Let's get away from the Israelites! The LORD is fighting for Israel against Egypt."

Then the LORD spoke to Moses. He said, "Reach out your hand over the sea. The waters will flow back over the Egyptians and their chariots and horsemen." So Moses reached out his hand over the sea. At sunrise the sea went back to its place. The Egyptians tried to run away from the sea. But the LORD swept them into it. The water flowed back and covered the chariots and horsemen. It covered the entire army of Pharaoh that had followed the people of Israel into the sea. Not one of the Egyptians was left.

But the Israelites went through the sea on dry ground. There was a wall of water on their right side and on their left. That day the LORD saved Israel from the power of Egypt. The Israelites saw the Egyptians lying dead on the shore. The Israelites saw the amazing power the LORD showed against the Egyptians. So the Israelites had great respect for the LORD and put their trust in him. They also put their trust in his servant Moses.

Aaron's sister Miriam was a prophet. She took a tambourine in her hand. All the women followed her. They played tambourines and danced. Miriam sang to them,

"Sing to the LORD.
   He is greatly honored.
He has thrown Pharaoh's horses and chariot drivers
   into the Red Sea."

remember what you read

1. What is something you noticed for the first time?

_____

_____

_____

_____

2. What questions did you have?

_____

_____

_____

_____

3. Was there anything that bothered you?

_____

_____

_____

_____

4. What did you learn about loving God?

_____

_____

_____

_____

5. What did you learn about loving others?

_____

_____

_____

_____

EXODUS, PART 5

introduction to Exodus, parts 5-7

God delivered his people from slavery in Egypt. Over the next three days, we will read how he took care of them in the wilderness after they left Egypt. We'll also see how God made a covenant, a very serious agreement, with his people. This covenant made them into God's special nation. And this nation would fulfill God's promise to Abraham that his people would bless all nations. But the people didn't always keep their part of the agreement. God even wanted to live with his people. He gave Moses plans for a beautiful tent that would be his house in the middle of the camp.

⟳⟳⟳

Then Moses led Israel away from the Red Sea. They went into the Desert of Shur. For three days they traveled in the desert. They didn't find any water there. When they came to Marah, they couldn't drink its water. It was bitter. That's why the place is named Marah. The people told Moses they weren't happy with him. They said, "What are we supposed to drink?"

Then Moses cried out to the LORD. The LORD showed him a stick. Moses threw it into the water. The water became fit to drink.

There the LORD gave a ruling and instruction for the people. And there he tested them. He said, "I am the LORD your God. Listen carefully to me. Do what is right in my eyes. Pay attention to my commands. Obey all my rules. If you do, I will not send on you any of the sicknesses I sent on the Egyptians. I am the LORD who heals you."

The people came to Elim. It had 12 springs and 70 palm trees. They camped there near the water.

The whole community of Israel started out from Elim. They came to the Desert of Sin. It was between Elim and Sinai. They arrived there on the 15th day of the second month after they had come out of Egypt. In the desert the whole community told Moses and Aaron they weren't happy with them. The Israelites said to them, "We wish the LORD had put us to death in Egypt. There we sat around pots of meat. We ate all the food we wanted. But you have brought us out into this desert. You must want this entire community to die of hunger."

Then the LORD spoke to Moses. He said, "I will rain down bread from heaven for you. The people must go out each day. Have them gather enough bread for that day. Here is how I will test them. I will see if they will follow my directions. On the sixth day they must prepare what they bring in. On that day they must gather twice as much as on the other days."

So Moses and Aaron spoke to all the people of Israel. They said, "In the evening you will know that the LORD brought you out of Egypt. And in the morning you will see the glory of the LORD. He has heard you say you aren't happy with him. Who are we? Why are you telling us you aren't happy with us?" Moses also said, "You will know that the LORD has heard you speak against him. He will give you meat to eat in the evening. He'll give you all the bread you want in the morning. But who are we? You aren't speaking against us. You are speaking against the LORD."

Then Moses told Aaron, "Talk to the whole community of Israel. Say to them, 'Come to the LORD. He has heard you speak against him.'"

While Aaron was talking to the whole community of Israel, they looked toward the desert. There was the glory of the LORD appearing in the cloud!

The LORD said to Moses, "I have heard the people of Israel talking about how unhappy they are. Tell them, 'When the sun goes down, you will eat meat. In the morning you will be filled with bread. Then you will know that I am the LORD your God.'"

That evening quail came and covered the camp. In the morning the ground around the camp was covered with dew. When the dew was gone, thin flakes appeared on the desert floor. They looked like frost on the ground. The people of Israel saw the flakes. They asked each other, "What's that?" They didn't know what it was.

Moses said to them, "It's the bread the LORD has given you to eat. Here is what the LORD has commanded. He has said, 'Everyone should gather as much as they need. Take three pounds for each person who lives in your tent.'"

The people of Israel did as they were told. Some gathered a lot, and some gathered a little. When they measured it out, the one who gathered a lot didn't have too much. And the one who gathered a little had enough. Everyone gathered only what they needed.

Then Moses said to them, "Don't keep any of it until morning."

Some of them didn't pay any attention to Moses. They kept part of it until morning. But it was full of maggots and began to stink. So Moses became angry with them.

Each morning everyone gathered as much as they needed. But by the hottest time of the day, the thin flakes had melted away. On the sixth day, the people gathered twice as much. It amounted to six pounds for each person. The leaders of the community came and reported that to Moses. He said to them, "Here is what the LORD commanded. He said, 'Tomorrow will be a day of rest. It will be a holy Sabbath day. It will be set apart for the LORD. So bake what you want to bake. Boil what you want to boil. Save what is left. Keep it until morning.'"

So they saved it until morning, just as Moses commanded. It didn't stink or get maggots in it. "Eat it today," Moses said. "Today is a Sabbath day to honor the LORD. You won't find any flakes on the ground today. Gather them for six days. But on the seventh day there won't be any. It's the Sabbath day."

The people of Israel called the bread manna. It was white like coriander seeds. It tasted like wafers made with honey. Moses said, "Here is what the LORD has commanded. He has said, 'Get three pounds of manna. Keep it for all time to come. Then those who live after you will see the bread I gave you to eat in the desert. I gave it to you when I brought you out of Egypt.'"

Aaron did exactly as the LORD had commanded Moses. He put the manna with the tablets of the covenant law. He put it there so it would be kept for all time to come. The Israelites ate manna for 40 years. They ate it until they came to a land where people were living. They ate it until they reached the border of Canaan.

The whole community of Israel started out from the Desert of Sin. They traveled from place to place, just as the LORD commanded. They camped at Rephidim. But there wasn't any water for the people to drink. So they argued with Moses. They said, "Give us water to drink."

Moses replied, "Why are you arguing with me? Why are you testing the LORD?"

But the people were thirsty for water there. So they told Moses they weren't happy with him. They said, "Why did you bring us up out of Egypt? Did you want us, our children and our livestock to die of thirst?"

Then Moses cried out to the LORD. He said, "What am I going to do with these people? They are almost ready to kill me by throwing stones at me."

The LORD answered Moses. "Go out in front of the people. Take some of the elders of Israel along with you. Take in your hand the walking stick you used when you struck the Nile River. Go. I will stand there in front of you by the rock at Mount Horeb. Hit the rock. Then water will come out of it for the people to drink." So Moses hit the rock while the elders of Israel watched. Moses called the place Massah and Meribah. That's because the people of Israel argued with him there. They also tested the LORD. They asked, "Is the LORD among us or not?"

The Amalekites came and attacked the Israelites at Rephidim. Moses said to Joshua, "Choose some of our men. Then go out and fight against the Amalekites. Tomorrow I will stand on top of the hill. I'll stand there holding the walking stick God gave me."

So Joshua fought against the Amalekites, just as Moses had ordered. Moses, Aaron and Hur went to the top of the hill. As long as Moses held up his hand, the Israelites were winning. But every time he lowered his hands, the Amalekites began to win. When Moses' arms got tired, Aaron and Hur got a stone and put it under him. Then he sat on it. Aaron and Hur held up his hands. Aaron was on one side, and Hur was on the other. Moses' hands remained steady until sunset. So Joshua destroyed the Amalekite army with swords.

Then the Lord said to Moses, "This is something to be remembered. So write it on a scroll. Make sure Joshua knows you have done it. I will completely erase the memory of the Amalekites from the earth."

Then Moses built an altar. He called it The Lord Is My Banner. He said, "The Amalekites opposed the authority of the Lord. So the Lord will fight against the Amalekites for all time to come."

Exactly three months after the people of Israel left Egypt, they came to the Desert of Sinai. After they started out from Rephidim, they entered the Desert of Sinai. They camped there in the desert in front of the mountain.

Then Moses went up to God. The Lord called out to him from the mountain. He said, "Here is what I want you to say to my people, who belong to Jacob's family. Tell the Israelites, 'You have seen for yourselves what I did to Egypt. You saw how I carried you on the wings of eagles and brought you to myself. Now obey me completely. Keep my covenant. If you do, then out of all the nations you will be my special treasure. The whole earth is mine. But you will be a kingdom of priests to serve me. You will be my holy nation.' That is what you must tell the Israelites."

So Moses went back. He sent for the elders of the people. He explained to them everything the Lord had commanded him to say. All the people answered together. They said, "We will do everything the Lord has said." So Moses brought their answer back to the Lord.

The Lord spoke to Moses. He said, "I am going to come to you in a thick cloud. The people will hear me speaking with you. They will always put their trust in you." Then Moses told the Lord what the people had said.

The Lord said to Moses, "Go to the people. Today and tomorrow set them apart for me. Have them wash their clothes. Have the people ready by the third day. On that day the Lord will come down on Mount Sinai. Everyone will see it. Put limits for the people around the mountain. Tell them, 'Be careful that you do not go near the mountain. Do not even touch the foot of it. Whoever touches the mountain must be put to death. Do not lay a hand on any of them. Kill them with stones or shoot them with arrows. Whether they are people or animals, do not let them live.' They may go near the mountain only when the ram's horn gives out a long blast."

Moses went down the mountain to the people. After he set them apart for the Lord, they washed their clothes. Then he spoke to the people. He said, "Get ready for the third day."

remember what you read

1. What is something you noticed for the first time?

_____

_____

_____

_____

2. What questions did you have?

_____

_____

_____

_____

3. Was there anything that bothered you?

_____

_____

_____

_____

4. What did you learn about loving God?

_____

_____

_____

_____

5. What did you learn about loving others?

_____

_____

_____

_____

On the morning of the third day there was thunder and lightning. A thick cloud covered the mountain. A trumpet gave out a very loud blast. Everyone in the camp trembled with fear. Then Moses led the people out of the camp to meet with God. They stood at the foot of the mountain. Smoke covered Mount Sinai, because the LORD came down on it in fire. The smoke rose up from it like smoke from a furnace. The whole mountain trembled and shook. The sound of the trumpet got louder and louder. Then Moses spoke. And the voice of God answered him.

The LORD came down to the top of Mount Sinai. He told Moses to come to the top of the mountain. So Moses went up. The LORD said to him, "Go down and warn the people. They must not force their way through to see the LORD. If they do, many of them will die. The priests approach the LORD when they serve him. But even they must set themselves apart for the LORD. If they do not, his anger will break out against them."

Moses said to the LORD, "The people can't come up Mount Sinai. You yourself warned us. You said, 'Put limits around the mountain. Set it apart as holy.'"

Here are all the words God spoke. He said,

"I am the LORD your God. I brought you out of Egypt. That is the land where you were slaves.

"Do not put any other gods in place of me.

"Do not make for yourself statues of gods that look like anything in the sky. They may not look like anything on the earth or in the waters either. Do not bow down to them or

103

worship them. I, the LORD your God, am a jealous God. I cause the sins of the parents to affect their children. I will cause the sins of those who hate me to affect even their grandchildren and great-grandchildren. But for all time to come I show love to all those who love me and keep my commandments.

"Do not misuse the name of the LORD your God. The LORD will find guilty anyone who misuses his name.

"Remember to keep the Sabbath day holy. Do all your work in six days. But the seventh day is a sabbath to honor the LORD your God. Do not do any work on that day. The same command applies to your sons and daughters, your male and female servants, and your animals. It also applies to any outsiders who live in your towns. In six days the LORD made the heavens, the earth, the sea and everything in them. But he rested on the seventh day. So the LORD blessed the Sabbath day and made it holy.

"Honor your father and mother. Then you will live a long time in the land the LORD your God is giving you.

"Do not murder.

"Do not commit adultery.

"Do not steal.

"Do not be a false witness against your neighbor.

"Do not want to have anything your neighbor owns. Do not want to have your neighbor's house, wife, male or female servant, ox or donkey."

The people saw the thunder and lightning. They heard the trumpet. They saw the mountain covered with smoke. They trembled with fear and stayed a long way off. They said to Moses, "Speak to us yourself. Then we'll listen. But don't let God speak to us. If he does, we'll die."

Moses said to the people, "Don't be afraid. God has come to test you. He wants you to have respect for him. That will keep you from sinning."

Moses approached the thick darkness where God was. But the people remained a long way off.

God gave Moses laws to make sure that servants were treated well, that people who hurt or killed others were punished, and that people paid fairly for damages or injuries they or their animals caused.

"I am sending an angel ahead of you. He will guard you along the way. He will bring you to the place I have prepared. Pay attention to him. Listen to what he says. Do not refuse to obey him. He will not forgive you if you turn against him. He has my full authority. Listen carefully to what he says. Do everything I say. Then I will be an enemy to your enemies. I will fight against those who fight against you. My angel will go ahead of you. He will bring you into the land of the Amorites, Hittites, Perizzites, Canaanites, Hivites and Jebusites. I will wipe them out. Do not do what they do. Do not bow down to their gods or worship them. You must destroy the statues of their gods. You must break their sacred stones to pieces. Worship the LORD your God. Then he will bless your food and water. I, the LORD, will take away any sickness you may have. In your land no woman will give birth to a dead baby. Every woman will be able to have children. I will give you a long life.

"I will send my terror ahead of you. I will throw every nation you meet into a panic. I will make all your enemies turn their backs and run away. I will send hornets ahead of you. They will drive the Hivites, Canaanites and Hittites out of your way. But I will not drive them out in just one year. If I did, the land would be deserted. There would be too many wild animals for you. I will drive them out ahead of you little by little. I will do that until there are enough of you to take control of the land.

"I will make your borders secure from the Red Sea to the Mediterranean Sea. They will go from the desert to the Euphrates River. I will hand over to you the people who live in the land. You will drive them out to make room for yourselves. Do not make a covenant with them or with their gods. Do not let them live in your land. If you do, they will cause you to sin against me. If you worship their gods, that will certainly be a trap for you."

Moses went and told the people all the LORD's words and laws. They answered with one voice. They said, "We will do everything the LORD has told us to do." Then Moses wrote down everything the LORD had said.

Moses got up early the next morning. He built an altar at the foot of the mountain. He set up 12 stone pillars. They stood for the 12 tribes of Israel. Then he sent young Israelite men to sacrifice burnt offerings. They also sacrificed young bulls as friendship offerings to the LORD. Moses put half of the blood in bowls. He splashed the other half against the altar. Then he took the Book of the Covenant and read it to the people. They answered, "We will do everything the LORD has told us to do. We will obey him."

Then Moses took the blood and sprinkled it on the people. He said, "This is the blood that puts the covenant into effect. The LORD has made this covenant with you in keeping with all these words."

Moses and Aaron, Nadab and Abihu, and the 70 elders of Israel went up. They saw the God of Israel. Under his feet was something like a street made out of lapis lazuli. It was as bright blue as the sky itself. But God didn't destroy those Israelite leaders when they saw him. They ate and drank.

The LORD said to Moses, "Come up to me on the mountain. Stay here. I will give you the stone tablets. They contain the law and commandments I have written to teach the people."

Then Moses and Joshua, his helper, started out. Moses went up on the mountain of God. He said to the elders, "Wait for us here until we come back to you. Aaron and Hur are with you. Anyone who has a problem can go to them."

Moses went up on the mountain. Then the cloud covered it. The glory of the LORD settled on Mount Sinai. The cloud covered the mountain for six days. On the seventh day the LORD called out to Moses from inside the cloud. The people of Israel saw the glory of the LORD. It looked like a fire burning on top of the mountain. Moses entered the cloud as he went on up the mountain. He stayed on the mountain for 40 days and 40 nights.

The LORD finished speaking to Moses on Mount Sinai. Then he gave him the two tablets of the covenant law. They were made out of stone. The words on them were written by the finger of God.

The people saw that Moses took a long time to come down from the mountain. So they gathered around Aaron. They said to him, "Come. Make us a god that will lead us. This fellow Moses brought us up out of Egypt. But we don't know what has happened to him."

Aaron answered them, "Take the gold earrings off your wives, your sons and your daughters. Bring the earrings to me." So all the people took off their earrings. They brought them to Aaron. He took what they gave him and made it into a metal statue of a god. It looked like a calf. Aaron shaped it with a tool. Then the people said, "Israel, here is your god who brought you up out of Egypt."

When Aaron saw what they were doing, he built an altar in front of the calf. He said, "Tomorrow will be a feast day to honor the Lord." So the next day the people got up early. They sacrificed burnt offerings and brought friendship offerings. They sat down to eat and drink. Then they got up to dance wildly in front of their god.

The Lord spoke to Moses. He said, "Go down. Your people you brought up out of Egypt have become very sinful. They have quickly turned away from what I commanded them. They have made themselves a metal statue of a god in the shape of a calf. They have bowed down and sacrificed to it. And they have said, 'Israel, here is your god who brought you up out of Egypt.'

"I have seen these people," the Lord said to Moses. "They are stubborn. Now leave me alone. I will destroy them because of my great anger. Then I will make you into a great nation."

But Moses asked the Lord his God to have mercy on the people. "Lord," he said, "why should you destroy your people in anger? You used your great power and mighty hand to bring them out of Egypt. Why should the Egyptians say, 'He brought them out to hurt them. He wanted to kill them in the mountains. He wanted to wipe them off the face of the earth'? Turn away from your great anger. Please take pity on your people. Don't destroy them! Remember your servants Abraham, Isaac and Israel. You made a promise to them in your own name. You said, 'I will make your children after you as many as the stars in the sky. I will give them all this land I promised them. It will belong to them forever.'" Then the Lord took pity on his people. He didn't destroy them as he had said he would.

Moses turned and went down the mountain. He had the two tablets of the covenant law in his hands. Words were written on both sides of the tablets, front and back. The tablets were the work of God. The words had been written by God. They had been carved on the tablets.

Joshua heard the noise of the people shouting. So he said to Moses, "It sounds like war in the camp."

Moses replied,

"It's not the sound of winning.
It's not the sound of losing.
It's the sound of singing that I hear."

remember what you read

1. What is something you noticed for the first time?

_____

_____

_____

_____

2. What questions did you have?

_____

_____

_____

_____

3. Was there anything that bothered you?

_____

_____

_____

_____

4. What did you learn about loving God?

_____

_____

_____

_____

5. What did you learn about loving others?

_____

_____

_____

_____

As Moses approached the camp, he saw the calf. He also saw the people dancing. So he was very angry. He threw the tablets out of his hands. They broke into pieces at the foot of the mountain. He took the calf the people had made. He burned it in the fire. Then he ground it into powder. He scattered it on the water. And he made the Israelites drink it.

He said to Aaron, "What did these people do to you? How did they make you lead them into such terrible sin?"

"Please don't be angry," Aaron answered. "You know how these people like to do what is evil. They said to me, 'Make us a god that will lead us. This fellow Moses brought us up out of Egypt. But we don't know what has happened to him.' So I told them, 'Anyone who has any gold jewelry, take it off.' They gave me the gold. I threw it into the fire. And out came this calf!"

So Moses went back to the LORD. He said, "These people have committed a terrible sin. They have made a god out of gold for themselves. Now please forgive their sin. But if you won't, then erase my name out of the book you have written."

The LORD replied to Moses. The LORD said, "I will erase out of my book only the names of those who have sinned against me. Now go. Lead the people to the place I spoke about. My angel will go ahead of you. But when the time comes for me to punish, I will punish them for their sin."

The LORD struck the people with a plague. That's because of what they did with the calf Aaron had made.

Then the LORD said to Moses, "Leave this place. You and the people you brought up out of Egypt must leave it. Go up to the land I promised to give to Abraham, Isaac and Jacob. I said to them, 'I will give it to your children after you.' I will send an angel ahead of you. I will drive out the Canaanites, Amorites, Hittites, Perizzites, Hivites and Jebusites. Go up to the land that has plenty of milk and honey. But I will not go with you. You are stubborn. I might destroy you on the way."

Moses said to the Lord, "You have been telling me, 'Lead these people.' But you haven't let me know whom you will send with me. You have said, 'I know your name. I know all about you. And I am pleased with you.' If you are pleased with me, teach me more about yourself. Then I can know you. And I can continue to please you. Remember that this nation is your people."

The Lord replied, "I will go with you. And I will give you rest."

Then Moses said to him, "If you don't go with us, don't send us up from here. How will anyone know that you are pleased with me and your people? You must go with us. How else will we be different from all the other people on the face of the earth?"

The Lord said to Moses, "I will do exactly what you have asked. I am pleased with you. And I know your name. I know all about you."

Then Moses said, "Now show me your glory."

The Lord said, "I will make all my goodness pass in front of you. And I will announce my name, the Lord, in front of you. I will have mercy on whom I have mercy. And I will show love to those I love. But you can't see my face," he said. "No one can see me and stay alive."

The Lord continued, "There is a place near me where you can stand on a rock. When my glory passes by, I will put you in an opening in the rock. I will cover you with my hand until I have passed by. Then I will remove my hand. You will see my back. But my face must not be seen."

The Lord said to Moses, "Cut out two stone tablets that are just like the first ones. I will write on them the words that were on the first tablets, which you broke. Be ready in the morning. Then come up on Mount Sinai. Meet with me there on top of the mountain. No one must come with you. No one must be seen anywhere on the mountain. Not even the flocks and herds must be allowed to eat grass in front of the mountain."

So Moses carved out two stone tablets just like the first ones. Early in the morning he went up Mount Sinai. He carried the two stone tablets in his hands. He did as the LORD had commanded him to do. Then the LORD came down in the cloud. He stood there with Moses and announced his name, the LORD. As he passed in front of Moses, he called out. He said, "I am the LORD, the LORD. I am the God who is tender and kind. I am gracious. I am slow to get angry. I am faithful and full of love. I continue to show my love to thousands of people. I forgive those who do evil. I forgive those who refuse to obey me. And I forgive those who sin. But I do not let guilty people go without punishing them. I cause the sins of the parents to affect their children, grandchildren and great-grandchildren."

Moses bowed down to the ground at once and worshiped. "Lord," he said, "if you are pleased with me, then go with us. Even though these people are stubborn, forgive the evil things we have done. Forgive our sin. And accept us as your people."

Moses came down from Mount Sinai. He had the two tablets of the covenant law in his hands. His face was shining because he had spoken with the LORD. But he didn't realize it. Aaron and all the people of Israel saw Moses. His face was shining. So they were afraid to come near him. But Moses called out to them. So Aaron and all the leaders of the community came to him. And Moses spoke to them. After that, all the Israelites came near him. And he gave them all the commands the LORD had given him on Mount Sinai.

Moses finished speaking to them. Then he covered his face with a veil. But when he would go to speak with the LORD, he would remove the veil. He would keep it off until he came out. Then he would tell the people what the LORD had commanded. They would see that his face was shining. So Moses would cover his face with the veil again. He would keep it on until he went in again to speak with the LORD.

Moses gathered the whole community of Israel together. He said to them, "Here are the things the LORD has commanded you to do. You must do your work in six days. But the seventh day will be your holy day. It will be a day of sabbath rest to honor the LORD.

You must rest on it. Anyone who does any work on it must be put to death. Do not even light a fire in any of your homes on the Sabbath day."

Moses spoke to the whole community of Israel. He said, "Here is what the LORD has commanded. Take an offering for the LORD from what you have. Those who want to can bring an offering to the LORD. Here is what they can bring.

"gold, silver and bronze
blue, purple and bright red yarn and fine linen
goat hair
ram skins that are dyed red
another kind of strong leather
acacia wood
olive oil for the lights
spices for the anointing oil and for the sweet-smelling incense
onyx stones and other jewels for the linen apron and the chest
    cloth

"All the skilled workers among you must come. They must make everything the LORD has commanded for the holy tent and its covering. Here is what they must make.

"hooks, frames, crossbars, posts and bases
the ark of the covenant law, the poles and cover for the ark,
    and the curtain that hides the ark
the table for the holy bread, the poles and all the things for the
    table, and the holy bread
the lampstand for light and everything used with it, the lamps,
    and the olive oil that gives light
the altar for burning incense, the poles for the altar, the
    anointing oil and the sweet-smelling incense
the curtain for the entrance to the holy tent
the altar for burnt offerings with its bronze grate, its poles and
    all its tools
the large bronze bowl with its stand
the curtains of the courtyard with their posts and bases, and
    the curtain for the entrance to the courtyard

the ropes and tent stakes for the holy tent and for the courtyard
and the sacred clothes for Aaron the priest and the clothes for
his sons when they serve as priests."

*The Israelites brought a huge amount of gifts to build the holy tent.
Moses made sure the workers made everything exactly as God had
commanded.*

remember what you read

1. What is something you noticed for the first time?

_____

_____

_____

_____

2. What questions did you have?

_____

_____

_____

_____

3. Was there anything that bothered you?

_____

_____

_____

_____

4. What did you learn about loving God?

_____

_____

_____

_____

5. What did you learn about loving others?

_____

_____

_____

_____

introduction to Leviticus

The book of Leviticus gives many rules about how to be God's people. His people were set apart to live well and not do evil things. The people were supposed to follow these rules to be God's special people. When the world saw how they lived, they could join them as God's single family.

෨෨෨

The LORD called out to Moses. He spoke to him from the tent of meeting.

He told Moses what kind of offerings the Israelites should bring when they wanted to be forgiven for their sins, or when they wanted to keep a promise they made when they asked for help, or when they wanted to share God's blessings with their family and friends and people in need.

The Lord also told Moses to make some special offerings and to put some special clothes on Aaron and his sons to set them apart as priests. He explained how Aaron should come into the Most Holy Room once a year with a sacrifice to pay for all the sin of the Israelites. He told Moses the priests should follow special rules about getting married, crying for the dead, and eating the meat from the sacred offerings. They should keep a lamp burning in the tent of meeting all the time. They should also put fresh bread there every day as a reminder that all good things come from the Lord.

While speaking to Moses from the tent of meeting, the Lord also explained what foods the Israelites should and shouldn't eat if they wanted to stay "clean." He said to take special care of a woman who'd just had a baby. The Lord also gave Moses and Aaron rules about skin diseases and about mold in clothes and in houses, and about people who had blood or other liquid flowing from their bodies.

The Lord told all the Israelites not to eat blood because "blood is life" and that's why it can pay for people's sins. The Lord also told Moses that married people should keep their promises to each other.

The LORD spoke to Moses. He said, "Speak to the whole community of Israel. Tell them, 'Be holy, because I am holy. I am the LORD your God.

" 'All of you must have respect for your mother and father. You must always keep my Sabbath days. I am the LORD your God.

" 'Do not turn away from me to worship statues of gods. Do not make for yourselves metal statues of gods. I am the LORD your God.

" 'Suppose you are harvesting your crops. Then do not harvest all the way to the edges of your field. And do not pick up the grain you missed. Do not go over your vineyard a second time. Do not pick up the grapes that have fallen to the ground. Leave them for poor people and outsiders. I am the LORD your God.

" 'Do not steal.

" 'Do not tell lies.

" 'Do not cheat one another.

" 'Do not give your word in my name and then be a false witness. That would be treating the name of your God as if it were not holy. I am the LORD.

" 'Do not cheat your neighbor. Do not rob him.

" 'Do not hold back the pay of a hired worker until morning.

" 'Do not ask for bad things to happen to deaf people. Do not put anything in front of blind people that will make them trip. Instead, have respect for me. I am the LORD your God.

" 'Do not make something wrong appear to be right. Treat poor people and rich people in the same way. Do not favor one person over another. Instead, judge everyone fairly.

" 'Do not go around spreading lies among your people.

" 'Do not do anything that puts your neighbor's life in danger. I am the LORD.

" 'Do not hate another Israelite in your heart. Correct your neighbor boldly when they do something wrong. Then you will not share their guilt.

" 'Do not try to get even. Do not hold anything against any of your people. Instead, love your neighbor as you love yourself. I am the LORD.

" 'When you enter the land, suppose you plant a fruit tree. Then do not eat its fruit for the first three years. The fruit is "unclean." In the fourth year all the fruit will be holy. Offer it as a way of showing praise to me. But in the fifth year you can eat the fruit. Then you will gather more and more fruit. I am the LORD your God.

" 'You must always keep my Sabbath days. Have respect for my sacred tent. I am the LORD.

" 'Do not look for advice from people who get messages from those who have died. Do not go to people who talk to the spirits of the dead. If you do, they will make you "unclean." I am the LORD your God.

" 'Stand up in order to show your respect for old people. Also have respect for me. I am the LORD your God.

" 'Suppose an outsider lives with you in your land. Then do not treat them badly. Treat them as if they were one of your own people. Love them as you love yourself. Remember that all of you were outsiders in Egypt. I am the LORD your God.

" 'Be honest when you measure lengths, weights or amounts. Use honest scales and honest weights. Use honest dry measures. And use honest liquid measures. I am the LORD your God. I brought you out of Egypt.

" 'Obey all my rules and laws. Follow them. I am the LORD.' "

The Lord told Moses to have the Israelites celebrate some special times. The seventh day of each week was a Sabbath day to honor the Lord. The people shouldn't work on that day. During the year they should also celebrate special holidays like Passover, the offering of the first grain, and the Feast of Booths. Every seventh year they should not farm the land so it could have a rest. Every 50 years all Hebrew servants would be set free and any land that had been sold would be returned to its first owner.

The Lord promised that if the Israelites worshiped only him and carefully obeyed his commands, they would have good crops and peace in their land. But if they didn't, they wouldn't have good crops, their enemies would attack them, and finally they would be taken away from the land. But even after all that, the Lord would still remember his covenant with Abraham and not give up on them.

The Lord told Moses all these things while speaking to him from the tent of meeting. It took a whole month for the Lord to tell him everything.

introduction to Numbers, part 1

The Book of Numbers tells more of the story of how God traveled with Israel in the wilderness.

♈︎

The Lord told Moses which tribes should camp on the different sides of the tent of meeting. He explained the order they should break camp and march out when they traveled from place to place.

The Lord told Moses how to handle cases where it wasn't clear whether a person was guilty or not. The Lord also explained how Israelites could make a special promise to draw close to him by setting themselves apart from regular living for a certain period of time.

The LORD spoke to Moses. He said, "Tell Aaron and his sons, 'Here is how I want you to bless the Israelites. Say to them,

"'"May the LORD bless you
  and take good care of you.
May the LORD smile on you
  and be gracious to you.
May the LORD look on you with favor
  and give you peace."'

"In that way they will put the blessing of my name on the Israelites. And I will bless them."

Outsiders could celebrate Passover with the Israelites. Anyone who wasn't "clean" could celebrate it the next month.

The holy tent was set up. It was the tent where the tablets of the covenant law were kept. On the day it was set up, the cloud covered it. From evening until morning the cloud above the tent looked like fire. That's what continued to happen. The cloud covered the tent. At night the cloud looked like fire. When the cloud lifted from its place above the tent, the Israelites started out. Where the cloud settled, the Israelites camped. When the Lord gave the command, the Israelites started out. And when he gave the command, they camped. As long as the cloud stayed above the holy tent, they remained in camp. Sometimes the cloud remained above the tent for a long time. Then the Israelites obeyed the Lord's order. They didn't start out. Sometimes the cloud was above the tent for only a few days. When the Lord would give the command, they would camp. And when he would give the command, they would start out. Sometimes the cloud stayed only from evening until morning. When it lifted in the morning, they started out. It didn't matter whether it was day or night. When the cloud lifted, the people started out. It didn't matter whether the cloud stayed above the holy tent for two days or a month or a year. The Israelites would remain in camp. They wouldn't start out. But when the cloud lifted, they would start out. When the Lord gave the command, they camped. And when he gave the command, they started out. They obeyed the Lord's order. They obeyed him, just as he had commanded them through Moses.

The Lord told Moses to make two silver trumpets and blow them to signal whenever the cloud lifted. The Israelites could also blow the trumpets to ask for God's help, and to celebrate special holidays.

It was the 20th day of the second month of the second year. On that day the cloud began to move. It went up from above the holy tent where the tablets of the covenant law were kept.

So they started out from the mountain of the Lord. They traveled for three days. The ark of the covenant of the Lord went in front of them during those three days. It went ahead of them to find a place for them to rest. They started out from the camp by day. And the cloud of the LORD was above them.

When the ark started out, Moses said,

"LORD, rise up!
    Let your enemies be scattered.
    Let them run away from you."

When the ark stopped, Moses said,

"LORD, return.
    Return to the many thousands of people in Israel."

*

The LORD said to Moses, "Send some men to check out the land of Canaan. I am giving it to the Israelites. Send one leader from each of Israel's tribes."

So Moses sent them out from the Desert of Paran.

He said, "Go up through the Negev Desert. Go on into the central hill country. See what the land is like. See whether the people who live there are strong or weak. See whether they are few or many. What kind of land do they live in? Is it good or bad? What kind of towns do they live in? Do the towns have high walls around them or not? How is the soil? Is it rich land or poor land? Are there trees in it or not? Do your best to bring back some of the fruit of the land." It was the season for the first ripe grapes.

The men came to the Valley of Eshkol. There they cut off a branch that had a single bunch of grapes on it. Two of them carried it on a pole between them. They carried some pomegranates and figs along with it. At the end of 40 days, the men returned from checking out the land.

The men came back to Moses, Aaron and the whole community of Israel. The people were at Kadesh in the Desert of Paran. There the men reported to Moses and Aaron and all the people. They showed them the fruit of the land. They gave Moses their report. They said, "We went into the land you sent us to. It really does have plenty of milk and honey! Here's some fruit from the land.

But the people who live there are powerful. Their cities have high walls around them and are very large. We even saw members of the family line of Anak there. The Amalekites live in the Negev Desert. The Hittites, Jebusites and Amorites live in the central hill country. The Canaanites live near the Mediterranean Sea. They also live along the Jordan River."

Then Caleb interrupted the men speaking to Moses. He said, "We should go up and take the land. We can certainly do it."

But the men who had gone up with him spoke. They said, "We can't attack those people. They are stronger than we are." The men spread a bad report about the land among the Israelites. They said, "The land we checked out destroys those who live in it. All the people we saw there are very big and tall. We saw the Nephilim there. We seemed like grasshoppers in our own eyes. And that's also how we seemed to them." The family line of Anak came from the Nephilim.

That night all the members of the community raised their voices. They wept out loud. The Israelites spoke against Moses and Aaron. The whole community said to them, "We wish we had died in Egypt or even in this desert. Why is the Lord bringing us to this land? We're going to be killed by swords. Our enemies will capture our wives and children. Wouldn't it be better for us to go back to Egypt?" They said to one another, "We should choose another leader. We should go back to Egypt."

Then Moses and Aaron fell with their faces to the ground. They did it in front of the whole community of Israel gathered there. Joshua, the son of Nun, tore his clothes. So did Caleb, the son of Jephunneh. Joshua and Caleb were two of the men who had checked out the land. They spoke to the whole community of Israel. They said, "We passed through the land and checked it out. It's very good. If the Lord is pleased with us, he'll lead us into that land. It's a land that has plenty of milk and honey. He'll give it to us. But don't refuse to obey him. And don't be afraid of the people of the land. We will swallow them up. The Lord is with us. So nothing can save them. Don't be afraid of them."

But all the people talked about killing Joshua and Caleb by throwing stones at them. Then the glory of the Lord appeared at the tent of meeting. All the Israelites saw it. The Lᴏʀᴅ said to Moses, "How long will these people not respect me? How long will they refuse to believe in me? They refuse even though I have done many signs among them. So I will strike them down with a plague. I will destroy them. But I will make you into a greater and stronger nation than they are."

remember what you read

1. What is something you noticed for the first time?

_____

_____

_____

_____

2. What questions did you have?

_____

_____

_____

_____

3. Was there anything that bothered you?

_____

_____

_____

_____

4. What did you learn about loving God?

_____

_____

_____

_____

5. What did you learn about loving others?

_____

_____

_____

_____

NuMBERS, PART 2

introduction to Numbers, parts 2-3

God was very angry when his people did not trust him. The next few sections tell what happened to the Israelites because they disobeyed God.

∽∾∾∾

The LORD said to Moses and Aaron, "How long will this evil community speak against me? I have heard these Israelites talk about how unhappy they are. So tell them, 'Here is what I am announcing. I am the LORD. You can be sure that I live. And here is what you can be just as sure of. I will do to you the very thing that I heard you say. You will die in this desert. Every one of you 20 years old or more will die. Every one of you who was counted in the list of the people will die. Every one of you who has spoken out against me will be wiped out. I lifted up my hand and promised to make this land your home. But now not all of you will enter the land. Caleb, the son of Jephunneh, will enter it. So will Joshua, the son of Nun. They are the only ones who will enter the land. You have said that your enemies would capture your children. But I will bring your children in to enjoy the land you have turned your backs on. As for you, you will die in the desert. Your children will be shepherds here for 40 years. They will suffer because you were not faithful. They will suffer until the last of your bodies lies here in the desert. For 40 years you will suffer for your sins. That is one year for each of the 40 days you checked out the land. You will know what it is like to have me against you.' I, the LORD, have spoken. I will surely do these things to this entire evil community of Israel. They have joined together against me. They will meet their end in this desert. They will die here."

So the LORD struck down the men Moses had sent to check out the land. They had returned and had spread a bad report about the land. And that had made the whole community speak out against Moses. Those men were to blame for spreading the bad report. So the LORD struck them down. They died of a plague. Only two of the men who went to check out the land remained alive. One of them was Joshua, the son of Nun. The other was Caleb, the son of Jephunneh.

Moses reported to all the Israelites what the LORD had said. And they became very sad. Early the next morning they set out for the highest point in the hill country. "We have sinned," they said. "Now we are ready to go up to the land the LORD promised to give us."

But Moses said, "Why aren't you obeying the LORD's command? You won't succeed. So don't go up. The LORD isn't with you. Your enemies will win the battle over you. The Amalekites and the Canaanites will meet you on the field of battle. You have turned away from the LORD. So he won't be with you. And you will be killed by swords."

But they wouldn't listen. They still went up toward the highest point in the hill country. They went up even though Moses didn't move from the camp. They went even though the ark of the LORD's covenant didn't move from the camp. Then the Amalekites and the Canaanites who lived in that hill country came down. They attacked the Israelites. They won the battle over them. They chased the Israelites all the way to Hormah.

Korah was the son of Izhar, the son of Kohath. Kohath was the son of Levi. Korah and certain men from the tribe of Reuben turned against Moses. The men from Reuben were Dathan, Abiram and On. Dathan and Abiram were the sons of Eliab. On was the son of Peleth. All those men rose up against Moses. And 250 men of Israel joined them. All of them were known as leaders in the community. They had been appointed as members of the ruling body. They came as a group to oppose Moses and Aaron. They said to Moses and Aaron, "You have gone too far! The whole community is holy. Every one in it is holy. And the Lord is with them. So why do you put yourselves above the Lord's people?"

When Moses heard what they said, he fell with his face to the ground. Then he spoke to Korah and all his followers. He said, "In the morning the Lord will show who belongs to him. He will show who is holy. He'll bring that person near him. He'll bring the man he chooses near him. Korah, here's what you and all your followers must do. Get some shallow cups for burning incense. Tomorrow put burning coals and incense in them. Offer it to the Lord. The man the Lord chooses will be the one who is holy. You Levites have gone too far!"

Moses also said to Korah, "Listen, you Levites! The God of Israel has separated you from the rest of the community of Israel. He has brought you near him to work at the Lord's holy tent. He has given you to the people so that you can serve them. Isn't all that enough for you? He has already brought you and all the other Levites near him. But now you want to be priests too. You and all your followers have joined together against the Lord. Why are you telling Aaron you aren't happy with him?"

Then Moses sent for Dathan and Abiram, the sons of Eliab. But they said, "We won't come! You have brought us up out of a land that has plenty of milk and honey. You have brought us here to kill us in this desert. Isn't that enough? Now do you also want to act as if you were ruling over us? Besides, you haven't brought us into a land that has plenty of milk and honey. You haven't given us fields and vineyards of our own. Do you want to treat these men like slaves? No! We won't come!"

Then Moses became very angry. He said to the Lord, "Don't accept their offering. I haven't taken even a donkey from them. In fact, I haven't done anything wrong to any of them."

Moses said to Korah, "You and all your followers must stand in front of the Lord tomorrow. You must appear there along with Aaron. Each man must get his shallow cup. He must put incense in it. There will be a total of 250 incense cups. Each man must bring his cup to the Lord. You and Aaron must also bring your cups." So each of them got his cup. He put burning coals and incense in it. All the men came with Moses and Aaron. They stood at the entrance to the tent of meeting. Korah gathered all his followers together at the entrance to the tent. They opposed Moses and Aaron. Then the glory of the LORD appeared to the whole community. The LORD said to Moses and Aaron, "Separate yourselves from these people. Then I can put an end to all of them at once."

But Moses and Aaron fell with their faces to the ground. They cried out, "God, you are the God who gives life and breath to all living things. Will you be angry with the whole community when only one man sins?"

Then the LORD spoke to Moses. He said, "Tell the community, 'Move away from the tents of Korah, Dathan and Abiram.'"

Moses got up. He went to Dathan and Abiram. The elders of Israel followed him. Moses warned the community. He said, "Move away from the tents of these evil men! Don't touch anything that belongs to them. If you do, the LORD will sweep you away because of all their sins." So they moved away from the tents of Korah, Dathan and Abiram. Dathan and Abiram had already come out. They were standing at the entrances to their tents. Their wives, children and little ones were standing there with them.

Then Moses said, "What is about to happen wasn't my idea. The LORD has sent me to do everything I'm doing. Here is how you will know I'm telling you the truth. These men won't die a natural death. Something will happen to them that doesn't usually happen to people. If what I'm telling you doesn't happen, then you will know that the LORD hasn't sent me. But the LORD will make something totally new happen. The ground will open its mouth and swallow them up. It will swallow up everything that belongs to them. They will be buried alive. When that happens, you will know that these men have disrespected the LORD."

As soon as Moses finished saying all these words, what he had said came true. The ground under them broke open. It opened its mouth. It swallowed up those men. In fact, it swallowed up everyone who lived in their houses. It swallowed all Korah's men. And it swallowed up everything they owned. They went down into the grave alive. Everything they owned went down with them. The ground closed over them and they died. And so they disappeared from the community. All the Israelites around them heard their cries. They ran away from them. They shouted, "The ground is going to swallow us up too!"

Then the LORD sent down fire. It burned up the 250 men offering the incense.

In the first month the whole community of Israel arrived at the Desert of Zin. They stayed at Kadesh. Miriam died and was buried there.

The people didn't have any water. So they gathered together to oppose Moses and Aaron. They argued with Moses. They said, "We wish we had died when our people fell dead in front of the LORD. Why did you bring the LORD's people into this desert? We and our livestock will die here. Why did you bring us up out of Egypt? Why did you bring us to this terrible place? It doesn't have any grain or figs. It doesn't have any grapes or pomegranates. There isn't even any water for us to drink!"

Moses and Aaron left the people. They went to the entrance to the tent of meeting. There they fell with their faces to the ground. Then the glory of the LORD appeared to them. The LORD said to Moses, "Get your walking stick. You and your brother Aaron gather the people together. Then speak to that rock while everyone is watching. It will pour out its water. You will bring water out of the rock for the community. Then they and their livestock can drink it."

So Moses took the walking stick from the tent. He did just as the LORD had commanded him. He and Aaron gathered the people together in front of the rock. Moses said to them, "Listen, you who refuse to obey! Do we have to bring water out of this rock for you?" Then Moses raised his arm. He hit the rock twice with his walking stick. Water poured out. And the people and their livestock drank it.

But the LORD spoke to Moses and Aaron. He said, "You did not trust in me enough to honor me. You did not honor me as the holy God in front of the Israelites. So you will not bring this community into the land I am giving them."

remember what you read

1. What is something you noticed for the first time?

_____

_____

_____

_____

2. What questions did you have?

_____

_____

_____

_____

3. Was there anything that bothered you?

_____

_____

_____

_____

4. What did you learn about loving God?

_____

_____

_____

_____

5. What did you learn about loving others?

_____

_____

_____

_____

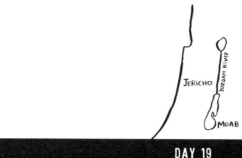

The Israelites traveled from Mount Hor along the way to the Red Sea. They wanted to go around Edom. But they grew tired on the way. So they spoke against God and against Moses. They said, "Why have you brought us up out of Egypt? Do you want us to die here in the desert? We don't have any bread! We don't have any water! And we hate this awful food!"

Then the Lord sent poisonous snakes among the Israelites. The snakes bit them. Many of the people died. The others came to Moses. They said, "We sinned when we spoke against the Lord and against you. Pray that the Lord will take the snakes away from us." So Moses prayed for the people.

The Lord said to Moses, "Make a snake. Put it up on a pole. Then anyone who is bitten can look at it and remain alive." So Moses made a bronze snake. He put it up on a pole. Then anyone who was bitten by a snake and looked at the bronze snake remained alive.

Finally, all the people who doubted died. They doubted that God could defeat the giants in the land he promised. God told Moses and the people to move toward the land. Several nations refused to let Israel pass through their land. Balak, the king of Moab, hired Balaam to curse Israel. But God would not let Balaam do this. However, the people of Israel made some terrible decisions, and many people died.

Then the Lord said to Moses, "Go up this mountain in the Abarim Range. See the land I have given the Israelites. After you have seen it, you too will join the members of your family who have already died. You will die, just as your brother Aaron did. The community refused to obey me at the waters of Meribah Kadesh in the Desert of Zin. At that time, you and Aaron did not obey my command. You did not honor me in front of them as the holy God."

Moses spoke to the LORD. He said, "LORD, you are the God who gives life and breath to all living things. Please put someone in charge of this community. Have that person lead them and take care of them. Then your people won't be like sheep without a shepherd."

So the LORD said to Moses, "Joshua, the son of Nun, has the ability to be a wise leader. Get him and place your hand on him. Have him stand in front of Eleazar the priest and the whole community. Put him in charge while everyone is watching. Give him some of your authority. Then the whole community of Israel will obey him. Joshua will stand in front of Eleazar the priest. Eleazar will help him make decisions. Eleazar will get help from me by using the Urim. Joshua and the whole community of Israel must not make any move at all unless I command them to."

The people of Gad and Reuben liked the land east of the Jordan River. They asked Moses to let them live there. They had to promise to cross the Jordan and help the rest of the tribes take the land God said he would give them. Then they could go back and live in their new home.

On the plains of Moab the LORD spoke to Moses. He spoke to him by the Jordan River across from Jericho. The LORD said, "Speak to the Israelites. Tell them, 'Go across the Jordan River into Canaan. Drive out all those living in the land. The statues of their gods are made out of stone and metal. Destroy all those statues. And destroy all the high places where they are worshiped. Take the land as your own. Make your homes in it. I have given it to you. Cast lots when you divide up the land. Do it based on the number of people in each tribe and family. Give a larger share to a larger group. And give a smaller group a smaller share. The share they receive by casting lots will belong to them. Give out the shares based on the number of people in Israel's tribes.

The Lord chose several men to help Joshua give out the land. He told the Israelites to pick several cities where people could go for safety if they killed someone by accident. If these cities weren't there, the family of the person who died could kill the accidental killer.

Introduction to Deuteronomy, parts 1-2

The book of Deuteronomy is several things. It is a long speech by Moses to the people before he died. He retold the story of Israel in the wilderness. So it is a reminder of the consequences when people do not trust God. Deuteronomy is also a "second law" or "second covenant." Moses renewed the first covenant with these children of the people who came out of Egypt. He wanted them to be faithful to God and the covenant when they finally made their homes in the land God promised.

∽∾∾∾

These are the words Moses spoke to all the Israelites. At that time, they were in the desert east of the Jordan River.

It was the 40th year since the Israelites had left Egypt. On the first day of the 11th month, Moses spoke to them. He told them everything the Lord had commanded him to tell them. They had already won the battle over Sihon. Sihon was the king of the Amorites. He had ruled in Heshbon. Israel had also won the battle over Og at Edrei. Og was the king of Bashan. He had ruled in Ashtaroth.

The people were east of the Jordan River in the territory of Moab. There Moses began to explain the law. Here is what he said.

The Lord our God spoke to us at Mount Horeb. He said, "You have stayed long enough at this mountain. Take your tents down. Go into the hill country of the Amorites. Go to all the people who are their neighbors. Go to the people who live in the Arabah Valley. Travel to the mountains and the western hills. Go to the people in the Negev Desert and along the coast. Travel to the land of Canaan and to Lebanon. Go as far as the great Euphrates River. I have given you all this land. Go in and take it as your own. The Lord promised he would give the land to your fathers. He promised it to Abraham,

Isaac and Jacob. He also said he would give it to their children after them."

Moses spoke for a long time about everything that happened in the desert. He reminded the Israelites how they disobeyed and doubted God. But he encouraged them that God was ready to keep all his promises if they would obey.

Ask now about the days of long ago. Find out what happened long before your time. Ask about what has happened since the time God created human beings on the earth. Ask from one end of the world to the other. Has anything as great as this ever happened? Has anything like it ever been heard of? You heard the voice of God speaking out of fire. And you lived! Has that happened to any other people? Has any god ever tried to take one nation out of another to be his own? Has any god done it by testing his people? Has any god done it with signs and amazing deeds or with war? Has any god reached out his mighty hand and powerful arm? Or has any god shown his people his great and wonderful acts? The Lord your God did all those things for you in Egypt. With your very own eyes you saw him do them.

The Lord showed you those things so that you might know he is God. There is no other God except him. From heaven he made you hear his voice. He wanted to teach you. On earth he showed you his great fire. You heard his words coming out of the fire. He loved your people of long ago. He chose their children after them. So he brought you out of Egypt. He used his great strength to do it. He drove out nations to make room for you. They were greater and stronger than you are. He will bring you into their land. He wants to give it to you as your very own. The whole land is as good as yours right now.

The Lord is God in heaven above and on the earth below. Today you must agree with that and take it to heart. There is no other God. I'm giving you his rules and commands today. Obey them. Then things will go well with you and your children after you. You will live a long time in the land. The Lord your God is giving you the land for all time to come.

Israel, listen to me. Here are the rules and laws I'm announcing to you today. Learn them well. Be sure to obey them. The LORD our God made a covenant with us at Mount Horeb. He didn't make it only with our people of long ago. He also made it with us. In fact, he made it with all of us who are alive here today. The LORD spoke to you face to face. His voice came out of the fire on the mountain. At that time I stood between the LORD and you. I announced to you the LORD's message. I did it because you were afraid of the fire. You didn't go up the mountain.

Moses reviewed the laws God gave to the people.

Later on, your child might ask you, "What is the meaning of the terms, rules and laws the LORD our God has commanded you to obey?" If they do ask you, tell them, "We were Pharaoh's slaves in Egypt. But the LORD used his mighty hand to bring us out of Egypt. With our own eyes we saw the LORD send amazing signs. They were great and terrible. He sent them on Egypt and Pharaoh and everyone in his house. But the LORD brought us out of Egypt. He planned to bring us into the land of Canaan and give it to us. It's the land he promised to our people of long ago. The LORD our God commanded us to obey all his rules. He commanded us to honor him. If we do, we will always succeed and be kept alive. That's what is happening today. We must make sure we obey the whole law in the sight of the LORD our God. That's what he has commanded us to do. If we obey his law, we'll be doing what he requires of us."

The LORD your God will bring you into the land. You are going to enter it and take it as your own. He'll drive out many nations to make room for you. He'll drive out the Hittites, Girgashites, Amorites, Canaanites, Perizzites, Hivites and Jebusites. Those seven nations are larger and stronger than you are. The LORD your God will hand them over to you. You will win the battle over them. You must completely destroy them. Don't make a peace treaty with them. Don't show them any mercy. Don't marry any of their people. Don't give your daughters to their sons. And don't take their daughters for your sons. If you do, those people will turn your children away from serving the LORD. Then your children will serve other gods. The LORD will be very angry with you. He will quickly destroy you. So here is what you must do to those people. Break down their altars. Smash their sacred stones. Cut down the poles they use to worship the female god named Asherah. Burn the statues of their gods in the fire. You are a holy nation. The LORD your God has set you apart for himself. He has chosen you to be his special treasure. He chose you out of all the nations on the face of the earth to be his people.

The LORD chose you because he loved you very much. He didn't choose you because you had more people than other nations. In fact, you had the smallest number of all. The LORD chose you because he loved you. He wanted to keep the promise he had made to your people of long ago. That's why he used his mighty hand to bring you out of Egypt. He bought you back from the land where you were slaves. He set you free from the power of Pharaoh, the king of Egypt.

remember what you read

1. What is something you noticed for the first time?

_____

_____

_____

_____

2. What questions did you have?

_____

_____

_____

_____

3. Was there anything that bothered you?

_____

_____

_____

_____

4. What did you learn about loving God?

_____

_____

_____

_____

5. What did you learn about loving others?

_____

_____

_____

_____

Obey the commands of the LORD your God. Live as he wants you to live. Have respect for him. The LORD your God is bringing you into a good land. It has brooks, streams and deep springs of water. Those springs flow in its valleys and hills. It has wheat, barley, vines, fig trees, pomegranates, olive oil and honey. There is plenty of food in that land. You will have everything you need. Its rocks have iron in them. And you can dig copper out of its hills.

When you have eaten and are satisfied, praise the LORD your God. Praise him for the good land he has given you. Make sure you don't forget the LORD your God. Don't fail to obey his commands, laws and rules. I'm giving them to you today. But suppose you don't obey his commands. And suppose you have plenty to eat. You build fine houses and live in them. The number of your herds and flocks increases. You also get more and more silver and gold. And everything you have multiplies. Then your hearts will become proud. And you will forget the LORD your God. The LORD brought you out of Egypt. That's the land where you were slaves. He led you through that huge and terrible desert. It was a dry land. It didn't have any water. It had poisonous snakes and scorpions. The LORD gave you water out of solid rock. He gave you manna to eat in the desert. Your people had never even known anything about manna before. The LORD took your pride away. He tested you. He did it so that things would go well with you in the end. You might say to yourself, "My power and my strong hands have made me rich." But remember the LORD your God. He gives you the ability to produce wealth. That shows he stands by the terms of the covenant he made with you. He promised it to your people of long ago. And he's still faithful to his covenant today.

Israel, listen to me. You are now about to go across the Jordan River. You will take over the land of the nations that live there. Those nations are greater and stronger than you are. Their large cities have walls that reach up to the sky. The people who live there are Anakites. They are strong and tall. You know all about them. You have heard people say, "Who can stand up against the Anakites?" But today you can be sure the LORD your God will go over there ahead of you. He is like a fire that will burn them up. He'll destroy them. He'll bring them under your control. You will drive them out. You will put an end to them quickly, just as the LORD has promised you.

The LORD your God will drive them out to make room for you. When he does, don't say to yourself, "The LORD has done it because I am godly. That's why he brought me here to take over this land." That isn't true. The LORD is going to drive out those nations to make room for you because they are very evil. You are not going in to take over their land because you have done what is right or honest. It's because those nations are so evil. That's why the LORD your God will drive them out to make room for you. He will do what he said he would do. He made a promise to your fathers, to Abraham, Isaac and Jacob. The LORD your God is giving you this good land to take as your own. But you must understand that it isn't because you are a godly nation. In fact, you are stubborn.

So be faithful. Obey the commands the LORD your God is giving you today. Love him. Serve him with all your heart and with all your soul. Then the LORD will send rain on your land at the right time. He'll send rain in the fall and in the spring. You will be able to gather your grain. You will also be able to make olive oil and fresh wine. He'll provide grass in the fields for your cattle. You will have plenty to eat.

Listen to me. I'm setting a blessing and a curse in front of you today. I'm giving you the commands of the LORD your God today. You will be blessed if you obey them. But you will be cursed if you don't obey them. So don't turn away from the path I'm now commanding you to take. Don't turn away by worshiping other gods you didn't know before. The LORD your God will bring you into the land to take it over. When he does, you must announce the blessings from Mount Gerizim. You must announce the curses from Mount Ebal. As you know, those mountains are across the Jordan River. They are on the west side of the Jordan toward the setting sun. They are near the large trees of Moreh. The mountains are in the territory of the Canaanites, who live in the Arabah Valley near Gilgal. You are about to go across the Jordan River. You will enter the land and take it over. The LORD your God is giving it to you. You will take it over and live there. When you do, make sure you obey all the rules and laws I'm giving you today.

Moses reminded the Israelites of all the laws that the Lord gave them at Mount Sinai, from the tent of meeting, and along their journey to Canaan.

Make sure you obey the LORD your God completely. Be careful to obey all his commands. I'm giving them to you today. If you do these things, the LORD will honor you more than all the other nations on earth. If you obey the LORD your God, here are the blessings that will come to you and remain with you.

You will be blessed in the cities. You will be blessed out in the country.

Your children will be blessed. Your crops will be blessed. The young animals among your livestock will be blessed. That includes your calves and lambs.

Your baskets and bread pans will be blessed.

You will be blessed no matter where you go.

But suppose you don't obey the LORD your God. And you aren't careful to obey all his commands and rules I'm giving you today. Then he will send curses on you. They'll catch up with you. Here are those curses.

You will be cursed in the cities. You will be cursed out in the country.

Your baskets and bread pans will be cursed.

Your children will be cursed. Your crops will be cursed. Your calves and lambs will be cursed.

You will be cursed no matter where you go.

What I'm commanding you today is not too hard for you. It isn't beyond your reach. It isn't up in heaven. So you don't have to ask, "Who will go up into heaven to get it? Who will announce it to us so we can obey it?" And it isn't beyond the ocean. So you don't have to ask, "Who will go across the ocean to get it? Who will announce it to us so we can obey it?" No, the message isn't far away at all. In fact, it's really near you. It's in your mouth and in your heart so that you can obey it.

Today I'm giving you a choice. You can have life and success. Or you can have death and harm. I'm commanding you today to love the Lord your God. I'm commanding you to live exactly as he wants you to live. You must obey his commands, rules and laws. Then you will live. There will be many of you. The Lord your God will bless you in the land you are entering to take as your own.

Don't let your hearts turn away from the Lord. Instead, obey him. Don't let yourselves be drawn away to other gods. And don't bow down to them and worship them. If you do, I announce to you this day that you will certainly be destroyed. You are about to go across the Jordan River and take over the land. But you won't live there very long.

I'm calling for the heavens and the earth to be witnesses against you this very day. I'm offering you the choice of life or death. You can choose either blessings or curses. But I want you to choose life. Then you and your children will live. And you will love the Lord your God. You will obey him. You will remain true to him. The Lord is your very life. He will give you many years in the land. He promised to give that land to your fathers, to Abraham, Isaac and Jacob.

The Lord gave a command to Joshua, the son of Nun. He said, "Be strong and brave. You will bring the Israelites into the land I promised them. I myself will be with you."

Moses finished writing the words of this law in a book. He wrote them down from beginning to end. Then he gave a command to the Levites who carried the ark of the covenant of the Lord. Moses said, "Take this Book of the Law. Place it beside the ark of the covenant of the Lord your God. It will remain there as a witness against you."

Moses, the man of God, gave a special blessing to each of the Israelite tribes before he died.

Moses climbed Mount Nebo. He went up from the plains of Moab to the highest slopes of Pisgah. It's across from Jericho. At Pisgah the LORD showed him the whole land from Gilead all the way to Dan. Moses saw the whole land of Naphtali. He saw the territory of Ephraim and Manasseh. The LORD showed him the whole land of Judah all the way to the Mediterranean Sea. Moses saw the Negev Desert. He saw the whole area from the Valley of Jericho all the way to Zoar. Jericho was also known as The City of Palm Trees. Then the LORD spoke to Moses. He said, "This is the land I promised to Abraham, Isaac and Jacob. I told them, 'I will give this land to your children and their children.' Moses, I have let you see it with your own eyes. But you will not go across the Jordan River to enter it."

Moses, the servant of the LORD, died there in Moab. It happened just as the LORD had said. The LORD buried the body of Moses in Moab. His grave is in the valley across from Beth Peor. But to this day no one knows where his grave is. Moses was 120 years old when he died. But his eyesight was still good. He was still very strong. The Israelites mourned over Moses on the plains of Moab for 30 days. They did it until their time for weeping and crying was over.

Joshua, the son of Nun, was filled with wisdom. That's because Moses had placed his hands on him. So the Israelites listened to Joshua. They did what the LORD had commanded Moses.

Since then, Israel has never had a prophet like Moses. The LORD knew him face to face. Moses did many signs and amazing things. The LORD had sent him to do them in Egypt. Moses did them against Pharaoh, against all his officials and against his whole land. No one has ever had the mighty power Moses had. No one has ever done the wonderful acts he did in the sight of all the Israelites.

remember what you read

1. What is something you noticed for the first time?

_____

_____

_____

_____

2. What questions did you have?

_____

_____

_____

_____

3. Was there anything that bothered you?

_____

_____

_____

_____

4. What did you learn about loving God?

_____

_____

_____

_____

5. What did you learn about loving others?

_____

_____

_____

_____

introduction to Joshua, parts 1-3

The book of Joshua begins right after Moses gave his great speech in Deuteronomy. Moses died, and God called Joshua to lead the people of Israel into the land he promised to give them. Joshua led Israel in battle, and he divided up the land among all the people.

Moses, the servant of the LORD, died. After that, the LORD spoke to Joshua, the son of Nun. Joshua was Moses' helper. The LORD said to Joshua, "My servant Moses is dead. Now then, I want you and all these people to get ready to go across the Jordan River. I want all of you to go into the land I am about to give to the Israelites. I will give all of you every place you walk on, just as I promised Moses. Your territory will reach from the Negev Desert all the way to Lebanon. The great Euphrates River will be to the east. The Mediterranean Sea will be to the west. Your territory will include all the Hittite country. Joshua, no one will be able to oppose you as long as you live. I will be with you, just as I was with Moses. I will never leave you. I will never desert you. Be strong and brave. You will lead these people. They will take the land as their very own. It is the land I promised to give their people of long ago.

"Be strong and very brave. Make sure you obey the whole law my servant Moses gave you. Do not turn away from it to the right or the left. Then you will have success everywhere you go. Never stop reading this Book of the Law. Day and night you must think about what it says. Make sure you do everything written in it. Then things will go well with you. And you will have great success. Here is what I am commanding you to do. Be strong and brave. Do not be afraid. Do not lose hope. I am the LORD your God. I will be with you everywhere you go."

Joshua, the son of Nun, sent two spies from Shittim. He sent them in secret. He said to them, "Go and look over the land. Most of all, check out Jericho." So they went to Jericho. They stayed at the house of a prostitute. Her name was Rahab.

The king of Jericho was told, "Look! Some of the Israelites have come here tonight. They've come to check out the land." So the king sent a message to Rahab. It said, "Bring out the men who came into your house. They've come to check out the whole land."

But the woman had hidden the two men. She said, "It's true that the men came here. But I didn't know where they had come from. They left at sunset, when it was time to close the city gate. I don't know which way they went. Go after them quickly. You might catch up with them." But in fact she had taken them up on the roof. There she had hidden them under some flax she had piled up. The king's men left to hunt down the spies. They took the road that leads to where the Jordan River can be crossed. As soon as they had gone out of the city, the gate was shut.

Rahab went up on the roof before the spies settled down for the night. She said to them, "I know that the LORD has given you this land. We are very much afraid of you. Everyone who lives in this country is weak with fear because of you. We've heard how the LORD dried up the Red Sea for you when you came out of Egypt. We've heard what you did to Sihon and Og, the two Amorite kings. They ruled east of the Jordan River. You completely destroyed them. When we heard about it, we were terrified. Because of you, we aren't brave anymore. The LORD your God is the God who rules in heaven above and on the earth below.

"Now then, please give me your word. Promise me in the name of the LORD that you will be kind to my family. I've been kind to you. Promise me that you will spare the lives of my father and mother.

Spare my brothers and sisters. Also spare everyone in their families. Promise that you won't put any of us to death."

So the men made a promise to her. "If you save our lives, we'll save yours," they said. "Just don't tell anyone what we're doing. Then we'll be kind and faithful to you when the Lord gives us the land."

The house Rahab lived in was part of the city wall. So she let the spies down by a rope through the window. She said to them, "Go up into the hills. The men chasing you won't be able to find you. Hide yourselves there for three days until they return. Then you can go on your way."

Joshua said to the people, "Set yourselves apart to the Lord. Tomorrow he'll do amazing things among you."

Joshua said to the priests, "Go and get the ark of the covenant. Walk on ahead of the people." So they went and got it. Then they walked on ahead of them.

The Lord said to Joshua, "Today I will begin to honor you in the eyes of all the Israelites. Then they will know that I am with you, just as I was with Moses. Speak to the priests who carry the ark of the covenant. Tell them, 'When you reach the edge of the Jordan River, go into the water and stand there.'"

Joshua said to the Israelites, "Come here. Listen to what the Lord your God is saying. You will soon know that the living God is among you. He will certainly drive out the people now living in the land. He'll do it to make room for you. He'll drive out the Canaanites, Hittites, Hivites, Perizzites, Girgashites, Amorites and Jebusites. The ark will go into the Jordan River ahead of you. It's the ark of the covenant of the Lord of the whole earth. Choose 12 men from the tribes of Israel. Choose one from each tribe. The priests will carry the ark of the Lord. He's the Lord of the whole earth. As soon as the priests step into the Jordan, it will stop flowing. The water that's coming down the river will pile up in one place. That's how you will know that the living God is among you."

So the people took their tents down. They prepared to go across the Jordan River. The priests carrying the ark of the covenant went ahead of them. The water of the Jordan was going over its banks.

It always does that at the time the crops are being gathered. The priests came to the river. Their feet touched the water's edge. Right away the water coming down the river stopped flowing. It piled up far away at a town called Adam near Zarethan. The water flowing down to the Dead Sea was completely cut off. So the people went across the Jordan River opposite Jericho. The priests carried the ark of the covenant of the LORD. They stopped in the middle of the river and stood on dry ground. They stayed there until the whole nation of Israel had gone across on dry ground.

So Joshua called together the 12 men he had appointed from among the Israelites. There was one man from each tribe. He said to them, "Go back to the middle of the Jordan River. Go to where the ark of the LORD your God is. Each one of you must pick up a stone. You must carry it on your shoulder. There will be as many stones as there are tribes in Israel. The stones will serve as a reminder to you. In days to come, your children will ask you, 'What do these stones mean?' Tell them that the LORD cut off the flow of water in the Jordan River. Tell them its water stopped flowing when the ark of the covenant of the LORD went across. The stones will always remind the Israelites of what happened there."

So the Israelites did as Joshua commanded them.

All the Amorite and Canaanite kings heard how the LORD had dried up the Jordan River. They heard how he had dried it up for the Israelites until they had gone across it. The Amorite kings lived west of the Jordan. The kings of Canaan lived along the Mediterranean Sea. When all those kings heard what the LORD had done, they were terrified. They weren't brave enough to face the Israelites anymore.

The Israelites celebrated the Passover Feast. They observed it on the evening of the 14th day of the month. They did it while they were camped at Gilgal on the plains around Jericho. The day after the Passover, they ate some of the food grown in the land. On that same day they ate grain that had been cooked. They also ate bread made without yeast. The manna stopped coming down the day after they ate the food grown in the land. The Israelites didn't have manna anymore. Instead, that year they ate food grown in Canaan.

When Joshua was near Jericho, he looked up and saw a man standing in front of him. The man was holding a sword. He was ready for battle. Joshua went up to him. He asked, "Are you on our side? Or are you on the side of our enemies?"

"I am not on either side," he replied. "I have come as the commander of the LORD's army." Then Joshua fell with his face to the ground. He asked the man, "What message does my Lord have for me?"

The commander of the LORD's army replied, "Take off your sandals. The place you are standing on is holy ground." So Joshua took them off.

The gates of Jericho were shut tight and guarded closely because of the Israelites. No one went out. No one came in.

Then the LORD said to Joshua, "I have handed Jericho over to you. I have also handed over to you its king and its fighting men. March around the city once with all your fighting men. In fact, do it for six days. Have seven priests get trumpets made out of rams' horns. They must carry them in front of the ark. On the seventh day, march around the city seven times. Tell the priests to blow the trumpets as you march. You will hear them blow a long blast on the trumpets. When you do, tell the whole army to give a loud shout. The wall of the city will fall down. Then the whole army will march up to the city. Everyone will go straight in."

So Joshua, the son of Nun, called for the priests. He said to them, "Go and get the ark of the covenant of the LORD. I want seven of you to carry trumpets in front of it." He gave an order to the army. He said, "Move out! March around the city. Some of the fighting men must march in front of the ark of the LORD."

When Joshua had spoken to the men, the seven priests went forward. They were carrying the seven trumpets as they marched in front of the ark of the LORD. They were blowing the trumpets. The ark of the LORD's covenant was carried behind the priests. Some of the fighting men marched ahead of the priests who were blowing the trumpets. The others followed behind the ark and guarded all the priests. That whole time the priests were blowing the trumpets. But Joshua had given an order to the army. He had said, "Don't give a war cry. Don't raise your voices. Don't say a word until the day I tell you to shout. Then shout!" So he had the ark of the LORD carried around the city once. Then the army returned to camp. They spent the night there.

remember what you read

1. What is something you noticed for the first time?

_____

_____

_____

_____

2. What questions did you have?

_____

_____

_____

_____

3. Was there anything that bothered you?

_____

_____

_____

_____

4. What did you learn about loving God?

_____

_____

_____

_____

5. What did you learn about loving others?

_____

_____

_____

_____

JOSHUA, PART 2

Joshua got up early the next morning. The priests went and got the ark of the LORD. The seven priests carrying the seven trumpets started out. They marched in front of the ark of the LORD. They blew the trumpets. Some of the fighting men marched ahead of them. The others followed behind the ark and guarded all of them. The priests kept blowing the trumpets. On the second day they marched around the city once. Then the army returned to camp. They did all those things for six days.

On the seventh day, they got up at sunrise. They marched around the city, just as they had done before. But on that day they went around it seven times. On the seventh time around, the priests blew a long blast on the trumpets. Then Joshua gave a command to the army. He said, "Shout! The LORD has given you the city! The city and everything in it must be set apart to the LORD to be destroyed. But the prostitute Rahab and all those with her in her house must be spared. That's because she hid the spies we sent. But keep away from the things that have been set apart to the LORD. If you take any of them, you will be destroyed. And you will bring trouble on the camp of Israel. You will cause it to be destroyed. All the silver and gold is holy. It is set apart to the LORD. So are all the things made out of bronze and iron. All those things must be added to the treasures kept in the LORD's house."

The priests blew the trumpets. As soon as the army heard the sound, they gave a loud shout. Then the wall fell down. Everyone charged straight in. So they took the city. They set it apart to the LORD to be destroyed. They destroyed every living thing in it with their swords. They killed men and women. They wiped out young people and old people. They destroyed cattle, sheep and donkeys.

Then Joshua spoke to the two men who had gone in to check out the land. He said, "Go into the prostitute's house. Bring her out. Also bring out everyone with her. That's what you promised her you would do." So the young men who had checked out the land went into Rahab's house. They brought her out along with her parents and brothers and sisters. They brought out everyone else there with her. They put them in a place outside the camp of Israel.

Then they burned the whole city and everything in it. But they added the silver and gold to the treasures kept in the LORD's house. They also put there the things made out of bronze and iron. But Joshua spared the prostitute Rahab. He spared her family. He also spared everyone else in the house with her. He did it because she hid the spies he had sent to Jericho. Rahab lives among the Israelites to this day.

Joshua sent men from Jericho to Ai. Ai is near Beth Aven east of Bethel. Joshua told the men, "Go up and check out the area around Ai." So the men went up and checked it out.

Then they returned to Joshua. They said, "The whole army doesn't have to go up and attack Ai. Send only two or three thousand men. They can take the city. Don't make the whole army go up there. Only a few people live in Ai." So only about 3,000 troops went up. But the men of Ai drove them away. They chased the Israelites from the city gate all the way to Shebarim. They killed about 36 of them on the way down. So the Israelites were terrified.

Joshua and the elders of Israel became sad. Joshua tore his clothes. He fell in front of the ark of the LORD with his face to the ground. He remained there until evening. The elders did the same thing. They also sprinkled dust on their heads. Joshua said, "LORD and King, why did you ever bring these people across the Jordan River? Did you want to hand us over to the Amorites? Did you want them to destroy us? I wish we had been content to stay on the other side of the Jordan! Lord, our enemies have driven us away. What can I say? The Canaanites will hear about it. So will everyone else in the country. They will surround us. They'll erase any mention of our name from the face of the earth. Then what will you do when people don't honor your great name anymore?"

The LORD said to Joshua, "Get up! What are you doing down there on your face? Israel has sinned. I made a covenant with them. I commanded them to keep it. But they have broken it. They have taken some of the things that had been set apart to me in a special way to be destroyed. They have stolen. They have lied. They have taken the things they stole and have put them with their own things. That is why the Israelites can't stand up against their enemies. They turn their backs and run. That's because I have decided to let them be destroyed. You must destroy the things you took that had been set apart to me. If you do not, I will not be with you anymore.

"Go and set the people apart. Tell them, 'Make yourselves pure. Get ready for tomorrow. Here is what the LORD, the God of Israel, wants you to do. He says, "People of Israel, you have kept some of the things that had been set apart to me to be destroyed. You can't stand up against your enemies until you get rid of those things."

" 'In the morning, come forward tribe by tribe. The tribe the LORD chooses will come forward group by group. The group the LORD chooses will come forward family by family. And the men in the family the LORD chooses will come forward one by one. Whoever is caught with the things that had been set apart to the LORD will be destroyed by fire. Everything that belongs to that person will also be destroyed. He has broken the LORD's covenant. He has done a very terrible thing in Israel!' "

Early the next morning Joshua had Israel come forward by tribes. The tribe of Judah was chosen. The groups of Judah came forward. The group of Zerah was chosen. Joshua had the group of Zerah come forward by families. The family of Zimri was chosen. He had their men come forward one by one. Achan was chosen. Achan was the son of Karmi. Karmi was the son of Zimri. And Zimri was the son of Zerah. Zerah was from the tribe of Judah.

Joshua said to Achan, "My son, the LORD is the God of Israel. So give him glory and honor him by telling the truth! Tell me what you have done. Don't hide it from me."

Achan replied, "It's true! I've sinned against the LORD, the God of Israel. Here is what I've done. I saw a beautiful robe from Babylonia among the things we had taken. I saw five pounds of silver.

And I saw a gold bar that weighed 20 ounces. I wanted them, so I took them. I hid them in the ground inside my tent. The silver is on the bottom."

So Joshua sent some messengers. They ran to Achan's tent. And there was everything, hidden in his tent! The silver was on the bottom. They brought the things out of the tent. They took them to Joshua and all the Israelites. And they spread them out in the sight of the LORD.

Then Joshua and all the people grabbed Achan, the son of Zerah. They took the silver, the robe and the gold bar. They took Achan's sons and daughters. They took his cattle, donkeys and sheep. They also took his tent and everything he had. They carried all of it out to the Valley of Achor. Joshua said to Achan, "Why have you brought this trouble on us? The LORD will bring trouble on you today."

Then all the people killed Achan by throwing stones at him. They also killed the rest of his family with stones. They burned all of them up. They placed a large pile of rocks on top of Achan's body. The place has been called the Valley of Achor ever since. That pile is still there to this day. After the people killed Achan, the LORD was no longer angry with them.

Then the LORD said to Joshua, "Do not be afraid. Do not lose hope. Go up and attack Ai. Take the whole army with you. I have handed the king of Ai over to you. I have given you his people, his city and his land. Remember what you did to Jericho and its king. You will do the same thing to Ai and its king. But this time you can keep for yourselves the livestock and everything else you take from them. Have some of your fighting men hide behind the city and take them by surprise."

So Joshua and the whole army moved out to attack Ai. He chose 30,000 of his best fighting men. He sent them out at night. He gave them orders. He said, "Listen carefully to what I'm saying. You must hide behind the city. Don't go very far away from it. All of you must be ready to attack it. I and all those with me will march up to the city. The men of Ai will come out to fight against us, just as they did before. Then we'll run away from them. They'll chase us until we've drawn them away from the city. They'll say, 'They are running away from us, just as they did before.' When we run away from them, come out of your hiding place. Capture the city. The LORD your God will hand it over to you. When you have taken it, set it on fire. Do what the LORD has commanded. Make sure you obey my orders."

Early the next morning Joshua brought together his army. He and the leaders of Israel marched in front of them to Ai. The whole army that was with him marched up to the city. They stopped in front of it. They set up camp north of Ai. There was a valley between them and the city. Joshua had chosen about 5,000 soldiers. He had ordered them to hide in a place west of Ai. It was between Bethel and Ai. The men took up their battle positions. All the men in the camp north of the city took up their positions. So did those who were supposed to hide west of the city. That night Joshua went into the valley.

The king of Ai saw what the troops with Joshua were doing. So the king and all his men hurried out of the city early in the morning. They marched out to meet Israel in battle. They went to a place that looked out over the Arabah Valley. The king didn't know that some of Israel's fighting men were hiding behind the city. Joshua and all his men let the men of Ai drive them back. The Israelites ran away toward the desert. All the men of Ai were called out to chase them. They chased Joshua. So they were drawn away from the city. Not even one man remained in Ai or Bethel. All of them went out to chase Israel. When they did, they left the city wide open.

remember what you read

1. What is something you noticed for the first time?

_____

_____

_____

_____

2. What questions did you have?

_____

_____

_____

_____

3. Was there anything that bothered you?

_____

_____

_____

_____

4. What did you learn about loving God?

_____

_____

_____

_____

5. What did you learn about loving others?

_____

_____

_____

_____

JOSHUA, PART 3

Then the LORD said to Joshua, "Hold out toward Ai the javelin that is in your hand. I will give the city to you." So Joshua held out toward the city the javelin in his hand. As soon as he did, the men hiding behind the city got up quickly. They came out of their hiding places and rushed forward. They entered the city and captured it. They quickly set it on fire.

The men of Ai looked back. They saw smoke rising up from the city into the sky. But they couldn't escape in any direction. The Israelites had been running away toward the desert. But now they turned around to face those chasing them. Joshua and all his men saw that the men who had been hiding behind the city had captured it. They also saw that smoke was going up from it. So they turned around and attacked the men of Ai. The men who had set Ai on fire came out of the city. They also fought against the men of Ai. So the men of Ai were caught in the middle. The army of Israel was on both sides of them. Israel struck them down. They didn't let anyone remain alive or get away. But they captured the king of Ai alive. They brought him to Joshua.

Israel finished killing all the men of Ai. They destroyed them in the fields and in the desert where they had chased them. They struck down every one of them with their swords. Then all the Israelites returned to Ai. And they killed those who were left in it. The total number of men and women they killed that day was 12,000. The Israelites put to death all the people of Ai. Joshua continued to hold out his javelin toward Ai. He didn't lower his hand until he and his men had totally destroyed everyone who lived there. But this time Israel kept for themselves the livestock and everything else they had taken from the city. The LORD had directed Joshua to let them do it.

Joshua built an altar to honor the LORD, the God of Israel. He built it on Mount Ebal. Moses, the servant of the LORD, had commanded the Israelites to do that. Joshua built the altar according to what is written in the Book of the Law of Moses. Joshua built the altar out of stones that iron tools had never touched. Then the people offered on the altar burnt offerings to the LORD. They also sacrificed friendship offerings on it. Joshua copied the law of Moses on stones. He did it while all the Israelites were watching. They were standing on both sides of the ark of the covenant of the LORD. All the Israelites, including outsiders and citizens, were there. Israel's elders, officials and judges were also there. All of them faced the priests, who were Levites. They were carrying the ark. Half of the people stood in front of Mount Gerizim. The other half stood in front of Mount Ebal. Moses, the servant of the LORD, had earlier told them to do it. Moses told them to do it when he had given directions to bless the Israelites.

Then Joshua read all the words of the law out loud. He read the blessings and the curses. He read them just as they are written in the Book of the Law. Joshua read every word Moses had commanded. He read them to the whole community of Israel. That included the women and children. It also included the outsiders living among them.

All the kings who ruled west of the Jordan River heard about the battles Israel had won. That included the kings who ruled in the central hill country and the western hills. It also included those who ruled along the entire coast of the Mediterranean Sea all the way to Lebanon. They were the kings of the Hittites, Amorites, Canaanites, Perizzites, Hivites and Jebusites. They brought their armies together to fight against Joshua and Israel.

People from the town of Gibeon were scared of Israel. They disguised themselves and pretended to come from a long way away. They asked Israel to make peace with them. Israel's leaders didn't ask God about Gibeon, so they signed a treaty. When they found out the people of

Gibeon were lying, they did not kill them. Israel made them cut wood and carry water. Five Amorite kings attacked Gibeon.

Joshua marched all night from Gilgal. He took the Amorite armies by surprise. The LORD threw them into a panic as Israel marched toward them. Then Joshua and the Israelites won a complete victory over them at Gibeon. Amorites tried to escape as Israel marched toward them. Then the LORD threw large hailstones down on them. The hailstones killed more of them than the swords of the Israelites did.

On that day Joshua spoke to the LORD while the Israelites were listening. He said,

"Sun, stand still over Gibeon.
    And you, moon, stand still over the Valley of Aijalon."
So the sun stood still.
    The moon stopped.
    They didn't move again until the nation won the battle over
        its enemies.

You can read about it in the Book of Jashar.

The sun stopped in the middle of the sky. It didn't go down for about a full day. There has never been a day like it before or since. It was a day when the LORD listened to a mere human being. Surely the LORD was fighting for Israel!

So Joshua and the men of Israel had complete victory over them. They also defeated and destroyed all the cities in the central part of Canaan that had high walls around them. Then the kings of the cities in the northern part of Canaan joined together to attack the Israelites. But Joshua defeated all of them, too.

So the LORD gave Israel all the land he had promised to give to Abraham, Isaac and Jacob. And Israel took it over. Then they made their homes there. The LORD gave them peace and rest on every side. He had promised their people of long ago that he would do that. Not one of Israel's enemies was able to fight against them and win. The LORD handed all their enemies over to them. The LORD kept all the good promises he had made to the Israelites. Every one of them came true.

☙✿❧

A long time had passed. The LORD had given Israel peace and rest from all their enemies around them. By that time Joshua was very old. So he sent for all the elders, leaders, judges and officials of Israel. He said to them, "I'm very old. You yourselves have seen everything the LORD your God has done. You have seen what he's done to all these nations because of you. The LORD your God fought for you. Remember how I've given you all the land of the nations that remain here. I've given each of your tribes a share of it. It's the land of the nations I conquered. It's between the Jordan River and the Mediterranean Sea in the west. The LORD your God himself will drive those nations out of your way. He will push them out to make room for you. You will take over their land, just as the LORD your God promised you.

"Be very strong. Be careful to obey everything written in the Book of the Law of Moses. Don't turn away from it to the right or the left. Don't have anything to do with the nations that remain among you. Don't use the names of their gods for any reason at all. Don't give your word and make promises in their names. You must not serve them. You must not bow down to them. You must remain true to the LORD your God, just as you have done until now.

"The LORD has driven out great and powerful nations to make room for you. To this day no one has been able to fight against you and win. One of you can chase a thousand away. That's because the LORD your God fights for you, just as he promised he would. So be very careful to love the LORD your God."

Joshua spoke to all the people. He said, "The LORD is the God of Israel. He says, 'Long ago your people lived east of the Euphrates River. They worshiped other gods there. Your people included Terah. He was the father of Abraham and Nahor. I took your father Abraham from the land east of the Euphrates. I led him all through

Canaan. I gave him many children and grandchildren. I gave him Isaac. To Isaac I gave Jacob and Esau. I gave the hill country of Seir to Esau. But Jacob and his family went down to Egypt.

" 'Then I sent Moses and Aaron. I made the people of Egypt suffer because of the plagues I sent on them. But I brought you out of Egypt. When I brought your people out, they came to the Red Sea. The people of Egypt chased them with chariots and with men on horses. They chased them all the way to the sea. But your people cried out to me for help. So I put darkness between you and the people of Egypt. I swept them into the sea. It completely covered them. Your own eyes saw what I did to them. After that, you lived in the desert for a long time.

" 'I brought you to the land of the Amorites. They lived east of the Jordan River. They fought against you. But I handed them over to you. I destroyed them to make room for you. Then you took over their land. Balak, the son of Zippor, prepared to fight against Israel. Balak was the king of Moab. He sent for Balaam, the son of Beor. Balak wanted Balaam to put a curse on you. But I would not listen to Balaam's curses. So he blessed you again and again. And I saved you from his power.

" 'Then you went across the Jordan River. You came to Jericho. Its people fought against you. So did the Amorites, Perizzites, Canaanites, Hittites, Girgashites, Hivites and Jebusites. But I handed them over to you. I sent hornets ahead of you. They drove your enemies out to make room for you. That included the two Amorite kings. You did not do that with your own swords and bows. So I gave you a land you had never farmed. I gave you cities you had not built. You are now living in them. And you are eating the fruit of vineyards and olive trees you did not plant.'

"So have respect for the LORD. Serve him. Be completely faithful to him. Throw away the gods your people worshiped east of the Euphrates River and in Egypt. Serve the LORD. But suppose you don't want to serve him. Then choose for yourselves right now whom you will serve. You can choose the gods your people served east of the Euphrates River. Or you can serve the gods of the Amorites. After all, you are living in their land. But as for me and my family, we will serve the LORD."

Then the people answered Joshua, "We would never desert the LORD! We would never serve other gods! The LORD our God himself brought us and our parents up out of Egypt. He brought us out of that land where we were slaves. With our own eyes, we saw those great signs he did. He kept us safe on our entire journey. He kept us safe as we traveled through all the nations. He drove them out to make room for us. That included the Amorites. They also lived in the land. We too will serve the LORD. That's because he is our God."

On that day Joshua made a covenant for the people. There at Shechem he reminded them of its rules and laws. He recorded these things in the Book of the Law of God. Then he got a large stone. He set it up in Shechem under the oak tree. It was near the place that had been set apart for the LORD.

"Look!" he said to all the people. "This stone will be a witness against us. It has heard all the words the LORD has spoken to us. Suppose you aren't faithful to your God. Then the stone will be a witness against you."

Joshua sent the people away. He sent all of them to their own shares of land.

Then Joshua, the servant of the LORD, died. He was the son of Nun. He was 110 years old when he died.

remember what you read

1. What is something you noticed for the first time?

_____

_____

_____

_____

2. What questions did you have?

_____

_____

_____

_____

3. Was there anything that bothered you?

_____

_____

_____

_____

4. What did you learn about loving God?

_____

_____

_____

_____

5. What did you learn about loving others?

_____

_____

_____

_____

JUDGES, PART I

introduction to Judges, parts 1-3

The people of Israel were no longer in a single camp with a leader among them. They started to turn away from God. So God gave "judges" or leaders to guide the people and save them from their enemies. But Israel kept going in circles of disobeying, crying out for help, being rescued, and disobeying again.

∽͡𝓎𝓎͡∼

All the people of Joshua's time joined the members of their families who had already died. Then those who were born after them grew up. They didn't know the LORD and what he had done for Israel. The Israelites did what was evil in the sight of the LORD. They served gods that were named Baal. They deserted the LORD, the God of their people. He had brought them out of Egypt. But now the Israelites served other gods and worshiped them. They served the gods of the nations that were around them. They made the LORD angry because they deserted him. They served Baal. They also served female gods that were named Ashtoreth. The LORD became angry with the Israelites. So he handed them over to robbers. The robbers stole everything from them. The LORD handed the Israelites over to their enemies all around them. Israel wasn't able to fight against them anymore and win. When the Israelites went out to fight, the LORD's power was against them. He let their enemies win the battle over them. The LORD had warned them that it would happen. And now they were suffering terribly.

Then the LORD gave them leaders. The leaders saved them from the power of those robbers. But the people wouldn't listen to their leaders. They weren't faithful to the LORD. They served other gods and worshiped them. They didn't obey the LORD's commands as their people before them had done. They quickly turned away from the path their people had taken. When the LORD gave them a leader, he was with that leader. The LORD saved the people from the power of their enemies. He did it as long as the leader lived. The LORD felt very sorry for the people. They groaned because of what their enemies did to them. Their enemies treated them badly. But when the leader died, the people returned to their evil ways. The things they did were even more sinful than the things their people before them had done. They served other gods and worshiped them. They refused to give up their evil practices. They wouldn't change their stubborn ways.

So the LORD became very angry with the Israelites. He said, "This nation has broken my covenant. I made it with their people of long ago. But this nation has not listened to me. Joshua left some nations in the land when he died. I will no longer drive out those nations to make room for Israel. I will use those nations to test Israel. I will see whether Israel will live the way I, the LORD, want them to. I will see whether they will be like their people of long ago. I will see whether they will follow my path."

The Israelites disobeyed God. But then they said they were sorry. God sent Othniel to save Israel from their enemies. But after he died, the people disobeyed again. The same happened with Ehud and Shamgar.

After Ehud died, the Israelites once again did what was evil in the sight of the LORD. So the LORD handed them over to the power of Jabin. He was a king in Canaan. He ruled in Hazor. The commander of his army was Sisera. Jabin had 900 chariots. He treated the Israelites very badly for 20 years. So they cried out to the LORD for help.

Deborah was a prophet. She was the wife of Lappidoth. She was leading Israel at that time. Under the Palm Tree of Deborah she served the people as their judge. The Israelites came to have her decide cases for them. Deborah sent for Barak and said, "The LORD, the God of Israel, is giving you a command. He says, 'Go! Take 10,000 men from the tribes of Naphtali and Zebulun with you. Then lead them up to Mount Tabor. I will lead Sisera into a trap. I will bring him, his chariots and his troops to the Kishon River. There I will hand him over to you.'"

Barak said to her, "If you go with me, I'll go. But if you don't go with me, I won't go."

"All right," Deborah said. "I'll go with you. But because of the way you are doing this, you won't receive any honor. Instead, the LORD will hand Sisera over to a woman." So Deborah went to Kedesh with Barak. There he sent for men from Zebulun and Naphtali. And 10,000 men followed him into battle.

Sisera was told that Barak, the son of Abinoam, had gone up to Mount Tabor. So Sisera gathered together his 900 chariots. He also gathered together all his men.

Then Deborah said to Barak, "Go! Today the LORD will hand Sisera over to you. Hasn't the LORD gone ahead of you?" So Barak went down Mount Tabor. His 10,000 men followed him. As Barak's men marched out, the LORD drove Sisera away from the field of battle. The LORD scattered all of Sisera's chariots. Barak's men struck down Sisera's army with their swords. Sisera got down from his chariot. He ran away on foot.

He ran to the tent of Jael. She was the wife of Heber, the Kenite. Sisera ran there because there was a treaty between Heber's family and Jabin, the king of Hazor.

Jael went out to meet Sisera. "Come in, sir," she said. "Come right in. Don't be afraid." So he entered her tent. Then she covered him with a blanket.

"I'm thirsty," he said. "Please give me some water." So Jael opened a bottle of milk. The bottle was made out of animal skin. She gave him a drink of milk. Then she covered him up again.

"Stand in the doorway of the tent," he told her. "Someone might come by and ask you, 'Is anyone in there?' If that happens, say 'No.'"

But Heber's wife Jael picked up a tent stake and a hammer. She went quietly over to Sisera. He was lying there, fast asleep. He was very tired. She drove the stake through his head right into the ground. So he died.

Just then Barak came by because he was chasing Sisera. Jael went out to meet him. "Come right in," she said. "I'll show you the man you are looking for." So he went in with her. Sisera was lying there with the stake through his head. He was dead.

On that day God brought Jabin under Israel's control. The Israelites became so strong that they destroyed him.

On that day Deborah and Barak sang a song. Barak was the son of Abinoam. Here is what Deborah and Barak sang.

"The princes in Israel lead the way.
   The people follow them just because they want to.
   When this happens, praise the Lord!

"Kings, hear this! Rulers, listen!
   I will sing to the Lord.
   I will praise the Lord in song. He is the God of Israel.

So the land was at peace for 40 years.

⁊⁊⁊

The Israelites did what was evil in the sight of the Lord. So for seven years he handed them over to the people of Midian. The Midianites treated the Israelites very badly. Each year the people planted their crops. When they did, the Midianites came into the country and attacked it. The Midianites made the Israelites very poor. So they cried out to the Lord for help.

The angel of the Lord came. He sat down under an oak tree in Ophrah that belonged to Joash. Gideon the son of Joash was threshing wheat in a winepress to hide the wheat from the Midianites. The angel of the Lord appeared to Gideon. He said, "Mighty warrior, the Lord is with you."

"Pardon me, sir," Gideon replied, "you say the Lord is with us. Then why has all this happened to us? Where are all the wonderful things he has done? Our people of long ago told us about them. They said, 'Didn't the Lord bring us up out of Egypt?' But now the Lord has deserted us. He has handed us over to Midian."

The Lord turned to Gideon. He said to him, "You are strong. Go and save Israel from the power of Midian. I am sending you."

"Pardon me, sir," Gideon replied, "but how can I possibly save Israel? My family group is the weakest in the tribe of Manasseh. And I'm the least important member of my family."

The Lord answered, "I will be with you. So you will strike down the Midianites."

Gideon replied, "If you are pleased with me, give me a special sign. Then I'll know that it's really you talking to me. Please don't go away until I come back. I'll bring my offering and set it down in front of you."

The Lord said, "I will wait until you return."

Gideon went inside and prepared a young goat. From 36 pounds of flour he made bread without using yeast. He put the meat in a basket. In a pot he put soup made from the meat. Then he brought all of it and offered it to the Lord under the oak tree.

The angel of God said to Gideon, "Take the meat and the bread. Place them on this rock. Then pour out the soup." So Gideon did it. The angel of the Lord had a walking stick in his hand. With the tip of the stick he touched the meat and the bread. Fire blazed out of the rock. It burned up the meat and the bread. Then the angel of the Lord disappeared. Gideon realized it was the angel of the Lord. He cried out, "Oh no, my Lord and King, I have seen the angel of the Lord face to face!"

But the Lord said to him, "May peace be with you! Do not be afraid. You are not going to die."

So Gideon built an altar there to honor the Lord. He called it The Lord Is Peace.

All the Midianites and Amalekites gathered their armies together. Other tribes from the east joined them. All of them went across the Jordan River. They camped in the Valley of Jezreel. Then the Spirit of the Lord came on Gideon. So Gideon blew a trumpet to send for the men of Abiezer. He told them to follow him. He sent messengers all through Manasseh's territory. He called for the men of Manasseh to fight. He also sent messengers to the men of Asher, Zebulun and Naphtali. So all those men went up to join the others.

Gideon said to God, "You promised you would use me to save Israel. Please do something for me. I'll put a piece of wool on the threshing floor. Suppose dew is only on the wool tomorrow morning. And suppose the ground all around it is dry. Then I will know that you will use me to save Israel. I'll know that your promise will come true." And that's what happened. Gideon got up early the next day. He squeezed the dew out of the wool. The water filled a bowl.

Then Gideon said to God, "Don't be angry with me. Let me ask you for just one more thing. Let me use the wool for one more test. But this time make the wool dry. And let the ground be covered with dew." So that night God did it. Only the wool was dry. The ground all around it was covered with dew.

Early in the morning Gideon and all his men camped at the spring of Harod. The LORD said to Gideon, "I want to hand Midian over to you. But you have too many men for me to do that. Then Israel might brag, 'My own strength has saved me.' So here is what I want you to announce to the army. Tell them, 'Those who tremble with fear can turn back. They can leave Mount Gilead.'" So 22,000 men left. But 10,000 remained.

The LORD said to Gideon, "There are still too many men. So take them down to the water. There I will reduce the number of them for you. If I say, 'This one will go with you,' he will go. But if I say, 'That one will not go with you,' he will not go."

remember what you read

1. What is something you noticed for the first time?

_____

_____

_____

_____

2. What questions did you have?

_____

_____

_____

_____

3. Was there anything that bothered you?

_____

_____

_____

_____

4. What did you learn about loving God?

_____

_____

_____

_____

5. What did you learn about loving others?

_____

_____

_____

_____

So Gideon took the men down to the water. There the Lord said to him, "Some men will drink the way dogs do. They will lap up the water with their tongues. Separate them from those who get down on their knees to drink." Three hundred men brought up the water to their mouths with their hands. And they lapped it up the way dogs do. All the rest got down on their knees to drink.

The Lord spoke to Gideon. He said, "With the help of the 300 men who lapped up the water I will save you. I will hand the Midianites over to you. Let all the other men go home." So Gideon sent those Israelites home. But he kept the 300 men. They took over the supplies and trumpets the others had left.

The Midianites had set up their camp in the valley below where Gideon was. During that night the Lord said to Gideon, "Get up. Go down against the camp. I am going to hand it over to you. But what if you are afraid to attack? Then go down to the camp with your servant Purah. Listen to what they are saying. After that, you will not be afraid to attack the camp." So Gideon and his servant Purah went down to the edge of the camp. The Midianites had set up their camp in the valley. So had the Amalekites and all the other tribes from the east. There were so many of them that they looked like huge numbers of locusts. Like the grains of sand on the seashore, their camels couldn't be counted.

Gideon arrived just as a man was telling a friend about his dream. "I had a dream," he was saying. "A round loaf of barley bread came rolling into the camp of Midian. It hit a tent with great force. The tent turned over and fell down flat."

His friend replied, "That can only be the sword of Gideon, the son of Joash. Gideon is from Israel. God has handed the Midianites over to him. He has given him the whole camp."

Gideon heard the man explain what the dream meant. Then Gideon bowed down and worshiped. He returned to the camp of Israel. He called out, "Get up! The Lord has handed the Midianites over to you." Gideon separated the 300 men into three fighting groups. He put a trumpet and an empty jar into the hands of each man. And he put a torch inside each jar.

"Watch me," he told them. "Do what I do. I'll go to the edge of the enemy camp. Then do exactly as I do. I and everyone with me will blow our trumpets. Then blow your trumpets from your positions all around the camp. And shout the battle cry, 'For the Lord and for Gideon!' "

Gideon and the 100 men with him reached the edge of the enemy camp. It was about ten o'clock at night. It was just after the guard had been changed. Gideon and his men blew their trumpets. They broke the jars that were in their hands. The three fighting groups blew their trumpets. They smashed their jars. They held their torches in their left hands. They held in their right hands the trumpets they were going to blow. Then they shouted the battle cry, "A sword for the Lord and for Gideon!" Each man stayed in his position around the camp. But all the Midianites ran away in fear. They were crying out as they ran.

When the 300 trumpets were blown, the Lord caused all the men in the enemy camp to start fighting one another. They attacked one another with their swords. The army ran away.

Israel brought Midian under their control. Midian wasn't able to attack Israel anymore. So the land was at peace for 40 years. The peace lasted as long as Gideon was living.

Several more leaders helped Israel: Tola, Jair, Jephthah, Ibzan, Elon, and Abdon. But after God saved his people, they always disobeyed again.

Once again the Israelites did what was evil in the sight of the Lord. So the Lord handed them over to the Philistines for 40 years.

A certain man from Zorah was named Manoah. He was from the tribe of Dan. Manoah had a wife who wasn't able to have children. The angel of the Lord appeared to Manoah's wife. He said, "You are not able to have children. But you are going to become pregnant. You will have a baby boy. Make sure you do not drink any kind of wine. Also make sure you do not eat anything that is 'unclean.' You will become pregnant. You will have a son. The hair on his head must never be cut. That is because the boy will be a Nazirite. He will be set apart to God from the day he is born. He will take the lead in saving Israel from the power of the Philistines."

Then the woman went to her husband. She told him, "A man of God came to me. He looked like an angel of God. His appearance was so amazing that it filled me with great wonder. I didn't ask him where he came from. And he didn't tell me his name. But he said to me, 'You will become pregnant. You will have a son. So do not drink any kind of wine. Do not eat anything that is "unclean." That is because the boy will be a Nazirite. He will belong to God in a special way from the day he is born until the day he dies.'"

Then Manoah prayed to the Lord. He said, "Pardon your servant, Lord. I beg you to let the man of God you sent to us come again. He told us we would have a son. We want the man of God to teach us how to bring up the boy."

God heard Manoah. And the angel of God came again to the woman. He came while she was out in the field. But her husband Manoah wasn't with her. The woman hurried to her husband. She told him, "He's here! The man who appeared to me the other day is here!"

Manoah got up and followed his wife. When he came to the man, he spoke to him. He said, "Are you the man who talked to my wife?"

"I am," he replied.

So Manoah asked him, "What will happen when your words come true? What rules should we follow for the boy's life and work?"

The angel of the Lord answered him. He said, "Your wife must do everything I have told her to do. She must not eat anything that comes from grapevines. She must not drink any kind of wine. She must not eat anything that is 'unclean.' She must do everything I have commanded her to do."

Manoah said to the angel of the LORD, "We would like you to stay and eat. We want to prepare a young goat for you."

The angel of the LORD replied, "Even if I stay, I will not eat any of your food. But if you still want to prepare a burnt offering, you must offer it to the LORD." Manoah didn't realize it was the angel of the LORD.

Then Manoah asked the angel of the LORD a question. "What is your name?" he said. "We want to honor you when your word comes true."

The angel replied, "Why are you asking me what my name is? You would not be able to understand it." Manoah got a young goat. He brought it along with the grain offering. He sacrificed it on a rock to the LORD. Then the LORD did an amazing thing. It happened while Manoah and his wife were watching. A flame blazed up from the altar toward heaven. The angel of the LORD rose up in the flame. When Manoah and his wife saw it, they fell with their faces to the ground. The angel of the LORD didn't show himself again to Manoah and his wife. Then Manoah realized it was the angel of the LORD.

"We're going to die!" he said to his wife. "We've seen God!"

But his wife answered, "The LORD doesn't want to kill us. If he did, he wouldn't have accepted a burnt offering and a grain offering from us. He wouldn't have shown us all these things. He wouldn't have told us we're going to have a son."

Later, the woman had a baby boy. She named him Samson. As he grew up, the LORD blessed him. The Spirit of the LORD began to work in his life. It happened while he was in Mahaneh Dan. That place is between Zorah and Eshtaol.

Samson went down to Timnah. There he saw a young Philistine woman. When he returned, he spoke to his father and mother. He said, "I've seen a Philistine woman in Timnah. Get her for me. I want her to be my wife."

His father and mother replied, "Can't we find a wife for you among your relatives? Isn't there one among any of our people?

Do you have to go to the Philistines to get a wife? They aren't God's people. They haven't even been circumcised."

But Samson said to his father, "Get her for me. She's the right one for me." Samson's parents didn't know that the LORD wanted things to happen this way. He was working out his plans against the Philistines. That's because the Philistines were ruling over Israel at that time.

Samson went down to Timnah. His father and mother went with him. They approached the vineyards of Timnah. Suddenly a young lion came roaring toward Samson. Then the Spirit of the LORD came powerfully on Samson. So he tore the lion apart with his bare hands. He did it as easily as he might have torn a young goat apart. But he didn't tell his father or mother what he had done. Then he went down and talked with the woman. He liked her.

Some time later, he was going back to marry her. But he turned off the road to look at the lion's dead body. He saw large numbers of bees and some honey in it. He dug out the honey with his hands. He ate it as he walked along. Then he joined his parents again. He gave them some honey. They ate it too. But he didn't tell them he had taken it from the lion's dead body.

Samson's father went down to see the woman. Samson had a feast prepared there. He was following the practice of young men when they married their wives. When the people saw Samson, they gave him 30 men to be his companions.

"Let me tell you a riddle," Samson said to the companions. "The feast will last for seven days. Give me the answer to the riddle before the feast ends. If you do, I'll give you 30 linen shirts. I'll also give you 30 sets of clothes. But suppose you can't give me the answer. Then you must give me 30 linen shirts. You must also give me 30 sets of clothes."

"Tell us your riddle," they said. "Let's hear it."

Samson replied,

"Out of the eater came something to eat.
  Out of the strong came something sweet."

For three days they couldn't give him the answer.

On the fourth day they spoke to Samson's wife. "Get your husband to explain the riddle for us," they said. "If you don't, we'll burn you to death. We'll burn up everyone in your family. Did you invite us here to steal our property?"

remember what you read

1. What is something you noticed for the first time?

_____

_____

_____

_____

2. What questions did you have?

_____

_____

_____

_____

3. Was there anything that bothered you?

_____

_____

_____

_____

4. What did you learn about loving God?

_____

_____

_____

_____

5. What did you learn about loving others?

_____

_____

_____

_____

Then Samson's wife threw herself on him. She sobbed, "You hate me! You don't really love me. You have given my people a riddle. But you haven't told me the answer."

"I haven't even explained it to my father or mother," he replied. "So why should I explain it to you?" She cried during the whole seven days the feast was going on. So on the seventh day he finally told her the answer to the riddle. That's because she kept on asking him to tell her. Then she explained the riddle to her people.

Before sunset on the seventh day of the feast the men of the town spoke to Samson. They said,

"What is sweeter than honey?
  What is stronger than a lion?"

Samson said to them,

"You have plowed with my young cow.
  If you hadn't, you wouldn't have known the answer to my
    riddle."

Then the Spirit of the LORD came powerfully on Samson. He went down to Ashkelon. He struck down 30 of their men. He took everything they had with them. And he gave their clothes to those who had explained the riddle. Samson was very angry as he returned to his father's home. Samson's wife was given to someone else. She was given to a companion of Samson. The companion had helped him at the feast.

Later on, Samson went to visit his wife. He took a young goat with him. He went at the time the wheat was being gathered. He said, "I'm going to my wife's room." But her father wouldn't let him go in.

Her father said, "I was sure you hated her. So I gave her to your companion. Isn't her younger sister more beautiful? Take her instead."

Samson said to them, "This time I have a right to get even with the Philistines. I'm going to hurt them badly." So he went out and caught 300 foxes. He tied them in pairs by their tails. Then he tied a torch to each pair of tails. He lit the torches. He let the foxes loose in the fields of grain that belonged to the Philistines. He burned up the grain that had been cut and stacked. He burned up the grain that was still growing. He also burned up the vineyards and olive trees.

The Philistines asked, "Who did this?" They were told, "Samson did. He's the son-in-law of the man from Timnah. Samson did it because his wife was given to his companion."

So the Philistines went up and burned the woman and her father to death. Samson said to the Philistines, "Is that how you act? Then I promise I won't stop until I pay you back." He struck them down with heavy blows. He killed many of them. Then he went down and stayed in a cave. It was in the rock of Etam.

The Philistines went up and camped in Judah. They spread out near Lehi. The people of Judah asked, "Why have you come to fight against us?"

"We've come to take Samson as our prisoner," they answered. "We want to do to him what he did to us."

Then 3,000 men from Judah went to get Samson. They went down to the cave in the rock of Etam. They said to Samson, "Don't you realize the Philistines are ruling over us? What have you done to us?"

Samson answered, "I only did to them what they did to me."

The men of Judah said to him, "We've come to tie you up. We're going to hand you over to the Philistines."

Samson said, "Promise me you won't kill me yourselves."

"We agree," they answered. "We'll only tie you up and hand you over to them. We won't kill you." So they tied him up with two new ropes. They led him up from the rock. Samson approached Lehi.

The Philistines came toward him shouting. Then the Spirit of the
LORD came powerfully on Samson. The ropes on his arms became
like burned thread. They dropped off his hands. He found a fresh
jawbone of a donkey. He grabbed it and struck down 1,000 men.

Then Samson said,

> "By using a donkey's jawbone
>   I've made them look like donkeys.
> By using a donkey's jawbone
>   I've struck down 1,000 men."

Some time later, Samson fell in love again. The woman lived in
the Valley of Sorek. Her name was Delilah. The rulers of the Philistines went to her. They said, "See if you can get him to tell you
the secret of why he's so strong. Find out how we can overpower
him. Then we can tie him up. We can bring him under our control.
Each of us will give you 28 pounds of silver."

So Delilah said to Samson, "Tell me the secret of why you are so
strong. Tell me how you can be tied up and controlled."

Samson answered her, "Let someone tie me up with seven new
bowstrings. They must be strings that aren't completely dry. Then
I'll become as weak as any other man."

So the Philistine rulers brought seven new bowstrings to her.
They weren't completely dry. Delilah tied Samson up with them.
Men were hiding in the room. She called out to him, "Samson!
The Philistines are attacking you!" But he snapped the bowstrings
easily. They were like pieces of string that had come too close to
a flame. So the secret of why he was so strong wasn't discovered.

Delilah spoke to Samson again. "You have made me look foolish," she said. "You told me a lie. Come on. Tell me how you can
be tied up."

Samson said, "Let someone tie me tightly with new ropes. They
must be ropes that have never been used. Then I'll become as
weak as any other man."

So Delilah got some new ropes. She tied him up with them. Men
were hiding in the room. She called out to him, "Samson! The Philistines are attacking you!" But he snapped the ropes off his arms.
They fell off just as if they were threads.

Delilah spoke to Samson again. "All this time you have been making me look foolish," she said. "You have been telling me lies. This time really tell me how you can be tied up."

He replied, "Weave the seven braids of my hair into the cloth on a loom. Then tighten the cloth with a pin. If you do, I'll become as weak as any other man." So while Samson was sleeping, Delilah took hold of the seven braids of his hair. She wove them into the cloth on a loom. Then she tightened the cloth with a pin.

Again she called out to him, "Samson! The Philistines are attacking you!" He woke up from his sleep. He pulled up the pin and the loom, together with the cloth.

Then she said to him, "How can you say, 'I love you'? You won't even share your secret with me. This is the third time you have made me look foolish. And you still haven't told me the secret of why you are so strong." She continued to pester him day after day. She nagged him until he was sick and tired of it.

So he told her everything. He said, "My hair has never been cut. That's because I've been a Nazirite since the day I was born. A Nazirite is set apart to God. If you shave my head, I won't be strong anymore. I'll become as weak as any other man."

Delilah realized he had told her everything. So she sent a message to the Philistine rulers. She said, "Come back one more time. He has told me everything." So the rulers returned. They brought the silver with them. Delilah got Samson to go to sleep on her lap. Then she called for someone to shave off the seven braids of his hair. That's how she began to bring Samson under her control. And he wasn't strong anymore.

She called out, "Samson! The Philistines are attacking you!"

He woke up from his sleep. He thought, "I'll go out just as I did before. I'll shake myself free." But he didn't know that the LORD had left him.

Then the Philistines grabbed him. They poked his eyes out. They took him down to Gaza. They put bronze chains around him. Then they made him grind grain in the prison. His head had been shaved. But the hair on it began to grow again.

The rulers of the Philistines gathered together. They were going to offer a great sacrifice to their god Dagon. They were going to celebrate. They said, "Our god has handed our enemy Samson over to us."

When the people saw Samson, they praised their god. They said,

"Our god has handed our enemy over to us.
  Our enemy has destroyed our land.
  He has killed large numbers of our people."

After they had drunk a lot of wine, they shouted, "Bring Samson out. Let him put on a show for us." So they called Samson out of the prison. He put on a show for them.

They had him stand near the temple pillars. Then he spoke to the servant who was holding his hand. He said, "Put me where I can feel the pillars. I'm talking about the ones that hold up the temple. I want to lean against them." The temple was crowded with men and women. All the Philistine rulers were there. About 3,000 men and women were on the roof. They were watching Samson put on a show. Then he prayed to the LORD. Samson said, "LORD and King, show me that you still have concern for me. Please, God, make me strong just one more time. Let me pay the Philistines back for what they did to my two eyes. Let me do it with only one blow." Then Samson reached toward the two pillars that were in the middle of the temple. They were the ones that held up the temple. He put his right hand on one of them. He put his left hand on the other. He leaned hard against them. Samson said, "Let me die together with the Philistines!" Then he pushed with all his might. The temple came down on the rulers. It fell on all the people in it. So Samson killed many more Philistines when he died than he did while he lived.

In those days Israel didn't have a king. The people did anything they thought was right.

introduction to Ruth, parts 1-2

The story of Ruth is beautiful. Most people in Israel were following the "gods" of other nations. Ruth is in a bad situation. See how she makes decisions based on her faith in God. One man in this story

followed God's covenant rules very carefully. How did he do that? Pay attention to Boaz's actions toward Ruth.

❧❧❧

There was a time when Israel didn't have kings to rule over them. But they had leaders to help them. This is a story about some things that happened during that time. There wasn't enough food in the land of Judah. So a man went to live for a while in the country of Moab. He was from Bethlehem in Judah. His wife and two sons went with him. The man's name was Elimelek. His wife's name was Naomi. The names of his two sons were Mahlon and Kilion. They were from the tribe of Ephraim. Their home had been in Bethlehem in Judah. They went to Moab and lived there.

Naomi's husband Elimelek died. So she was left with her two sons. They married women from Moab. One was named Orpah. The other was named Ruth. Naomi's family lived in Moab for about ten years. Then Mahlon and Kilion also died. So Naomi was left without her two sons and her husband.

While Naomi was in Moab, she heard that the LORD had helped his people. He had begun to provide food for them again. So Naomi and her two daughters-in-law prepared to go from Moab back to her home. She left the place where she had been living. Her daughters-in-law went with her. They started out on the road that would take them back to the land of Judah.

remember what you read

1. What is something you noticed for the first time?

_____

_____

_____

_____

2. What questions did you have?

_____

_____

_____

_____

3. Was there anything that bothered you?

_____

_____

_____

_____

4. What did you learn about loving God?

_____

_____

_____

_____

5. What did you learn about loving others?

_____

_____

_____

_____

Naomi said to her two daughters-in-law, "Both of you go back. Each of you go to your own mother's home. You were kind to your husbands, who have died. You have also been kind to me. So may the Lord be just as kind to you. May the Lord help each of you find rest in the home of another husband."

Then she kissed them goodbye. They broke down and wept loudly. They said to her, "We'll go back to your people with you."

But Naomi said, "Go home, my daughters. Why would you want to come with me? Am I going to have any more sons who could become your husbands? Go home, my daughters. I'm too old to have another husband. Suppose I thought there was still some hope for me. Suppose I married a man tonight. And later I had sons by him. Would you wait until they grew up? Would you stay single until you could marry them? No, my daughters. My life is more bitter than yours. The Lord's power has turned against me!"

When they heard that, they broke down and wept again. Then Orpah kissed her mother-in-law goodbye. But Ruth held on to her.

"Look," said Naomi. "Your sister-in-law is going back to her people and her gods. Go back with her."

But Ruth replied, "Don't try to make me leave you and go back. Where you go I'll go. Where you stay I'll stay. Your people will be my people. Your God will be my God. Where you die I'll die. And there my body will be buried. I won't let even death separate you from me. If I do, may the Lord punish me greatly." Naomi realized that Ruth had made up her mind to go with her. So she stopped trying to make her go back.

The two women continued on their way. At last they arrived in

Bethlehem. The whole town was stirred up because of them. The women in the town asked, "Can this possibly be Naomi?"

"Don't call me Naomi," she told them. "Call me Mara. The Mighty One has made my life very bitter. I was full when I went away. But the Lord has brought me back empty. So why are you calling me Naomi? The Lord has made me suffer. The Mighty One has brought trouble on me."

Ruth, who was from Moab, spoke to Naomi. Ruth said, "Let me go out to the fields. I'll pick up the grain that has been left. I'll do it behind anyone who is pleased with me."

Naomi said to her, "My daughter, go ahead." So Ruth went out to a field and began to pick up grain. She worked behind those cutting and gathering the grain. As it turned out, she was working in a field that belonged to Boaz. He was from the family of Elimelek.

Just then Boaz arrived from Bethlehem. He greeted those cutting and gathering the grain. He said, "May the Lord be with you!"

"And may the Lord bless you!" they replied.

Boaz spoke to the man in charge of his workers. He asked, "Who does that young woman belong to?"

The man replied, "She's from Moab. She came back from there with Naomi. The young woman said, 'Please let me walk behind the workers. Let me pick up the grain that is left.' She came into the field. She has kept on working here from morning until now. She took only one short rest in the shade."

So Boaz said to Ruth, "Dear woman, listen to me. Don't pick up grain in any other field. Don't go anywhere else. Stay here with the women who work for me. Keep your eye on the field where the men are cutting grain. Walk behind the women who are gathering it. Pick up the grain that is left. I've told the men not to bother you. When you are thirsty, go and get a drink. Take water from the jars the men have filled."

When Ruth heard that, she bowed down with her face to the ground. She asked him, "Why are you being so kind to me? In fact, why are you even noticing me? I'm from another country."

Boaz replied, "I've been told all about you. I've heard about everything you have done for your mother-in-law since your husband died. I know that you left your father and mother. I know that you left your country. You came to live with people you didn't know before. May the LORD reward you for what you have done. May the LORD, the God of Israel, bless you richly. You have come to him to find safety under his care."

"Sir, I hope you will continue to be kind to me," Ruth said. "You have made me feel safe. You have spoken kindly to me. And I'm not even as important as one of your servants!"

When it was time to eat, Boaz spoke to Ruth again. "Come over here," he said. "Have some bread. Dip it in the wine vinegar."

So Ruth picked up grain in the field until evening. Then she separated the barley from the straw. The barley weighed 30 pounds. She carried it back to town. Her mother-in-law saw how much she had gathered. Ruth also brought out the food left over from the lunch Boaz had given her. She gave it to Naomi.

Her mother-in-law asked her, "Where did you pick up grain today? Where did you work? May the man who noticed you be blessed!"

Then Ruth told her about the man whose field she had worked in. "The name of the man I worked with today is Boaz," she said.

"May the LORD bless him!" Naomi said to her daughter-in-law. "The LORD is still being kind to those who are living and those who are dead." She continued, "That man is a close relative of ours. He's one of our family protectors."

Then Ruth, who was from Moab, said, "He told me more. He even said, 'Stay with my workers until they have finished bringing in all my grain.'"

Naomi replied to her daughter-in-law Ruth. She said, "That will be good for you, my daughter. Go with the women who work for him. You might be harmed if you go to someone else's field."

One day Ruth's mother-in-law Naomi spoke to her. She said, "My daughter, I must find a home for you. It should be a place where you will be provided for. You have been working with the women who work for Boaz. He's a relative of ours. Tonight he'll be separating the straw from his barley on the threshing floor. So wash yourself. Put on some perfume. And put on your best clothes. Then go down to the threshing floor. But don't let Boaz know you are there.

Wait until he has finished eating and drinking. Notice where he lies down. Then go over and uncover his feet. Lie down there. He'll tell you what to do."

"I'll do everything you say," Ruth answered. So she went down to the threshing floor. She did everything her mother-in-law had told her to do.

When Boaz had finished eating and drinking, he was in a good mood. He went over to lie down at the far end of the grain pile. Then Ruth approached quietly. She uncovered his feet and lay down there. In the middle of the night, something surprised Boaz and woke him up. He turned and found a woman lying there at his feet!

"Who are you?" he asked.

"I'm Ruth," she said. "You are my family protector. So take good care of me by making me your wife."

"Dear woman, may the LORD bless you," he replied. "You are showing even more kindness now than you did earlier. You didn't run after the younger men, whether they were rich or poor. Dear woman, don't be afraid. I'll do for you everything you ask. All the people of my town know that you are an excellent woman. It's true that I'm a relative of yours. But there's a family protector who is more closely related to you than I am. So stay here for the night. In the morning if he wants to help you, good. Let him help you. But if he doesn't want to, then I'll do it. You can be sure that the LORD lives. And you can be just as sure that I'll help you. Lie down here until morning."

So she stayed at his feet until morning. But she got up before anyone could be recognized. Boaz thought, "No one must know that a woman came to the threshing floor."

He said to Ruth, "Bring me the coat you have around you. Hold it out." So she did. He poured more than fifty pounds of barley into it and helped her pick it up. Then he went back to town.

Ruth came to her mother-in-law. Naomi asked, "How did it go, my daughter?"

Then Ruth told her everything Boaz had done for her. She said, "He gave me all this barley. He said, 'Don't go back to your mother-in-law with your hands empty.'"

Naomi said, "My daughter, sit down until you find out what happens. The man won't rest until he settles the whole matter today."

Boaz went up to the town gate and sat down there. Right then, the family protector he had talked about came by. Then Boaz said, "Come over here, my friend. Sit down." So the man went over and sat down.

Boaz brought ten of the elders of the town together. He said, "Sit down here." So they did. Then he spoke to the family protector. He said, "Naomi has come back from Moab. She's selling the piece of land that belonged to our relative Elimelek. I thought I should bring the matter to your attention. I suggest that you buy the land. Buy it while those sitting here and the elders of my people are looking on as witnesses. If you are willing to buy it back, do it. But if you aren't, tell me. Then I'll know. No one has the right to buy it back except you. And I'm next in line."

"I'll buy it," he said.

Then Boaz said, "When you buy the property from Naomi, you must also marry Ruth. She is from Moab and is the dead man's widow. So you must marry her. That's because his property must continue to belong to his family."

When the family protector heard that, he said, "Then I can't buy the land. If I did, I might put my own property in danger. So you buy it. I can't do it. Buy it yourself."

Then Boaz said to the elders and all the people, "Today you are witnesses. You have seen that I have bought land from Naomi. I have bought all the property that had belonged to Elimelek, Kilion and Mahlon. I've also taken Ruth, who is from Moab, to become my wife. She is Mahlon's widow. I've decided to marry her so the dead man's name will stay with his property. Now his name won't disappear from his family line or from his hometown. Today you are witnesses!"

So Boaz married Ruth. The LORD blessed her so that she became pregnant. And she had a son. The women said to Naomi, "We praise the LORD. Today he has provided a family protector for you. May this child become famous all over Israel! He will make your life new again. He'll take care of you when you are old. He's the son of your very own daughter-in-law. She loves you. She is better to you than seven sons."

Then Naomi took the child in her arms and took care of him. The women living there said, "Naomi has a son!" They named him Obed. He was the father of Jesse. Jesse was the father of David.

remember what you read

1. What is something you noticed for the first time?

_____

_____

_____

_____

2. What questions did you have?

_____

_____

_____

_____

3. Was there anything that bothered you?

_____

_____

_____

_____

4. What did you learn about loving God?

_____

_____

_____

_____

5. What did you learn about loving others?

_____

_____

_____

_____

SAMUEL-KINGS, PART 1

introduction to Samuel-Kings, parts 1-13

Samuel–Kings is usually listed as 1 Samuel, 2 Samuel, 1 Kings, and 2 Kings. But it is really one big book. It is one story starting with the end of the time of the "judges" or leaders. Samuel was a leader who heard from God often. He shared God's words with the people. The people asked for a king, and God gave one to them. The rest of Samuel–Kings tells the story of Israel's and Judah's kings for about 450 years.

∽∿∿↷

A certain man from Ramathaim in the hill country of Ephraim was named Elkanah. He was the son of Jeroham. Jeroham was the son of Elihu. Elihu was the son of Tohu. Tohu was the son of Zuph. Elkanah belonged to the family line of Zuph. Elkanah lived in the territory of Ephraim. Elkanah had two wives. One was named Hannah. The other was named Peninnah. Peninnah had children, but Hannah didn't.

Year after year Elkanah went up from his town to Shiloh. He went there to worship and sacrifice to the Lord who rules over all. Hophni and Phinehas served as priests of the Lord at Shiloh. They were the two sons of Eli. Every year at Shiloh, the day would come for Elkanah to offer a sacrifice. On that day, he would give a share of the meat to his wife Peninnah. He would also give a share to each of her sons and daughters. But he would give two shares of meat to Hannah. That's because he loved her. He also gave her two shares because the Lord had kept her from having children. Peninnah teased Hannah to make her angry. She did it because the LORD had kept Hannah from having children. Peninnah teased Hannah year after year. Every time Hannah would go up to the house of the LORD, Elkanah's other wife would tease her. She would keep doing it until Hannah cried and wouldn't eat. Her husband Elkanah would say to her, "Hannah, why are you crying? Why don't you eat? Why are you so unhappy? Don't I mean more to you than ten sons?"

One time when they had finished eating and drinking in Shiloh, Hannah stood up. Eli the priest was sitting on his chair by the doorpost of the LORD's house. Hannah was very sad. She wept and wept. She prayed to the LORD. She made a promise to him. She said, "LORD, you rule over all. Please see how I'm suffering! Show concern for me! Don't forget about me! Please give me a son! If you do, I'll give him back to the LORD. Then he will serve the LORD all the days of his life. He'll never use a razor on his head. He'll never cut his hair."

As Hannah kept on praying to the LORD, Eli watched her lips. She was praying in her heart. Her lips were moving. But she wasn't making a sound. Eli thought Hannah was drunk. He said to her, "How long are you going to stay drunk? Stop drinking your wine."

"That's not true, sir," Hannah replied. "I'm a woman who is deeply troubled. I haven't been drinking wine or beer. I was telling the LORD all my troubles. Don't think of me as an evil woman. I've been praying here because I'm very sad. My pain is so great."

Eli answered, "Go in peace. May the God of Israel give you what you have asked him for."

She said, "May you be pleased with me." Then she left and had something to eat. Her face wasn't sad anymore.

Early the next morning Elkanah and his family got up. They worshiped the LORD. Then they went back to their home in Ramah. And the LORD blessed her. So after some time, Hannah became pregnant. She had a baby boy. She said, "I asked the LORD for him." So she named him Samuel.

When the boy didn't need her to breast-feed him anymore, she took him with her to Shiloh. She took him there even though he was still very young. She brought him to the LORD's house.

She brought along a bull that was three years old. She brought 36 pounds of flour. She also brought a bottle of wine. The bottle was made out of animal skin. After the bull was sacrificed, Elkanah and Hannah brought the boy to Eli. Hannah said to Eli, "Pardon me, sir. I'm the woman who stood here beside you praying to the Lord. And that's just as sure as you are alive. I prayed for this child. The Lord has given me what I asked him for. So now I'm giving him to the Lord. As long as he lives he'll be given to the Lord." And there Eli worshiped the Lord.

Then Hannah prayed. She said,

"The Lord has filled my heart with joy.
    He has made me strong.
I can laugh at my enemies.
    I'm so glad he saved me.

"There isn't anyone holy like the Lord.
    There isn't anyone except him.
    There isn't any Rock like our God.

"People don't win just because they are strong.
    Those who oppose the Lord will be totally destroyed.
The Most High God will thunder from heaven.
    The Lord will judge the earth from one end to the other.

"He will give power to his king.
    He will give honor to his anointed one."

Then Elkanah went home to Ramah. But the boy Samuel served the Lord under the direction of Eli the priest.

He wore a sacred linen apron. Each year his mother made him a little robe. She took it to him when she went up to Shiloh with her husband. She did it when her husband went to offer the yearly sacrifice. Eli would bless Elkanah and his wife. He would say, "May the Lord give you children by this woman. May they take the place of the boy she prayed for and gave to the Lord." Then they would go home. The Lord was gracious to Hannah. Over a period of years she had three more sons and two daughters. During that whole time the boy Samuel grew up serving the Lord.

In those days the LORD didn't give many messages to his people. He didn't give them many visions.

One night Eli was lying down in his usual place. His eyes were becoming so weak he couldn't see very well. Samuel was lying down in the LORD's house. That's where the ark of God was kept. The lamp of God was still burning. The LORD called out to Samuel.

Samuel answered, "Here I am." He ran over to Eli and said, "Here I am. You called out to me."

But Eli said, "I didn't call you. Go back and lie down." So he went and lay down.

Again the LORD called out, "Samuel!" Samuel got up and went to Eli. He said, "Here I am. You called out to me."

"My son," Eli said, "I didn't call you. Go back and lie down."

Samuel didn't know the LORD yet. That's because the LORD still hadn't given him a message.

The LORD called out for the third time. He said, "Samuel!" Samuel got up and went to Eli. He said, "Here I am. You called out to me."

Then Eli realized that the LORD was calling the boy. So Eli told Samuel, "Go and lie down. If someone calls out to you again, say, 'Speak, LORD. I'm listening.'" So Samuel went and lay down in his place.

The LORD came and stood there. He called out, just as he had done the other times. He said, "Samuel! Samuel!"

Then Samuel replied, "Speak. I'm listening."

The LORD said to Samuel, "Pay attention! I am about to do something terrible in Israel. It will make the ears of everyone who hears about it tingle. At that time I will do everything to Eli and his family that I said I would. I will finish what I have started. I told Eli I would punish his family forever. He knew his sons were sinning. He knew they were saying bad things about me. In spite of that, he did not stop them. So I made a promise to the family of Eli. I said, 'The sins of Eli's family will never be paid for by bringing sacrifices or offerings.'"

Samuel lay down until morning. Then he opened the doors of the LORD's house. He was afraid to tell Eli about the vision he had received. But Eli called out to him. He said, "Samuel, my son."

Samuel answered, "Here I am."

"What did the LORD say to you?" Eli asked. "Don't hide from me anything he told you. If you do, may God punish you greatly." So Samuel told him everything. He didn't hide anything from him. Then Eli said, "He is the LORD. Let him do what he thinks is best."

As Samuel grew up, the LORD was with him. He made everything Samuel said come true. So all the Israelites recognized that Samuel really was a prophet of the LORD. Everyone from Dan all the way to Beersheba knew it. The LORD continued to appear at Shiloh. There he made himself known to Samuel through the messages he gave him.

And Samuel gave those messages to all the Israelites.

The Israelites lost a battle with the Philistines. They thought they would win the next battle if they brought the ark of God with them. Eli's sons came with the ark. But the Israelites lost again and Eli's sons were killed. When Eli heard the news, he fell over, broke his neck, and died.

Then all the Israelites turned back to the LORD. So Samuel spoke to all the Israelites. He said, "Do you really want to return to the LORD with all your hearts? If you do, get rid of your false gods." So the Israelites served the LORD only.

Then Samuel said, "Gather all the Israelites together at Mizpah. I will pray to the LORD for you." When the people had come together at Mizpah, they went to the well and got water. They poured it out in front of the LORD. On that day they didn't eat any food. They admitted they had sinned.

The Philistines heard that Israel had gathered together at Mizpah. So the Philistine rulers came up to attack them. When the Israelites heard about it, they were afraid. They said to Samuel, "Don't stop crying out to the LORD our God to help us. Keep praying that he'll save us from the power of the Philistines." Then Samuel got a very young lamb. He sacrificed it as a whole burnt offering to the LORD. He cried out to the LORD to help Israel. And the LORD answered his prayer.

The Philistines came near to attack Israel. At that time Samuel was sacrificing the burnt offering. But that day the Lord thundered loudly against the Philistines. He threw them into such a panic that the Israelites were able to chase them away. The men of Israel rushed out of Mizpah. They chased the Philistines all the way to a point below Beth Kar. They killed them all along the way.

Then Samuel got a big stone. He set it up between Mizpah and Shen. He named it Ebenezer. He said, "The Lord has helped us every step of the way."

So the Philistines were brought under Israel's control. The Philistines didn't attack their territory again. The Lord used his power against the Philistines as long as Samuel lived. The Philistines had captured many towns between Ekron and Gath. But they had to give all of them back.

Samuel continued to lead Israel all the days of his life.

remember what you read

1. What is something you noticed for the first time?

_____

_____

_____

_____

2. What questions did you have?

_____

_____

_____

_____

3. Was there anything that bothered you?

_____

_____

_____

_____

4. What did you learn about loving God?

_____

_____

_____

_____

5. What did you learn about loving others?

_____

_____

_____

_____

When Samuel became old, all the elders of Israel gathered together. They came to Samuel at Ramah. They said to him, "You are old. Your sons don't live as you do. So appoint a king to lead us. We want a king just like the kings all the other nations have."

Samuel wasn't pleased when they said, "Give us a king to lead us." So he prayed to the LORD. The LORD told him, "Listen to everything the people are saying to you. You are not the one they have turned their backs on. I am the one they do not want as their king. They are doing just as they have always done. They have deserted me and served other gods. They have done that from the time I brought them up out of Egypt until this day. Now they are deserting you too. Let them have what they want. But give them a strong warning. Let them know what the king who rules over them will expect to be done for him."

Samuel told the people who were asking him for a king everything the LORD had said.

In spite of what Samuel said, the people refused to listen to him. "No!" they said. "We want a king to rule over us. Then we'll be like all the other nations. We'll have a king to lead us. He'll go out at the head of our armies and fight our battles."

Samuel heard everything the people said. He told the LORD about it. The LORD answered, "Listen to them. Give them a king."

Then Samuel said to the Israelites, "Each of you go back to your own town."

Samuel sent a message to the Israelites. He told them to meet with the LORD at Mizpah. He said to them, "The LORD is the God of Israel. He says, 'Israel, I brought you up out of Egypt. I saved you from their power. I also saved you from the power of all the kingdoms that had treated you badly.' But now you have turned your backs on your God. He saves you out of all your trouble and suffering. In spite of that, you have said, 'We refuse to listen. Place a king over us.' So now gather together to meet with the LORD. Do it tribe by tribe and family group by family group."

Then Samuel had each tribe of Israel come forward. The tribe of Benjamin was chosen by casting lots. Next he had the tribe of Benjamin come forward, family group by family group. Matri's group was chosen. Finally Saul, the son of Kish, was chosen. But when people looked for him, they realized he wasn't there. They needed more help from the LORD. So they asked him, "Has the man come here yet?"

The LORD said, "Yes. He has hidden himself among the supplies."

So they ran over there and brought him out. When he stood up, the people saw that he was a head taller than any of them. Samuel spoke to all the people. He said, "Look at the man the LORD has chosen! There isn't anyone like him among all the people."

Then the people shouted, "May the king live a long time!"

Samuel explained to the people the rights and duties of the king who ruled over them. He wrote them down in a book. He placed it in front of the LORD in the holy tent. Then he sent the people away. He sent each of them to their own homes.

Saul led the armies of Israel to defeat Nahash, the king of Ammon, and rescue the city of Jabesh Gilead.

❧

Saul was 30 years old when he became king. He ruled over Israel for 42 years.

Saul fought several battles against the Philistines. God won great victories through Saul's son Jonathan. One time, the prophet Samuel told Saul to wait seven days until Samuel came to offer a sacrifice to God. But the soldiers were afraid of the enemy, and Saul offered the sacrifice to encourage them. God was very angry that Saul disobeyed him.

After Saul became the king of Israel, he fought against Israel's enemies who were all around them. He went to war against Moab, Ammon and Edom. He fought against the kings of Zobah and the Philistines. No matter where he went, he punished his enemies. He fought bravely. He won the battle over the Amalekites. He saved Israel from the power of those who had carried off what belonged to Israel.

Samuel said to Saul, "The Lord sent me to anoint you as king over his people Israel. So listen now to a message from him. The Lord who rules over all says, 'I will punish the Amalekites because of what they did to Israel. As the Israelites came up from Egypt, the Amalekites attacked them. Now go. Attack the Amalekites.'"

Saul attacked the Amalekites. But he and his men kept the best of everything for themselves.

Then the Lord gave Samuel a message. He said, "I am very sad I have made Saul king. He has turned away from me. He has not done what I directed him to do." When Samuel heard that, he was angry. He cried out to the Lord during that whole night.

The Lord said to Samuel, "How long will you be filled with sorrow because of Saul? I have refused to have him as king over Israel. Fill your animal horn with olive oil and go on your way. I am sending you to Jesse in Bethlehem. I have chosen one of his sons to be king."

Samuel did what the Lord said. He arrived at Bethlehem. The elders of the town met him. They were trembling with fear. They asked, "Have you come in peace?"

Samuel replied, "Yes, I've come in peace. I've come to offer a sacrifice to the Lord. Set yourselves apart to him and come to the sacrifice with me." Then he set Jesse and his sons apart to the Lord. He invited them to the sacrifice.

When they arrived, Samuel saw Eliab. He thought, "This has to be the one the Lord wants me to anoint for him."

But the Lord said to Samuel, "Do not consider how handsome or tall he is. I have not chosen him. The Lord does not look at the things people look at. People look at the outside of a person. But the Lord looks at what is in the heart."

Then Jesse called for Abinadab. He had him walk in front of

Samuel. But Samuel said, "The LORD hasn't chosen him either." Then Jesse had Shammah walk by. But Samuel said, "The LORD hasn't chosen him either." Jesse had seven of his sons walk in front of Samuel. But Samuel said to him, "The LORD hasn't chosen any of them." So he asked Jesse, "Are these the only sons you have?"

"No," Jesse answered. "My youngest son is taking care of the sheep."

Samuel said, "Send for him. We won't sit down to eat until he arrives."

So Jesse sent for his son and had him brought in. He looked very healthy. He had a fine appearance and handsome features.

Then the LORD said, "Get up and anoint him. This is the one."

So Samuel got the animal horn that was filled with olive oil. He anointed David in front of his brothers. From that day on, the Spirit of the LORD came powerfully on David. Samuel went back to Ramah.

The Philistines gathered their army together for war. Saul and the army of Israel gathered together. The Philistine army was camped on one hill. Israel's army was on another. The valley was between them.

A mighty hero named Goliath came out of the Philistine camp. He was from Gath. He was more than nine feet tall. He had a bronze helmet on his head. He wore bronze armor that weighed 125 pounds. On his legs he wore bronze guards. He carried a bronze javelin on his back. His spear was as big as a weaver's rod. Its iron point weighed 15 pounds. The man who carried his shield walked along in front of him.

Goliath stood there and shouted to the soldiers of Israel. He said, "Why do you come out and line up for battle? I'm a Philistine. You are servants of Saul. Choose one of your men. Have him come down and face me. If he's able to fight and kill me, we'll become your slaves. But if I win and kill him, you will become our slaves and serve us." Goliath continued, "This day I dare the soldiers of Israel to send a man down to fight against me." Saul and the whole army of Israel heard what the Philistine said. They were terrified.

Jesse's three oldest sons had followed Saul into battle. But David went back and forth from Saul's camp to Bethlehem. He went to Bethlehem to take care of his father's sheep.

Jesse said to his son David, "Get at least half a bushel of grain that has been cooked. Also get ten loaves of bread. Take all of it to your brothers. Hurry to their camp. Take along these ten chunks of cheese to the commander of their military group. Find out how your brothers are doing. Bring me back some word about them. They are with Saul and all the men of Israel. They are in the Valley of Elah. They are fighting against the Philistines."

Early in the morning David left his father's flock in the care of a shepherd. David loaded up the food and started out, just as Jesse had directed. David reached the camp as the army was going out to its battle positions. The soldiers were shouting the war cry. The Israelites and the Philistines were lining up their armies for battle. The armies were facing each other. David left what he had brought with the man who took care of the supplies. He ran to the battle lines and asked his brothers how they were. As David was talking with them, Goliath stepped forward from his line. He again dared someone to fight him, and David heard it.

The Israelites had been saying, "Just look at how this man keeps daring Israel to fight him! The king will make the man who kills Goliath very wealthy. The king will also give his own daughter to be that man's wife. The king won't require anyone in the man's family to pay any taxes in Israel."

David spoke to the men standing near him. He asked them, "What will be done for the man who kills this Philistine? Goliath is bringing shame on Israel. What will be done for the one who removes it? This Philistine isn't even circumcised. He dares the armies of the living God to fight him. Who does he think he is?"

Someone heard what David said and reported it to Saul. So Saul sent for David.

David said to Saul, "Don't let anyone lose hope because of that Philistine. I'll go out and fight him."

Saul replied, "You aren't able to go out there and fight that Philistine. You are too young. He's been a warrior ever since he was a boy."

But David said to Saul, "I've been taking care of my father's sheep. Sometimes a lion or a bear would come and carry off a sheep from the flock. Then I would go after it and hit it. I would save the sheep it was carrying in its mouth. If it turned around to attack me, I would grab its hair. I would strike it down and kill it. In fact, I've killed both a lion and a bear. I'll do the same thing to this Philistine. He isn't even circumcised. He has dared the armies of the living God to fight him. The Lord saved me from the paw of the lion. He saved me from the paw of the bear. And he'll save me from the powerful hand of this Philistine too."

Saul said to David, "Go. And may the Lord be with you."

remember what you read

1. What is something you noticed for the first time?

_____

_____

_____

_____

2. What questions did you have?

_____

_____

_____

_____

3. Was there anything that bothered you?

_____

_____

_____

_____

4. What did you learn about loving God?

_____

_____

_____

_____

5. What did you learn about loving others?

_____

_____

_____

_____

Then Saul dressed David in his own military clothes. He put a coat of armor on him. He put a bronze helmet on his head. David put on Saul's sword over his clothes. He walked around for a while in all that armor because he wasn't used to it.

"I can't go out there in all this armor," he said to Saul. "I'm not used to it." So he took it off. Then David picked up his wooden staff. He went down to a stream and chose five smooth stones. He put them in the pocket of his shepherd's bag. Then he took his sling in his hand and approached Goliath.

At that same time, the Philistine kept coming closer to David. The man carrying Goliath's shield walked along in front of him. Goliath looked David over. He saw how young he was. He also saw how healthy and handsome he was. And he hated him. He said to David, "Why are you coming at me with sticks? Do you think I'm only a dog?" The Philistine cursed David in the name of his gods. "Come over here," he said. "I'll feed your body to the birds and wild animals!"

David said to Goliath, "You are coming to fight against me with a sword, a spear and a javelin. But I'm coming against you in the name of the LORD who rules over all. He is the God of the armies of Israel. He's the one you have dared to fight against. This day the LORD will give me the victory over you. I'll strike you down. I'll cut your head off. This day I'll feed the bodies of the Philistine army to the birds and wild animals. Then the whole world will know there is a God in Israel. The LORD doesn't rescue people by using a sword or a spear. And everyone here will know it. The battle belongs to the LORD. He will hand all of you over to us."

As the Philistine moved closer to attack him, David ran quickly to the battle line to meet him. He reached into his bag. He took out a stone. He put it in his sling. He slung it at Goliath. The stone hit him on the forehead and sank into it. He fell to the ground on his face.

So David won the fight against Goliath with a sling and a stone. He struck down the Philistine and killed him. He did it without even using a sword.

David ran and stood over him. He picked up Goliath's sword and cut off his head with it.

The Philistines saw that their hero was dead. So they turned around and ran away. Then the men of Israel and Judah shouted and rushed forward. They chased the Philistines to the entrance of Gath. They chased them to the gates of Ekron. Israel's army returned from chasing the Philistines. They had taken everything from the Philistine camp.

After David killed Goliath, he returned to the camp. Then Abner brought him to Saul. David was still carrying Goliath's head.

"Young man, whose son are you?" Saul asked him.

David said, "I'm the son of Jesse from Bethlehem."

David finished talking with Saul. After that, Jonathan and David became close friends. Jonathan loved David just as he loved himself. From that time on, Saul kept David with him. He didn't let him return home to his family. Jonathan made a covenant with David because he loved him just as he loved himself. Jonathan took off the robe he was wearing and gave it to David. He also gave him his military clothes. He even gave him his sword, his bow and his belt.

David did everything Saul sent him to do. He did it so well that Saul gave him a high rank in the army. That pleased Saul's whole army, including his officers.

After David had killed Goliath, the men of Israel returned home. The women came out of all the towns of Israel to meet King Saul. They danced and sang joyful songs. They played harps and tambourines. As they danced, they sang,

"Saul has killed thousands of men.
  David has killed tens of thousands."

That song made Saul very angry. It really upset him. He said to himself, "They are saying David has killed tens of thousands of men. But they are saying I've killed only thousands. The only thing left for him to get is the kingdom itself." From that time on, Saul watched David closely.

Saul sent some men to watch David's house. He told them to kill David the next morning. But David's wife Michal warned him. She said, "You must run for your life tonight. If you don't, tomorrow you will be killed." So Michal helped David escape through a window. He ran and got away.

David was best friends with Saul's son Jonathan. Jonathan helped David escape from Saul. Saul was so angry with him, he even tried to kill his own son!

But the prophet Gad spoke to David. He said, "Don't stay in your usual place of safety. Go into the land of Judah." So David left and went to the forest of Hereth.

Saul heard that the place where David and his men were hiding had been discovered. Saul was sitting under a tamarisk tree on the hill at Gibeah. He was holding his spear. All his officials were standing at his side. Saul said to them, "Men of Benjamin, listen to me! Do you think Jesse's son will give all of you fields and vineyards? Do you think he'll make some of you commanders of thousands of men? Do you think he'll make the rest of you commanders of hundreds? Is that why all of you have joined together against me? No one tells me when my son makes a covenant with Jesse's son. None of you is concerned about me. No one tells me that my son has stirred up Jesse's son to hide and wait to attack me. But that's exactly what's happening now."

Sometimes David stayed in places of safety in the desert. At other times he stayed in the hills of the Desert of Ziph. Day after day Saul looked for him. But God didn't hand David over to him.

David was at Horesh in the Desert of Ziph. There he learned that Saul had come out to kill him. Saul's son Jonathan went to David at Horesh. He told David that God would make him strong. "Don't be afraid," he said. "My father Saul won't harm you. You will be king over Israel. And I will be next in command. Even my father Saul knows this." The two of them made a covenant of friendship in front of the LORD. Then Jonathan went home. But David remained at Horesh.

The people of Ziph went up to Saul at Gibeah. They said, "David is hiding among us. He's hiding in places of safety at Horesh. Horesh is south of Jeshimon on the hill of Hakilah. Your Majesty, come down when it pleases you to come. It will be our duty to hand David over to you."

Saul replied, "May the LORD bless you because you were concerned about me. Make sure you are right. Go and check things out again. Find out where David usually goes. Find out who has seen him there. People tell me he's very tricky. Find out about all the hiding places he uses. Come back to me with all the facts. I'll go with you. Suppose he's in the area. Then I'll track him down among all the family groups of Judah."

So they started out. They went to Ziph ahead of Saul. David and his men were in the Desert of Maon. Maon is south of Jeshimon in the Arabah Valley. Saul and his men started out to look for David. David was told about it. So he went down to a rock in the Desert of Maon to hide. Saul heard he was there. So he went into the Desert of Maon to chase David.

Saul was going along one side of the mountain. David and his men were on the other side. They were hurrying to get away from Saul. Saul and his army were closing in on David and his men. They were about to capture them. Just then a messenger came to Saul. He said, "Come quickly! The Philistines are attacking the land." So Saul stopped chasing David. He went to fight against the Philistines. That's why they call that place Sela Hammahlekoth. David left that place. He went and lived in places of safety near En Gedi.

Saul returned from chasing the Philistines. Then he was told, "David is in the Desert of En Gedi." So Saul took 3,000 of the best soldiers from the whole nation of Israel. He started out to look for David and his men. He planned to look near the Rocky Cliffs of the Wild Goats.

He came to some sheep pens along the way. A cave was there.

Saul went in to go to the toilet. David and his men were far back in the cave. David's men said, "This is the day the LORD told you about. He said to you, 'I will hand your enemy over to you. Then you can deal with him as you want to.'" So David came up close to Saul without being seen. He cut off a corner of Saul's robe.

Later, David felt sorry that he had cut off a corner of Saul's robe. He said to his men, "May the LORD keep me from doing a thing like that again to my master. He is the LORD's anointed king. So I promise that I will never lay my hand on him. The LORD has anointed him." David said that to correct his men. He wanted them to know that they should never suggest harming the king. He didn't allow them to attack Saul. So Saul left the cave and went on his way.

Then David went out of the cave. He called out to Saul, "King Saul! My master!" When Saul looked behind him, David bowed down. He lay down flat with his face toward the ground. He said to Saul, "Why do you listen when men say, 'David is trying to harm you'? This day you have seen with your own eyes how the LORD handed you over to me in the cave. Some of my men begged me to kill you. But I didn't. I said, 'I will never lay my hand on my master. He is the LORD's anointed king.' Look, my father! Look at this piece of your robe in my hand! I cut off the corner of your robe. But I didn't kill you. See, there is nothing in my hand that shows I am guilty of doing anything wrong. I haven't turned against you. I haven't done anything to harm you. But you are hunting me down. You want to kill me. May the LORD judge between you and me. And may the LORD pay you back because of the wrong things you have done to me. But I won't do anything to hurt you. People say, 'Evil acts come from those who do evil.' So I won't do anything to hurt you.

"King Saul, who are you trying to catch? Who do you think you are chasing? I'm nothing but a dead dog or a flea! May the LORD be our judge. May he decide between us. May he consider my case and stand up for me. May he show that I'm not guilty of doing anything wrong. May he save me from you."

remember what you read

1. What is something you noticed for the first time?

_____

_____

_____

_____

2. What questions did you have?

_____

_____

_____

_____

3. Was there anything that bothered you?

_____

_____

_____

_____

4. What did you learn about loving God?

_____

_____

_____

_____

5. What did you learn about loving others?

_____

_____

_____

_____

SAMUEL-KINGS, PART 4

When David finished speaking, Saul asked him a question. He said, "My son David, is that your voice?" And Saul wept out loud. "You are a better person than I am," he said. "You have treated me well. But I've treated you badly. You have just now told me about the good things you did to me. The LORD handed me over to you. But you didn't kill me. Suppose a man finds his enemy. He doesn't let him get away without harming him. May the LORD reward you with many good things. May he do it because of the way you treated me today. I know for sure that you will be king. I know that the kingdom of Israel will be made secure under your control. Now make a promise in the name of the LORD. Promise me that you won't kill the children of my family. Also promise me that you won't wipe out my name from my family line."

So David made that promise to Saul. Then Saul returned home. But David and his men went up to his usual place of safety.

When Samuel died, the whole nation of Israel gathered together. They were filled with sorrow because he was dead. They buried him at his home in Ramah. Then David went down into the Desert of Paran.

Some people from Ziph went to Saul at Gibeah. They said, "David is hiding on the hill of Hakilah. It faces Jeshimon."

So Saul went down to the Desert of Ziph. He took 3,000 of the best soldiers in Israel with him. They went to the desert to look for David. Saul set up his camp beside the road. It was on the hill of Hakilah facing Jeshimon. But David stayed in the desert. He saw that Saul had followed him there. So he sent out scouts. From them he learned that Saul had arrived.

Then David started out. He went to the place where Saul had camped. He saw where Saul and Abner were lying down. Saul was lying inside the camp. The army was camped all around him. Abner was commander of the army. He was the son of Ner.

Then David spoke to Ahimelek, the Hittite. He also spoke to Joab's brother Abishai, the son of Zeruiah. He asked them, "Who will go down with me into the camp to Saul?"

"I'll go with you," said Abishai.

So that night David and Abishai went into the camp. They found Saul lying asleep inside the camp. His spear was stuck in the ground near his head. Abner and the soldiers were lying asleep around him.

Abishai said to David, "Today God has handed your enemy over to you. So let me pin him to the ground. I can do it with one jab of the spear. I won't even have to strike him twice."

But David said to Abishai, "Don't destroy him! No one can do any harm to the LORD's anointed king and not be guilty. You can be sure that the LORD lives," he said. "And you can be just as sure that the LORD himself will strike Saul down. Perhaps he'll die a natural death. Or perhaps he'll go into battle and be killed. May the LORD keep me from doing anything to harm his anointed king. Now get the spear and water jug that are near his head. Then let's leave."

So David took the spear and water jug that were near Saul's head. Then he and Abishai left. No one saw them. No one knew about what they had done. In fact, no one even woke up. Everyone was sleeping. That's because the LORD had put them into a deep sleep.

David went across to the other side of the valley. He stood on top of a hill far away from Saul's camp. There was a wide space between them. He called out to the army and to Abner, the son of Ner. He said, "Abner! Aren't you going to answer me?"

Abner replied, "Who is calling out to the king?"

David said, "You are a great soldier, aren't you? There isn't anyone else like you in Israel. So why didn't you guard the king? He's your master, isn't he? Someone came into the camp to destroy him. You didn't guard him. And that isn't good. You can be sure that the LORD lives. And you can be just as sure that you and your men must die. That's because you didn't guard your master. He's the LORD's anointed king. Look around you. Where are the king's spear and water jug that were near his head?"

Saul recognized David's voice. He said, "My son David, is that your voice?"

David replied, "Yes it is, King Saul, my master." He continued, "Why are you chasing me? What evil thing have I done? What am I guilty of? King Saul, please listen to what I'm saying. Was it the LORD who made you angry with me? If it was, may he accept my offering. Was it people who made you angry at me? If it was, may the LORD see them cursed. They have driven me today from my share of the LORD's land. By doing that, they might as well have said, 'Go and serve other gods.' Don't spill my blood on the ground far away from where the LORD lives. King Saul, you have come out to look for nothing but a flea. It's as if you were hunting a partridge in the mountains."

Then Saul said, "I have sinned. My son David, come back. Today you thought my life was very special. So I won't try to harm you again. I've really acted like a foolish person. I've made a huge mistake."

"Here's your spear," David answered. "Send one of your young men over to get it. The LORD rewards everyone for doing what is right and being faithful. He handed you over to me today. But I wouldn't harm you. You are the LORD's anointed king. Today I thought your life had great value. In the same way, may the LORD think of my life as having great value. May he save me from all trouble."

Then Saul said to David, "May the LORD bless you, David my son. You will do great things. You will also have great success."

So David went on his way. And Saul returned home.

The Philistines fought against the Israelites. The Israelites ran away from them. But many Israelites were killed on Mount Gilboa. The Philistines kept chasing Saul and his sons. They killed his sons Jonathan, Abinadab and Malki-Shua. The fighting was heavy around Saul. Men who were armed with bows and arrows caught up with him. They shot their arrows at him and wounded him badly.

Saul spoke to the man carrying his armor. He said, "Pull out your sword. Stick it through me. If you don't, these fellows who aren't circumcised will come. They'll stick their swords through me and hurt me badly."

But the man was terrified. He wouldn't do it. So Saul took his own sword and fell on it. The man saw that Saul was dead. So he fell on his own sword and died with him. Saul and his three sons died together that same day. The man who carried his armor also died with them that day. So did all of Saul's men.

After Saul died, David returned to Ziklag. He had won the battle over the Amalekites. He stayed in Ziklag for two days. On the third day a man arrived from Saul's camp. His clothes were torn. He had dust on his head. When he came to David, he fell to the ground to show him respect.

"Where have you come from?" David asked him.

He answered, "I've escaped from Israel's camp."

"What happened?" David asked. "Tell me."

He said, "Israel's men ran away from the battle. Many of them were killed. Saul and his son Jonathan are dead."

David sang a song of sadness about Saul and his son Jonathan. He ordered that it be taught to the people of Judah. It is a song that is played on a stringed instrument. It is written down in the Book of Jashar. David sang,

"Israel, a gazelle lies dead on your hills.
    Your mighty men have fallen.

"When they lived, Saul and Jonathan were loved and
        respected.
    When they died, they were not parted.
They were faster than eagles.
    They were stronger than lions.

"Israel's mighty men have fallen.
    Their weapons of war are broken."

After Saul and Jonathan died, David asked the LORD for advice. "Should I go up to one of the towns of Judah?" he asked.

The LORD said, "Go up."

David asked, "Where should I go?"

"To Hebron," the LORD answered.

So David went up there with his two wives. David also took his men and their families with him. They made their homes in Hebron and its towns. Then the men of Judah came to Hebron. There they anointed David to be king over the people of Judah.

Saul's son Ish-Bosheth became king over the rest of Israel. For two years people did sneaky things to try to make one king more powerful than the other. Finally, two men killed Ish-Bosheth, and David became king over all of Israel.

All the tribes of Israel came to see David at Hebron. They said, "We are your own flesh and blood. In the past, Saul was our king. But you led Israel on their military campaigns. And the LORD said to you, 'You will be the shepherd over my people Israel. You will become their ruler.'"

All the elders of Israel came to see King David at Hebron. There the king made a covenant with them in front of the LORD. They anointed David as king over Israel.

David was 30 years old when he became king. He ruled for 40 years. In Hebron he ruled over Judah for seven and a half years. In Jerusalem he ruled over all of Israel and Judah for 33 years.

The king and his men marched to Jerusalem. They went to attack the Jebusites who lived there. The Jebusites said to David, "You won't get in here." But David captured the fort of Zion. It became known as the City of David.

He built up the area around the fort. He filled in the low places. He started at the bottom and worked his way up. David became more and more powerful. That's because the LORD God who rules over all was with him.

King David was told, "The LORD has blessed the family of Obed-Edom. He has also blessed everything that belongs to him. That's because the ark of God is in Obed-Edom's house." So David went down there to bring up the ark. With great joy he brought it up from the house of Obed-Edom. He took it to the City of David. Those carrying the ark of the Lord took six steps forward. Then David sacrificed a bull and a fat calf. David was wearing a sacred linen apron. He danced in front of the Lord with all his might. He did it while he was bringing up the ark of the Lord. The whole community of Israel helped him bring it up. They shouted. They blew trumpets.

The ark of the Lord was brought into Jerusalem. It was put in its place in the tent David had set up for it. David sacrificed burnt offerings and friendship offerings to the Lord. After he finished sacrificing those offerings, he blessed the people in the name of the Lord who rules over all. He gave to each Israelite man and woman a loaf of bread. He also gave each one a date cake and a raisin cake. Then all the people went home.

The king moved into his palace. The Lord had given him peace and rest from all his enemies around him. Then the king spoke to Nathan the prophet. He said, "Here I am, living in a house that has beautiful cedar walls. But the ark of God remains in a tent."

Nathan replied to the king, "Go ahead and do what you want to. The Lord is with you."

remember what you read

1. What is something you noticed for the first time?

_____

_____

_____

_____

2. What questions did you have?

_____

_____

_____

_____

3. Was there anything that bothered you?

_____

_____

_____

_____

4. What did you learn about loving God?

_____

_____

_____

_____

5. What did you learn about loving others?

_____

_____

_____

_____

But that night the word of the LORD came to Nathan. The LORD said,

"Go and speak to my servant David. Tell him, 'The LORD says, "Are you the one to build me a house to live in? I brought the Israelites up out of Egypt. But I have not lived in a house from then until now. I have been moving from place to place. I have been living in a tent. I have moved from place to place with all the Israelites. I commanded their rulers to be shepherds over them. I never asked any of those rulers, 'Why haven't you built me a house that has beautiful cedar walls?'"'"

"So tell my servant David, 'The LORD who rules over all says, "I took you away from the grasslands. That's where you were taking care of your father's sheep and goats. I made you ruler over my people Israel. I have been with you everywhere you have gone. I have destroyed all your enemies. Now I will make you famous. Your name will be just as respected as the names of the most important people on earth. I will provide a place where my people Israel can live. I will plant them in the land. Then they will have a home of their own. They will not be bothered anymore. Evil people will no longer crush them, as they did at first. That is what your enemies have done ever since I appointed leaders over my people Israel. But I will give you peace and rest from all of them.

"'"I tell you that I, the LORD, will set up a royal house for you. Some day your life will come to an end. You will join the members of your family who have already died. Then I will make one of your own sons the next king after you. And

I will make his kingdom secure. He is the one who will build a house where I will put my Name. I will set up the throne of his kingdom. It will last forever. I will be his father. And he will be my son. When he does what is wrong, I will use other men to beat him with rods and whips. I took my love away from Saul. I removed him from being king. You were there when I did it. But I will never take my love away from your son. Your royal house and your kingdom will last forever in my sight. Your throne will last forever." ' "

Nathan reported to David all the words that the Lord had spoken to him.

Then King David went into the holy tent. He sat down in front of the Lord. He said,

"Lord and King, who am I? My family isn't important. So why have you brought me this far? I would have thought that you had already done more than enough for me. But now, Lord and King, you have also said what will happen to my royal house in days to come. And, my Lord and King, this promise is for a mere human being!

"Lord and King, how great you are! There isn't anyone like you. There isn't any God but you. We have heard about it with our own ears. Who is like your people Israel? God, we are the one nation on earth you have saved. You have set us free for yourself. Your name has become famous. You have done great and wonderful things. You have driven out nations and their gods to make room for your people. You saved us when you set us free from Egypt. You made Israel your very own people forever. Lord, you have become our God.

"And now, Lord God, keep forever the promise you have made to me and my royal house. Do exactly as you promised. Then your name will be honored forever. People will say, 'The Lord rules over all. He is God over Israel.' My royal house will be made secure in your sight.

"Lord who rules over all, you are the God of Israel. Here's what you have shown me. You told me, 'I will build you a royal house.' So I can boldly pray this prayer to you. Lord and King, you are God! Your covenant can be trusted. You have promised many good things to me. Now please bless my royal house. Then it will continue forever in your sight. LORD and King, you have spoken. Because you have given my royal house your blessing, it will be blessed forever."

David ruled over the whole nation of Israel. He did what was fair and right for all his people.

David asked, "Is anyone left from the royal house of Saul? If there is, I want to be kind to him because of Jonathan."

Ziba was a servant in Saul's family. David sent for him to come and see him. The king said to him, "Are you Ziba?"

"I'm ready to serve you," he replied.

The king asked, "Isn't there anyone still alive from the royal house of Saul? God has been very kind to me. I would like to be kind to that person in the same way."

Ziba answered the king, "A son of Jonathan is still living. Both of his feet were hurt so that he can't walk."

"Where is he?" the king asked.

Ziba answered, "He's in the town of Lo Debar. He's staying at the house of Makir, the son of Ammiel."

Mephibosheth came to David. He was the son of Jonathan, the son of Saul. Mephibosheth bowed down to David to show him respect.

David said, "Mephibosheth!"

"I'm ready to serve you," he replied.

"Don't be afraid," David told him. "You can be sure that I will be kind to you because of your father Jonathan. I'll give back to you all the land that belonged to your grandfather Saul. And I'll always provide what you need."

Mephibosheth bowed down to David. He said, "Who am I? Why should you pay attention to me? I'm nothing but a dead dog."

Then the king sent for Saul's servant Ziba. He said to him, "I'm giving your master's grandson everything that belonged to Saul and his family. You and your sons and your servants must farm the land for him. You must bring in the crops. Then he'll be taken care of. I'll always provide what he needs." Ziba had 15 sons and 20 servants.

Then Ziba said to the king, "I'll do anything you command me to do. You are my king and master." So David provided what Mephibosheth needed. He treated him like one of the king's sons.

It was spring. It was the time when kings go off to war. So David sent Joab out with the king's special troops and the whole army of Israel. They destroyed the Ammonites. They marched to the city of Rabbah. They surrounded it and got ready to attack it. But David remained in Jerusalem.

One evening David got up from his bed. He walked around on the roof of his palace. From the roof he saw a beautiful woman. He wanted her to be his wife. But she was already married. Her husband was named Uriah. He was one of David's best soldiers. David did a very bad thing. He sent a message to Joab. David told him, "Put Uriah out in front. That's where the fighting is the heaviest. Then pull your men back from him. When you do, the Ammonites will strike him down and kill him." And that's what Joab did.

Uriah's wife heard that her husband was dead. She mourned over him. When her time of sadness was over, David had her brought to his house. She became his wife. And she had a son by him. But the Lord wasn't pleased with what David had done.

The Lord sent the prophet Nathan to David. When Nathan came to him, he said, "Two men lived in the same town. One was rich. The other was poor. The rich man had a very large number of sheep and cattle. But all the poor man had was one little female lamb. He had bought it. He raised it. It grew up with him and his children. It shared his food. It drank from his cup. It even slept in his arms. It was just like a daughter to him.

"One day a traveler came to the rich man. The rich man wanted to prepare a meal for him. But he didn't want to kill one of his own sheep or cattle. Instead, he took the little female lamb that belonged to the poor man. Then the rich man cooked it for the traveler who had come to him."

David was very angry with the rich man. He said to Nathan, "The man who did this must die! And that's just as sure as the LORD is alive. The man must pay back four times as much as that lamb was worth. How could he do such a thing? And he wasn't even sorry he had done it."

Then Nathan said to David, "You are the man! The LORD, the God of Israel, says, 'I anointed you king over Israel. I saved you from Saul. I gave you everything that belonged to your master Saul. I made you king over all the people of Israel and Judah. And if all of that had not been enough for you, I would have given you even more. Why did you turn your back on what I told you to do? You did what is evil in my sight. You made sure that Uriah, the Hittite, would be killed in battle. You took his wife to be your own. You let the men of Ammon kill him with their swords. So time after time members of your own royal house will be killed with swords. That's because you turned your back on me. You took the wife of Uriah, the Hittite, to be your own.'

Then David said to Nathan, "I have sinned against the LORD."

Nathan replied, "The LORD has taken away your sin. You aren't going to die. But you have dared to show great disrespect for the LORD. So the son who has been born to you will die."

Nathan went home. Then the LORD made David's child very sick. That was the child David had by Uriah's wife. David begged God to heal the child. David didn't eat anything. He spent his nights lying on the ground. He put on the rough clothes people wear when they're sad. His most trusted servants stood beside him. They wanted him to get up from the ground. But he refused to do it. And he wouldn't eat any food with them.

On the seventh day the child died. David's attendants were afraid to tell him the child was dead. They thought, "While the child was still alive, we spoke to David. But he wouldn't listen to us. So how can we now tell him the child is dead? He might do something terrible to himself."

David saw that his attendants were whispering to one another. Then he realized the child was dead. "Has the child died?" he asked.

"Yes," they replied. "He's dead."

Then David got up from the ground. After he washed himself, he put on lotions. He changed his clothes. He went into the house of the Lord and worshiped him. Then he went to his own house. He asked for some food. They served it to him. And he ate it.

His attendants asked him, "Why are you acting like this? While the child was still alive, you wouldn't eat anything. You cried a lot. But now that the child is dead, you get up and eat!"

He answered, "While the child was still alive, I didn't eat anything. And I cried a lot. I thought, 'Who knows? The Lord might have mercy on me. He might let the child live.' But now he's dead. So why should I continue to go without food? Can I bring him back to life again? Someday I'll go to him. But he won't return to me."

Then David comforted his wife Bathsheba. Some time later she had a son. He was given the name Solomon. The Lord loved him. So the Lord sent a message through Nathan the prophet. The Lord said, "Name the boy Jedidiah."

remember what you read

1. What is something you noticed for the first time?

_____

_____

_____

_____

2. What questions did you have?

_____

_____

_____

_____

3. Was there anything that bothered you?

_____

_____

_____

_____

4. What did you learn about loving God?

_____

_____

_____

_____

5. What did you learn about loving others?

_____

_____

_____

_____

Some time later, David's son Absalom got a chariot and horses for himself. He also got 50 men to run in front of him. He would get up early. He would stand by the side of the road that led to the city gate. Sometimes a person would come with a case for the king to decide. Then Absalom would call out to him, "What town are you from?" He would answer, "I'm from one of the tribes of Israel." Absalom would say, "Look, your claims are based on the law. So you have every right to make them. But the king doesn't have anyone here who can listen to your case." Absalom would continue, "I wish I were appointed judge in the land! Then anyone who has a case or a claim could come to me. I would make sure they are treated fairly."

Sometimes people would approach Absalom and bow down to him. Then he would reach out his hand. He would take hold of them and kiss them. Absalom did that to all the Israelites who came to the king with their cases or claims. That's why the hearts of the people were turned toward him.

Absalom got the people of Israel to make him king. David had to run away for safety. Many soldiers stayed loyal to David and went with him. Absalom gathered the rest of Israel's armies and chased after him. But David's men won the battle, and Absalom was killed. All of this made David very sad. He went to his room and wept. As he went, he said, "My son Absalom! My son, my son Absalom! I wish I had died instead of you. Absalom! My son, my son!"

David sang the words of this song to the LORD. He sang them when the LORD saved him from the power of all his enemies and of Saul. He said,

"The LORD is my rock and my fort. He is the God who
        saves me.
    My God is my rock. I go to him for safety.
    He is like a shield to me. He's the power that saves me.
He's my place of safety. I go to him for help. He's my
        Savior.
    He saves me from those who want to hurt me.
I called out to the LORD. He is worthy of praise.
    He saved me from my enemies.

"The waves of death were all around me.
    A destroying flood swept over me.
The ropes of the grave were tight around me.
    Death set its trap in front of me.
When I was in trouble I called out to the LORD.
    I called out to my God.
From his temple he heard my voice.
    My cry for help reached his ears.

"The earth trembled and shook.
    The pillars of the heavens rocked back and forth.
    They trembled because the LORD was angry.
Smoke came out of his nose.
    Flames of fire came out of his mouth.
    Burning coals blazed out of it.
He opened the heavens and came down.
    Dark clouds were under his feet.
He got on the cherubim and flew.
    The wings of the wind lifted him up.
He covered himself with darkness.
    The dark rain clouds of the sky were like a tent
        around him.
From the brightness all around him
    flashes of lightning blazed out.
The LORD thundered from heaven.
    The voice of the Most High God was heard.
He shot his arrows and scattered the enemy.
    He sent flashes of lightning and chased them away.

The bottom of the sea could be seen.
 The foundations of the earth were uncovered.
It happened when the LORD's anger blazed out.
 It came like a blast of breath from his nose.

"He reached down from heaven. He took hold of me.
 He lifted me out of deep waters.
He saved me from my powerful enemies.
 He set me free from those who were too strong
  for me.
They stood up to me when I was in trouble.
 But the LORD helped me.
He brought me out into a wide and safe place.
 He saved me because he was pleased with me.

"The LORD lives! Give praise to my Rock!
 Give honor to my God, the Rock! He is my
  Savior!
He is the God who pays back my enemies.
 He brings the nations under my control.
 He sets me free from my enemies.
You have honored me more than them.
 You have saved me from a man who wanted to
  hurt me.
LORD, I will praise you among the nations.
 I will sing your praise.
He gives his king great victories.
 He shows his faithful love to his anointed king.
 He shows it to David and his family forever."
Here are David's last words. He said,

"I am David, the son of Jesse. God has given me a
  message.
 The Most High God has greatly honored me.
The God of Jacob anointed me as king.
 I am the hero of Israel's songs.

"The Spirit of the LORD spoke through me.
 I spoke his word with my tongue.

The God of Israel spoke.
  The Rock of Israel said to me,
'A king must rule over people in a way that is right.
  He must have respect for God when he rules.
Then he will be like the light of morning at sunrise
  when there aren't any clouds.
He will be like the bright sun after rain
  that makes grass grow on the earth.'

"Suppose my royal family was not right with God.
  Then he would not have made a covenant with me
      that will last forever.
  Every part of it was well prepared and made secure.
Then God would not have saved me completely
  or given me everything I longed for.
But evil people are like thorns that are thrown away.
  You can't pick them up with your hands.
Even if you touch them,
  you must use an iron tool or a spear.
  Thorns are burned up right where they are."

Here are the names of David's mighty warriors.

Josheb-Basshebeth was chief of the three mighty warriors. He was a Tahkemonite. He used his spear against 800 men. He killed all of them at one time.

Next to him was Eleazar. He was one of the three mighty warriors. He was the son of Dodai, the Ahohite. Eleazar was with David at Pas Dammim. That's where Israel's army made fun of the Philistines who were gathered there for battle. Then the Israelites pulled back. But Eleazar stayed right where he was. He struck down the Philistines until his hand grew tired. But he still held on to his sword. The Lord helped him win a great battle that day. The troops returned to Eleazar. They came back to him only to take what they wanted from the dead bodies.

Next to him was Shammah, the son of Agee. Shammah was a Hararite. The Philistines gathered together at a place where there was a field full of lentils. Israel's troops ran away from the

Philistines. But Shammah took his stand in the middle of the field. He didn't let the Philistines capture it. He struck them down. The Lord helped him win a great battle.

Abishai was chief over the three mighty warriors. He was the brother of Joab, the son of Zeruiah. He used his spear against 300 men. He killed all of them. So he became as famous as the three mighty warriors were. In fact, he was even more honored than the three mighty warriors. He became their commander. But he wasn't included among them.

Benaiah was a great hero from Kabzeel. He was the son of Jehoiada. Benaiah did many brave things. He struck down two of Moab's best warriors. He also went down into a pit on a snowy day. He killed a lion there. And he struck down a huge Egyptian. The Egyptian was holding a spear. Benaiah went out to fight against him with a club. He grabbed the spear out of the Egyptian's hand. Then he killed him with it. Those were some of the brave things Benaiah, the son of Jehoiada, did. He too was as famous as the three mighty warriors were. He was honored more than any of the thirty chief warriors. But he wasn't included among the three mighty warriors. David put him in charge of his own personal guards.

David became proud. He told Joab to go count all the soldiers in Israel. Joab didn't want to do this, but he obeyed the king anyway. God was very angry with David for not trusting him to protect Israel.

David felt sorry that he had counted the fighting men. So he said to the Lord, "I committed a great sin when I counted Judah and Israel's men. Lord, I beg you to take away my guilt. I've done a very foolish thing."

Before David got up the next morning, a message from the Lord came to Gad the prophet. He was David's seer. The message said, "Go and tell David, 'The Lord says, "I could punish you in three different ways. Choose one of them for me to use against you."'"

So Gad went to David. He said to him, "Take your choice. Do you want three years when there won't be enough food in your land? Or do you want three months when you will run away from your enemies while they chase you? Or do you want three days when there will be a plague in your land? Think it over. Then take your pick. Tell me how to answer the one who sent me."

David said to Gad, "I'm suffering terribly. Let us fall into the hands of the Lord. His mercy is great. But don't let me fall into human hands."

So the Lord sent a plague on Israel. It lasted from that morning until he decided to end it. From Dan all the way to Beersheba 70,000 people died. The angel reached his hand out to destroy Jerusalem. But the Lord stopped sending the plague. So he spoke to the angel who was making the people suffer. He said, "That is enough! Do not kill any more people." The angel of the Lord was at Araunah's threshing floor. Araunah was from the city of Jebus.

David saw the angel who was striking down the people. David said to the Lord, "I'm the one who has sinned. I'm the one who has done what is wrong. I'm like a shepherd for these people. These people are like sheep. What have they done? Let your judgment be on me and my family."

On that day Gad went to David. Gad said to him, "Go up to the threshing floor of Araunah, the Jebusite. Build an altar there to honor the Lord." So David went up and did it. He did what the Lord had commanded through Gad. Araunah looked and saw the king and his officials coming toward him. So he went out to welcome them. He bowed down to the king with his face toward the ground.

Araunah said, "King David, you are my master. Why have you come to see me?"

"To buy your threshing floor," David answered. "I want to build an altar there to honor the Lord. When I do, the plague on the people will be stopped."

Araunah said to David, "Take anything you wish. Offer it up. Here are oxen for the burnt offering. Here are threshing sleds. And here are wooden collars from the necks of the oxen. Use all the wood to burn the offering. Your Majesty, I'll give all of it to you." Araunah continued, "And may the Lord your God accept you."

But the king replied to Araunah, "No. I want to pay you for it. I won't sacrifice to the LORD my God burnt offerings that haven't cost me anything."

So David bought the threshing floor and the oxen. He paid 20 ounces of silver for them. David built an altar there to honor the LORD. He sacrificed burnt offerings and friendship offerings. Then the LORD answered David's prayer and blessed the land. The plague on Israel was stopped.

remember what you read

1. What is something you noticed for the first time?

_____

_____

_____

_____

2. What questions did you have?

_____

_____

_____

_____

3. Was there anything that bothered you?

_____

_____

_____

_____

4. What did you learn about loving God?

_____

_____

_____

_____

5. What did you learn about loving others?

_____

_____

_____

_____

WISDOM

The time came near for David to die. So he gave orders to his son Solomon.

He said, "I'm about to die, just as everyone else on earth does. So be strong. Show how brave you are. Do everything the LORD your God requires. Live the way he wants you to. Obey his orders and commands. Keep his laws and rules. Do everything written in the Law of Moses. Then you will have success in everything you do. You will succeed everywhere you go. The LORD will keep the promise he made to me. He said, 'Your sons must be careful about how they live. They must be faithful to me with all their heart and soul. Then you will always have a son from your family line to sit on the throne of Israel.'

David joined the members of his family who had already died. He was buried in the City of David. He had ruled over Israel for 40 years. He ruled for seven years in Hebron. Then he ruled for 33 years in Jerusalem. So Solomon sat on the throne of his father David. His position as king was made secure.

King Solomon went to the city of Gibeon to offer sacrifices. That's where the most important high place was. There he offered 1,000 burnt offerings on the altar. The LORD appeared to Solomon at Gibeon. He spoke to him in a dream during the night. God said, "Ask for anything you want me to give you."

Solomon answered, "You have been very kind to my father David, your servant. That's because he was faithful to you. He did what was right. His heart was honest. And you have continued to be very kind to him. You have given him a son to sit on his throne this day.

"LORD my God, you have now made me king. You have put me in the place of my father David. But I'm only a little child. I don't know how to carry out my duties. I'm here among the people you have chosen. They are a great nation. They are more than anyone can count. So give me a heart that understands. Then I can rule over your people. I can tell the difference between what is right and what is wrong. Who can possibly rule over this great nation of yours?"

The Lord was pleased that Solomon had asked for that. So God said to him, "You have not asked to live for a long time. You have not asked to be wealthy. You have not even asked to have your enemies killed. Instead, you have asked for wisdom. You want to do what is right and fair when you judge people. Because that is what you have asked for, I will give it to you. I will give you a wise and understanding heart. So here is what will be true of you. There has never been anyone like you. And there never will be. And that is not all. I will give you what you have not asked for. I will give you wealth and honor. As long as you live, no other king will be as great as you are. Live the way I want you to. Obey my laws and commands, just as your father David did. Then I will let you live for a long time." Solomon woke up. He realized he had been dreaming.

He returned to Jerusalem. He stood in front of the ark of the Lord's covenant. He sacrificed burnt offerings and friendship offerings. Then he gave a feast for all his officials.

God made Solomon very wise. His understanding couldn't even be measured. It was like the sand on the seashore. Solomon became famous in all the nations around him. He spoke 3,000 proverbs. He wrote 1,005 songs. He spoke about plants. He knew everything about them, from the cedar trees in Lebanon to the hyssop plants that grow out of walls. He spoke about animals and birds. He also spoke about reptiles and fish. The kings of all the world's nations heard about how wise Solomon was. So they sent their people to listen to him.

Solomon began to build the temple of the LORD. It was 480 years after the Israelites came out of Egypt. It was in the fourth year of Solomon's rule over Israel.

All the stones used for building the temple were shaped where they were cut. So hammers, chisels and other iron tools couldn't be heard where the temple was being built.

King Solomon finished all the work for the LORD's temple. Then he brought in the things his father David had set apart for the LORD. They included the silver and gold and all the other things for the LORD's temple. Solomon placed them with the other treasures that were there.

Then King Solomon sent for the elders of Israel. He told them to come to him in Jerusalem. They included all the leaders of the tribes. They also included the chiefs of the families of Israel. Solomon wanted them to bring up the ark of the LORD's covenant from Zion. Zion was the City of David. All the Israelites came together to where King Solomon was. It was at the time of the Feast of Booths. The feast was held in the month of Ethanim. That's the seventh month.

All the elders of Israel arrived. Then the priests picked up the ark and carried it. They brought up the ark of the LORD. They also brought up the tent of meeting and all the sacred things in the tent. The priests and Levites carried everything up. The entire community of Israel had gathered around King Solomon. All of them were in front of the ark. They sacrificed huge numbers of sheep and cattle. There were so many animals that they couldn't be recorded. In fact, they couldn't even be counted.

The priests brought the ark of the LORD's covenant law to its place in the Most Holy Room of the temple. They put it under the wings of the cherubim. Their wings were spread out over the place where the ark was. They covered the ark. They also covered the poles used to carry it. The poles were very long. Their ends could be seen from the Holy Room in front of the Most Holy Room. But they couldn't be seen from outside the Holy Room. They are still there to this day. There wasn't anything in the ark except the two stone tablets. Moses had placed them in it at Mount Horeb. That's where the LORD had made a covenant with the Israelites. He made it after they came out of Egypt.

The priests left the Holy Room. Then the cloud filled the temple of the LORD. The priests couldn't do their work because of it. That's because the glory of the LORD filled his temple.

Then Solomon said, "LORD, you have said you would live in a dark cloud. As you can see, I've built a beautiful temple for you. You can live in it forever."

The whole community of Israel was standing there. The king turned around and gave them his blessing.

Then Solomon stood in front of the LORD's altar. He stood in front of the whole community of Israel. He spread out his hands toward heaven. He said,

"LORD, you are the God of Israel. There is no God like you in heaven above or on earth below. You keep the covenant you made with us. You show us your love. You do that when we follow you with all our hearts. You have kept your promise to my father David. He was your servant. With your mouth you made a promise. With your powerful hand you have made it come true. And today we can see it.

"But will you really live on earth? After all, the heavens can't hold you. In fact, even the highest heavens can't hold you. So this temple I've built certainly can't hold you! But please pay attention to my prayer. LORD my God, be ready to help me as I make my appeal to you. Listen to my cry for help. Hear the prayer I'm praying to you today. Let your eyes look toward this temple night and day. You said, 'I will put my Name there.' So please listen to the prayer I'm praying toward this place. Hear me when I ask you to help us. Listen to your people Israel when they pray toward this place. Listen to us from heaven. It's the place where you live. When you hear us, forgive us.

"Suppose your people have sinned against you. And because of that, the sky is closed up and there isn't any rain. But your people pray toward this place. They praise you by admitting they've sinned. And they turn away from their sin because you have made them suffer. Then listen to them from heaven.

Forgive the sin of your people Israel. Teach them the right way to live. Send rain on the land you gave them as their share.

"Suppose there are outsiders who don't belong to your people Israel. And they have come from a land far away. They've come because they've heard about your name. When they get here, they will find out even more about your great name. They'll hear about how you reached out your mighty hand and powerful arm. So they'll come and pray toward this temple. Then listen to them from heaven. It's the place where you live. Do what those outsiders ask you to do. Then all the nations on earth will know you. They will have respect for you. They'll respect you just as your own people Israel do. They'll know that your Name is in this house I've built.

"Let your eyes be open to me when I ask you to help us. Let them be open to your people Israel when they ask you to help them. Pay attention to them every time they cry out to you. After all, you chose them out of all the nations in the world. You made them your very own people. You did it just as you had announced through your servant Moses. That's when you brought out of Egypt our people of long ago. You are our Lord and King."

Solomon finished praying. He finished asking the Lord to help his people. Then he got up from in front of the Lord's altar. He had been down on his knees with his hands spread out toward heaven. He stood in front of the whole community of Israel. He blessed them with a loud voice. He said,

"I praise the Lord. He has given peace and rest to his people Israel. That's exactly what he promised to do. He gave his people good promises through his servant Moses. Every single word of those promises has come true. May the Lord our God be with us, just as he was with our people who lived long ago. May he never leave us. May he never desert us. May he turn our hearts to him. Then we will live the way he wants us to. We'll obey the commands, rules and directions he gave our people of long ago. I've prayed these words to the Lord our God. May he keep them close to him day and night. May he stand up for me. May he also stand up for his people Israel. May he give us what we need every day. Then all the nations on earth will know that the LORD is God. They'll know that there isn't any other god. And may you commit your lives completely to the LORD our God. May you live by his rules. May you obey his commands. May you always do as you are doing now."

remember what you read

1. What is something you noticed for the first time?

_____

_____

_____

_____

2. What questions did you have?

_____

_____

_____

_____

3. Was there anything that bothered you?

_____

_____

_____

_____

4. What did you learn about loving God?

_____

_____

_____

_____

5. What did you learn about loving others?

_____

_____

_____

_____

SAMUEL-KINGS, PART 8

The queen of Sheba heard about how famous Solomon was. She also heard about how he served and worshiped the Lord. So she came to test Solomon with hard questions. She arrived in Jerusalem with a very large group of attendants. Her camels were carrying spices, huge amounts of gold, and valuable jewels. She came to Solomon and asked him about everything she wanted to know. Solomon answered all her questions. There wasn't anything too hard for the king to explain to her. So the queen of Sheba saw how very wise Solomon was. She saw the palace he had built. She saw the food on his table. She saw his officials sitting there. She saw the robes of the servants who waited on everyone. She saw his wine tasters. And she saw the burnt offerings Solomon sacrificed at the Lord's temple. She could hardly believe everything she had seen.

She said to the king, "Back in my own country I heard a report about you. I heard about how much you had accomplished. I also heard about how wise you are. Everything I heard is true. But I didn't believe those things. So I came to see for myself. And now I believe it! You are twice as wise and wealthy as people say you are. The report I heard doesn't even begin to tell the whole story about you. How happy your people must be! How happy your officials must be! They always get to serve you and hear the wise things you say. May the Lord your God be praised. He takes great delight in you. He placed you on the throne of Israel. The Lord will love Israel for all time to come. That's why he has made you king. He knows that you will do what is fair and right."

Each year Solomon received 25 tons of gold. That didn't include the money brought in by business and trade. It also didn't include the money from all the kings of Arabia and the governors of the territories.

King Solomon was richer than all the other kings on earth. He was also wiser than they were. People from the whole world wanted to meet Solomon in person. They wanted to see for themselves how wise God had made him. Year after year, everyone who came to him brought a gift. They brought gifts made out of silver and gold. They brought robes, weapons and spices. They also brought horses and mules.

King Solomon loved many women besides Pharaoh's daughter. They were from other lands. They were Moabites, Ammonites, Edomites, Sidonians and Hittites. The Lord had warned Israel about women from other nations. He had said, "You must not marry them. If you do, you can be sure they will turn your hearts toward their gods." But Solomon continued to love them anyway. He wouldn't give them up. He had 700 wives who came from royal families. And he had 300 concubines. His wives led him astray. As Solomon grew older, his wives turned his heart toward other gods. He didn't follow the Lord his God with all his heart. So he wasn't like his father David. Solomon worshiped Ashtoreth. Ashtoreth was the female god of the Sidonians. He also worshiped Molek. Molek was the god of the Ammonites. The Lord hated that god. Solomon did what was evil in the sight of the Lord. He didn't completely obey the Lord. He didn't do what his father David had done.

There is a hill east of Jerusalem. Solomon built a high place for worshiping Chemosh there. He built a high place for worshiping Molek there too. Chemosh was the god of Moab. Molek was the god of Ammon. The Lord hated both of those gods. Solomon also built high places so that all his wives from other nations could worship their gods. Those women burned incense and offered sacrifices to their gods.

The Lord became angry with Solomon. That's because his heart had turned away from the Lord, the God of Israel. He had appeared to Solomon twice. He had commanded Solomon not to worship other gods. But Solomon didn't obey the Lord. So the Lord said to Solomon, "You have chosen not to keep my covenant. You have decided not to obey my rules. I commanded you to do what I told you. But you did not do it. So you can be absolutely sure I will tear the kingdom away from you. I will give it to one of your officials. But I will not do that while you are still living. Because of your father David I will wait. I will tear the kingdom out of your son's hand. But I will not tear the whole kingdom away from him. I will give him one of the tribes because of my servant David. I will also do it because of Jerusalem. That is the city I have chosen."

Jeroboam refused to follow King Solomon. He was one of Solomon's officials.

Jeroboam was a very important young man. Solomon saw how well he did his work. So he put him in charge of all the workers in northern Israel.

About that time Jeroboam was going out of Jerusalem. Ahijah the prophet met him on the road. Ahijah was from Shiloh. He was wearing a new coat. The two of them were all alone out in the country. Ahijah grabbed the new coat he had on. He tore it up into 12 pieces. Then he said to Jeroboam, "Take ten pieces for yourself. The Lord is the God of Israel. He says, 'I am going to tear the kingdom out of Solomon's hand. I will give you ten of its tribes. Solomon will have one of its tribes. I will let him keep it because of my servant David and because of Jerusalem. I have chosen that city out of all the cities in the tribes of Israel. I will do these things because the tribes have deserted me. They have worshiped Ashtoreth, the female god of the people of Sidon. They have worshiped Chemosh, the god of the people of Moab. And they have worshiped Molek, the god of the people of Ammon. They have not lived the way I wanted them to. They have not done what is right in my eyes. They have not obeyed my rules and laws as Solomon's father David did.

" 'But I will not take the whole kingdom out of Solomon's hand. I have made him ruler all the days of his life. I have done it because of my servant David. I chose him, and he obeyed my commands and rules. I will take the kingdom out of his son's hands. And I will give you ten of the tribes. I will give one of the tribes to David's son. Then my servant David will always have a son on his throne in Jerusalem. The lamp of David's kingdom will always burn brightly in my sight. Jerusalem is the city I chose for my Name. But I will make you king over Israel. You will rule over everything your heart desires. So you will be the king of Israel. Do everything I command you to do. Live the way I want you to. Do what is right in my eyes. Obey my rules and commands. That is what my servant David did. If you do those things, I will be with you. I will build you a kingdom. It will last as long as the one I built for David. I will give Israel to you. I will punish David's family because of what Solomon has done. But I will not punish them forever.' "

Solomon tried to kill Jeroboam. But Jeroboam ran away to Egypt. He went to Shishak, the king of Egypt. He stayed there until Solomon died.

The other events of Solomon's rule are written down. Everything he did and the wisdom he showed are written down. They are written in the official records of Solomon. Solomon ruled in Jerusalem over the whole nation of Israel for 40 years. Then he joined the members of his family who had already died. He was buried in the city of his father David. Solomon's son Rehoboam became the next king after him.

～✶～

Rehoboam went to the city of Shechem. All the Israelites had gone there to make him king. Jeroboam heard about it. He was the son of Nebat. Jeroboam was still in Egypt at that time. He had gone there for safety. He wanted to get away from King Solomon. But now he returned from Egypt. So the people sent for Jeroboam. He and the whole community of Israel went to Rehoboam. They said to him, "Your father put a heavy load on our shoulders. But now make our hard work easier. Make the heavy load on us lighter. Then we'll serve you."

Rehoboam answered, "Go away for three days. Then come back to me." So the people went away.

King Rehoboam asked the elders for advice. They had served his father Solomon while he was still living. Rehoboam asked them, "What advice can you give me? How should I answer these people?"

They replied, "Serve them today. Give them what they are asking for. Then they'll always serve you."

But Rehoboam didn't accept the advice the elders gave him. Instead, he asked for advice from the young men. They had grown up with him and were now serving him. He asked them, "What's your advice? How should I answer these people? They say to me, 'Make the load your father put on our shoulders lighter.'"

The young men who had grown up with him gave their answer. They replied, "These people have said to you, 'Your father put a heavy load on our shoulders. Make it lighter.' Now tell them, 'My little finger is stronger than my father's legs. My father put a heavy load on your shoulders. But I'll make it even heavier. My father beat you with whips. But I'll beat you with bigger whips.'"

Three days later Jeroboam and all the people returned to Rehoboam. That's because the king had said, "Come back to me in three days." The king answered the people in a mean way. He didn't accept the advice the elders had given him. Instead, he followed the advice of the young men. He said, "My father put a heavy load on your shoulders. But I'll make it even heavier. My father beat you with whips. But I'll beat you with bigger whips." So the king didn't listen to the people. That's because the LORD had planned it that way. What he had said through Ahijah came true. Ahijah had spoken the LORD's message to Jeroboam, the son of Nebat. Ahijah was from Shiloh.

All the Israelites saw that the king refused to listen to them. So they answered the king. They said,

"We don't have any share in David's royal family.
　　We don't have any share in Jesse's son.
People of Israel, let's go back to our homes.
　　David's royal family, take care of your own kingdom!"

So the Israelites went home. But Rehoboam still ruled over the Israelites living in the towns of Judah.

remember what you read

1. What is something you noticed for the first time?

_____

_____

_____

_____

2. What questions did you have?

_____

_____

_____

_____

3. Was there anything that bothered you?

_____

_____

_____

_____

4. What did you learn about loving God?

_____

_____

_____

_____

5. What did you learn about loving others?

_____

_____

_____

_____

Jeroboam thought, "My kingdom still isn't secure. It could very easily go back to the royal family of David. Suppose the Israelites go up to Jerusalem to offer sacrifices at the LORD's temple. If they do, they will again decide to follow Rehoboam as their master. Then they'll kill me. They'll return to King Rehoboam. He is king of Judah."

So King Jeroboam asked for advice. Then he made two golden statues that looked like calves. He said to the people, "It's too hard for you to go up to Jerusalem. Israel, here are your gods who brought you up out of Egypt." He set up one statue in Bethel. He set up the other one in Dan. What Jeroboam did was sinful. And it caused Israel to sin. The people came to worship the statue at Bethel. They went all the way to Dan to worship the statue that was there.

Jeroboam built temples for worshiping gods on high places. He appointed all kinds of people as priests. They didn't even have to be Levites. He established a feast. It was on the 15th day of the eighth month. He wanted to make it like the Feast of Booths that was held in Judah. Jeroboam built an altar at Bethel. He offered sacrifices on it. He sacrificed to the calves he had made. He also put priests in Bethel. He did it at the high places he had made. He offered sacrifices on the altar he had built at Bethel. It was on the 15th day of the eighth month. That's the month he had chosen for it. So he established the feast for the Israelites. And he went up to the altar to sacrifice offerings.

A man of God went from Judah to Bethel. He had received a message from the LORD. He arrived in Bethel just as Jeroboam was standing by the altar to offer a sacrifice. The man cried out. He shouted a message from the LORD against the altar. He said, "Altar! Altar! The LORD says, 'A son named Josiah will be born into the royal family of David. Altar, listen to me! Josiah will sacrifice the priests of the high places on you. They will be the children of the priests who are offering sacrifices here. So human bones will be burned on you.'" That same day the man of God spoke about a miraculous sign. He said, "Here is the sign the LORD has announced. This altar will be broken to pieces. The ashes on it will be spilled out."

The man of God announced that message against the altar at Bethel. When King Jeroboam heard it, he reached out his hand from the altar. He said, "Grab him!" But as he reached out his hand toward the man, it dried up. He couldn't even pull it back. Also, the altar broke into pieces. Its ashes spilled out. That happened in keeping with the miraculous sign the man of God had announced. He had received a message from the LORD.

King Jeroboam spoke to the man of God. He said, "Pray to the LORD your God for me. Pray that my hand will be as good as new again." So the man of God prayed to the LORD for the king. And the king's hand became as good as new. It was just as healthy as it had been before.

Even after all of that happened, Jeroboam still didn't change his evil ways. Once more he appointed priests for the high places. He made priests out of all kinds of people. In fact, he let anyone become a priest who wanted to. He set them apart to serve at the high places. All of that was the great sin the royal family of Jeroboam committed. It led to their fall from power. Because of it, they were destroyed from the face of the earth.

෴

Rehoboam was king in Judah. He was the son of Solomon. Rehoboam was 41 years old when he became king. He ruled for 17 years in Jerusalem. It was the city the LORD had chosen out of all the cities in the tribes of Israel. He wanted to put his Name there. Rehoboam's mother was Naamah from Ammon.

The people of Judah did what was evil in the sight of the LORD.

The sins they had committed made the LORD angry. The LORD was angry because they refused to worship only him. They did more to make him angry than their people who lived before them had done. Judah also set up for themselves high places for worship. They set up sacred stones. They set up poles used to worship the female god named Asherah. They did it on every high hill and under every green tree. There were even male prostitutes at the temples in the land. The people took part in all the practices of other nations. The LORD hated those practices. He had driven those nations out to make room for the Israelites.

Shishak attacked Jerusalem. It was in the fifth year that Rehoboam was king. Shishak was king of Egypt. He carried away the treasures of the LORD's temple. He also carried away the treasures of the royal palace. He took everything. That included all the gold shields Solomon had made. So King Rehoboam made bronze shields to take their place. He gave them to the commanders of the guards on duty at the entrance to the royal palace. Every time the king went to the LORD's temple, the guards carried the shields. Later, they took them back to the room where they were kept.

The other events of Rehoboam's rule are written down. Everything he did is written in the official records of the kings of Judah. Rehoboam and Jeroboam were always at war with each other. Rehoboam joined the members of his family who had already died. He was buried in his family tomb in the City of David. His mother was Naamah from Ammon. Rehoboam's son Abijah became the next king after him.

Several kings ruled over Judah. Some disobeyed God. But others obeyed God. The kings of Israel did not care about following God. They did whatever they wanted, and this made God very angry.

Ahab became king of Israel. It was in the 38th year that Asa was king of Judah. Ahab ruled over Israel in Samaria for 22 years. He was the son of Omri. Ahab, the son of Omri, did what was evil in the sight of the LORD. He did more evil things than any of the kings who had ruled before him. He thought it was only a small thing to commit the sins Jeroboam, the son of Nebat, had committed. Ahab also married Jezebel. She was Ethbaal's daughter. Ethbaal was king of the people of Sidon. Ahab began to serve the god named Baal and worship him. He set up an altar to honor Baal. He set it up in the temple of Baal that he built in Samaria. Ahab also made a pole used to worship the female god named Asherah. He made the Lord very angry. Ahab did more to make him angry than all the kings of Israel had done before him. The Lord is the God of Israel.

Elijah was from Tishbe in the land of Gilead. He said to Ahab, "I serve the Lord. He is the God of Israel. You can be sure that he lives. And you can be just as sure that there won't be any dew or rain on the whole land. There won't be any during the next few years. It won't come until I say so."

Then a message came to Elijah from the Lord. He said, "Leave this place. Go east and hide in the Kerith Valley. It is east of the Jordan River. You will drink water from the brook. I have directed some ravens to supply you with food there."

So Elijah did what the Lord had told him to do. He went to the Kerith Valley. It was east of the Jordan River. He stayed there. The ravens brought him bread and meat in the morning. They also brought him bread and meat in the evening. He drank water from the brook.

Some time later the brook dried up. It hadn't rained in the land for quite a while. A message came to Elijah from the Lord. He said, "Go right away to Zarephath in the region of Sidon. Stay there. I have directed a widow there to supply you with food." So Elijah went to Zarephath. He came to the town gate. A widow was there gathering sticks. He called out to her. He asked, "Would you bring me a little water in a jar? I need a drink." She went to get the water. Then he called out to her, "Please bring me a piece of bread too."

"I don't have any bread," she replied. "And that's just as sure as the Lord your God is alive. All I have is a small amount of flour in a jar and a little olive oil in a jug. I'm gathering a few sticks to take home. I'll make one last meal for myself and my son. We'll eat it. After that, we'll die."

Elijah said to her, "Don't be afraid. Go home. Do what you have said. But first make a small loaf of bread for me. Make it out of what you have. Bring it to me. Then make some for yourself and your son. The Lord is the God of Israel. He says, 'The jar of flour will not be used up. The jug will always have oil in it. You will have flour and oil until the day the Lord sends rain on the land.'"

She went away and did what Elijah had told her to do. So Elijah had food every day. There was also food for the woman and her family. The jar of flour wasn't used up. The jug always had oil in it. That's what the Lord had said would happen. He had spoken that message through Elijah.

Some time later the son of the woman who owned the house became sick. He got worse and worse. Finally he stopped breathing. The woman said to Elijah, "You are a man of God. What do you have against me? Did you come to bring my sin out into the open? Did you come to kill my son?"

"Give me your son," Elijah replied. He took him from her arms. He carried him to the upstairs room where he was staying. He put him down on his bed. Then Elijah cried out to the Lord. He said, "Lord my God, I'm staying with this widow. Have you brought pain and sorrow even to her? Have you caused her son to die?" Then he lay down on the boy three times. He cried out to the Lord. He said, "Lord my God, give this boy's life back to him!"

The Lord answered Elijah's prayer. He gave the boy's life back to him. So the boy lived. Elijah picked up the boy. He carried him down from the upstairs room into the house. He gave him to his mother. He said, "Look! Your son is alive!"

Then the woman said to Elijah, "Now I know that you are a man of God. I know that the message you have brought from the Lord is true."

It was now three years since it had rained. A message came to Elijah from the Lord. He said, "Go. Speak to Ahab. Then I will send rain on the land." So Elijah went to speak to Ahab.

When he saw Elijah, he said to him, "Is that you? You are always stirring up trouble in Israel."

"I haven't made trouble for Israel," Elijah replied. "But you and your father's family have. You have turned away from the Lord's commands. You have followed gods that are named Baal. Now send for people from all over Israel. Tell them to meet me on Mount Carmel. And bring the 450 prophets of the god named Baal. Also bring the 400 prophets of the female god named Asherah. All of them eat at Jezebel's table."

remember what you read

1. What is something you noticed for the first time?

_____

_____

_____

_____

2. What questions did you have?

_____

_____

_____

_____

3. Was there anything that bothered you?

_____

_____

_____

_____

4. What did you learn about loving God?

_____

_____

_____

_____

5. What did you learn about loving others?

_____

_____

_____

_____

So Ahab sent that message all through Israel. He gathered the prophets together on Mount Carmel. Elijah went there and stood in front of the people. He said, "How long will it take you to make up your minds? If the LORD is the one and only God, worship him. But if Baal is the one and only God, worship him."

The people didn't say anything.

Then Elijah said to them, "I'm the only one of the LORD's prophets left. But Baal has 450 prophets. Get two bulls for us. Let Baal's prophets choose one for themselves. Let them cut it into pieces. Then let them put it on the wood. But don't let them set fire to it. I'll prepare the other bull. I'll put it on the wood. But I won't set fire to it. Then you pray to your god. And I'll pray to the LORD. The god who answers by sending fire down is the one and only God."

Then all the people said, "What you are saying is good."

Elijah said to the prophets of Baal, "Choose one of the bulls. There are many of you. So prepare your bull first. Pray to your god. But don't light the fire." So they prepared the bull they had been given.

They prayed to Baal from morning until noon. "Baal! Answer us!" they shouted. But there wasn't any reply. No one answered. Then they danced around the altar they had made.

At noon Elijah began to tease them. "Shout louder!" he said. "I'm sure Baal is a god! Perhaps he has too much to think about. Or maybe he has gone to the toilet. Or perhaps he's away on a trip. Maybe he's sleeping. You might have to wake him up." So they shouted louder. They cut themselves with swords and spears until their blood flowed. That's what they usually did when things really looked hopeless. It was now past noon. The prophets of Baal continued to prophesy with all their might. They did it until the time came to offer the evening sacrifice. But there wasn't any reply. No one answered. No one paid any attention.

Then Elijah said to all the people, "Come here to me." So they went to him. He rebuilt the altar of the Lord. It had been torn down. Elijah got 12 stones. There was one for each tribe in the family line of Jacob. The Lord's message had come to Jacob. It had said, "Your name will be Israel." Elijah used the stones to build an altar to honor the Lord. He dug a ditch around it. The ditch was large enough to hold 24 pounds of seeds. He arranged the wood for the fire. He cut the bull into pieces. He placed the pieces on the wood. Then he said to some of the people, "Fill four large jars with water. Pour it on the offering and the wood." So they did.

"Do it again," he said. So they did it again.

"Do it a third time," he ordered. And they did it the third time. The water ran down around the altar. It even filled the ditch.

When it was time to offer the evening sacrifice, the prophet Elijah stepped forward. He prayed, "Lord, you are the God of Abraham, Isaac and Israel. Today let everyone know that you are God in Israel. Let them know I'm your servant. Let them know I've done all these things because you commanded me to. Answer me. Lord, answer me. Then these people will know that you are the one and only God. They'll know that you are turning their hearts back to you again."

The fire of the Lord came down. It burned up the sacrifice. It burned up the wood and the stones and the soil. It even dried up the water in the ditch.

All the people saw it. Then they fell down flat with their faces toward the ground. They cried out, "The Lord is the one and only God! The Lord is the one and only God!"

Then Elijah commanded them, "Grab the prophets of Baal. Don't let a single one of them get away!" So they grabbed them. Elijah had them brought down to the Kishon Valley. There he had them put to death.

Elijah said to Ahab, "Go. Eat and drink. I can hear the sound of a heavy rain." So Ahab went off to eat and drink. But Elijah climbed to the top of Mount Carmel. He bent down toward the ground. Then he put his face between his knees.

"Go and look toward the sea," he told his servant. So he went up and looked.

"I don't see anything there," he said.

Seven times Elijah said, "Go back."

The seventh time the servant said, "I see a cloud. It's as small as a man's hand. It's coming up over the sea."

Elijah said, "Go to Ahab. Tell him, 'Tie your chariot to your horse. Go down to Jezreel before the rain stops you.'"

Black clouds filled the sky. The wind came up, and a heavy rain began to fall. Ahab rode off to Jezreel. The power of the LORD came on Elijah. He tucked his coat into his belt. And he ran ahead of Ahab all the way to Jezreel.

Ahab told Jezebel everything Elijah had done. He told her how Elijah had killed all the prophets of Baal with his sword. So Jezebel sent a message to Elijah. She said, "You can be sure that I will kill you, just as I killed the other prophets. I'll do it by this time tomorrow. If I don't, may the gods punish me greatly."

Elijah was afraid. So he ran for his life. He came to Beersheba in Judah. He left his servant there. Then he traveled for one day into the desert. He came to a small bush. He sat down under it. He prayed that he would die. "LORD, I've had enough," he said. "Take my life. I'm no better than my people of long ago." Then he lay down under the bush. And he fell asleep.

Suddenly an angel touched him. The angel said, "Get up and eat." Elijah looked around. Near his head he saw some bread. It had been baked over hot coals. A jar of water was also there. So Elijah ate and drank. Then he lay down again.

The angel of the LORD came to him a second time. He touched him and said, "Get up and eat. Your journey will be long and hard." So he got up. He ate and drank. The food gave him new strength. He traveled for 40 days and 40 nights. He kept going until he arrived at Horeb. It was the mountain of God. There he went into a cave and spent the night.

A message came to Elijah from the LORD. He said, "Elijah, what are you doing here?"

He replied, "LORD God who rules over all, I've been very committed to you. The Israelites have turned their backs on your covenant. They have torn down your altars. They've put your prophets to death with their swords. I'm the only one left. And they are trying to kill me."

The LORD said, "Go out. Stand on the mountain in front of me. I am going to pass by."

As the LORD approached, a very powerful wind tore the mountains apart. It broke up the rocks. But the LORD wasn't in the wind. After the wind there was an earthquake. But the LORD wasn't in the earthquake. After the earthquake a fire came. But the LORD wasn't in the fire. And after the fire there was only a gentle whisper. When Elijah heard it, he pulled his coat over his face. He went out and stood at the entrance to the cave.

The LORD said to him, "Go back the way you came. Go to the Desert of Damascus. When you get there, anoint Hazael as king over Aram. Also anoint Jehu as king over Israel. He is the son of Nimshi. And anoint Elisha from Abel Meholah as the next prophet after you. He is the son of Shaphat. Jehu will put to death anyone who escapes Hazael's sword. And Elisha will put to death anyone who escapes Jehu's sword. But I will keep 7,000 people in Israel for myself. They have not bowed down to Baal. And they have not kissed him."

Elijah left Mount Horeb. He saw Elisha, the son of Shaphat. Elisha was plowing in a field. He was driving the last of 12 pairs of oxen. Elijah went up to him. He threw his coat around him. Then Elisha left his oxen. He ran after Elijah. "Let me kiss my father and mother goodbye," he said. "Then I'll come with you."

"Go back," Elijah replied. "What have I done to you?"

So Elisha left him and went back. He got his two oxen and killed them. He burned the plow to cook the meat. He gave it to the people, and they ate it. Then he started to follow Elijah. He became Elijah's servant.

Ahab saw a vineyard that he wanted to buy. But the owner Naboth would not sell it. So Ahab pouted. Jezebel, the evil queen, hired bad people to lie about Naboth in court. Naboth was killed for crimes he did not commit. And Ahab took his vineyard. Elijah told Ahab how angry God was about this. He told him that his family would be destroyed as a consequence of his evil actions.

The other events of Ahab's rule are written down. Everything he did is written down. That includes the palace he built and decorated with ivory. It also includes the cities he built up and put high walls around. All these things are written in the official records of the kings of Israel. Ahab joined the members of his family who had already died. Ahab's son Ahaziah became the next king after him.

Elijah and Elisha were on their way from Gilgal. The LORD was going to use a strong wind to take Elijah up to heaven. Elijah said to Elisha, "Stay here. The LORD has sent me to Bethel."

But Elisha said, "I won't leave you. And that's just as sure as the LORD and you are alive." So they went down to Bethel.

There was a group of prophets at Bethel. They came out to where Elisha was. They asked him, "Do you know what the LORD is going to do? He's going to take your master away from you today."

"Yes, I know," Elisha replied. "So be quiet."

Then Elijah said to him, "Stay here, Elisha. The LORD has sent me to Jericho."

Elisha replied, "I won't leave you. And that's just as sure as the LORD and you are alive." So they went to Jericho.

There was a group of prophets at Jericho. They went up to where Elisha was. They asked him, "Do you know what the LORD is going to do? He's going to take your master away from you today."

"Yes, I know," Elisha replied. "So be quiet."

Then Elijah said to him, "Stay here. The LORD has sent me to the Jordan River."

Elisha replied, "I won't leave you. And that's just as sure as the LORD and you are alive." So the two of them walked on.

Fifty men from the group of prophets followed them. The men stopped and stood not far away from them. They faced the place where Elijah and Elisha had stopped at the Jordan River. Elijah rolled up his coat. Then he struck the water with it. The water parted to the right and to the left. The two of them went across the river on dry ground.

After they had gone across, Elijah said to Elisha, "Tell me. What can I do for you before I'm taken away from you?"

"Please give me a double share of your spirit," Elisha replied.

"You have asked me for something that's very hard to do," Elijah said. "But suppose you see me when I'm taken away from you. Then you will receive what you have asked for. If you don't see me, you won't receive it."

remember what you read

1. What is something you noticed for the first time?

_____

_____

_____

_____

2. What questions did you have?

_____

_____

_____

_____

3. Was there anything that bothered you?

_____

_____

_____

_____

4. What did you learn about loving God?

_____

_____

_____

_____

5. What did you learn about loving others?

_____

_____

_____

_____

SAMUEL-KINGS, PART II

They kept walking along and talking together. Suddenly there appeared a chariot and horses made of fire. The chariot and horses came between the two men. Then Elijah went up to heaven in a strong wind. Elisha saw it and cried out to Elijah, "My father! You are like a father to me! You, Elijah, are the true chariots and horsemen of Israel!" Elisha didn't see Elijah anymore. Then Elisha took hold of his own garment and tore it in two.

He picked up the coat that had fallen from Elijah. He went back and stood on the bank of the Jordan River. Then he struck the water with Elijah's coat. "Where is the power of the LORD?" he asked. "Where is the power of the God of Elijah?" When Elisha struck the water, it parted to the right and to the left. He went across the river.

The group of prophets from Jericho were watching. They said, "The spirit of Elijah has been given to Elisha." They went over to Elisha. They bowed down to him with their faces toward the ground.

The people of Jericho said to Elisha, "Look. This town has a good location. You can see that for yourself. But the spring of water here is bad. So the land doesn't produce anything."

"Bring me a new bowl," Elisha said. "Put some salt in it." So they brought it to him.

Then he went out to the spring. He threw the salt into it. He told the people, "The LORD says, 'I have made this water pure. It will never cause death again. It will never keep the land from producing crops again.'" The water has stayed pure to this day. That's what Elisha had said would happen.

The wife of a man from the group of the prophets cried out to Elisha. She said, "My husband is dead. You know how much respect he had for the LORD. But he owed money to someone. And now that person is coming to take my two boys away. They will become his slaves."

Elisha replied to her, "How can I help you? Tell me. What do you have in your house?"

"I don't have anything there at all," she said. "All I have is a small jar of olive oil."

Elisha said, "Go around to all your neighbors. Ask them for empty jars. Get as many as you can. Then go inside your house. Shut the door behind you and your sons. Pour oil into all the jars. As each jar is filled, put it over to one side."

The woman left him. Then she shut the door behind her and her sons. They brought the jars to her. And she kept pouring. When all the jars were full, she spoke to one of her sons. She said, "Bring me another jar."

But he replied, "There aren't any more left." Then the oil stopped flowing.

She went and told the man of God about it. He said, "Go and sell the oil. Pay what you owe. You and your sons can live on what is left."

Elisha returned to Gilgal. There wasn't enough food to eat in that area. The group of the prophets was meeting with Elisha. So he said to his servant, "Put the large pot over the fire. Cook some stew for these prophets."

One of them went out into the fields to gather herbs. He found a wild vine and picked some of its gourds. He picked as many as he could fit in his coat. Then he cut them up and put them into the pot of stew. But no one knew what they were. The stew was poured out for the men. They began to eat it. But then they cried out, "Man of God, the food in that pot will kill us!" They couldn't eat it.

Elisha said, "Get some flour." He put it in the pot. He said, "Serve it to the men to eat." Then there wasn't anything in the pot that could harm them.

A man came from Baal Shalishah. He brought the man of God 20 loaves of barley bread. They had been baked from the first grain that had ripened. The man also brought some heads of new grain. "Give this food to the people to eat," Elisha said.

"How can I put this in front of 100 men?" his servant asked.

But Elisha answered, "Give it to the people to eat. Do it because the LORD says, 'They will eat and have some left over.'" Then the servant put the food in front of them. They ate it and had some left over. It happened just as the LORD had said it would.

The group of the prophets said to Elisha, "Look. The place where we meet with you is too small for us. We would like to go to the Jordan River. Each of us can get some wood there. We want to build a place there for us to meet."

Elisha said, "Go."

Then one of them said, "Won't you please come with us?"

"I will," Elisha replied. And he went with them.

They went to the Jordan River. There they began to cut down trees. One of them was cutting down a tree. The iron blade of his ax fell into the water. "Oh no, master!" he cried out. "This ax was borrowed!"

The man of God asked, "Where did the blade fall?" He showed Elisha the place. Then Elisha cut a stick and threw it there. That made the iron blade float. "Take it out of the water," he said. So the man reached out and took it.

❧

Ahaziah began to rule as king over Judah. It was in the 12th year that Joram was king of Israel. Joram was the son of Ahab. Ahaziah was the son of Jehoram. Ahaziah was 22 years old when he became king. He ruled in Jerusalem for one year. His mother's name was Athaliah. She was a granddaughter of Omri. Omri had been the king of Israel. Ahaziah followed the ways of the royal family of

Ahab. Ahaziah did what was evil in the sight of the LORD, just as the family of Ahab had done. That's because he had married into Ahab's family.

Ahaziah joined forces with Joram. They went to war against Hazael at Ramoth Gilead. Joram was the son of Ahab. Hazael was king of Aram. The soldiers of Aram wounded King Joram. So he returned to Jezreel to give his wounds time to heal.

Ahaziah, the son of Jehoram, went down to Jezreel. He went there to see Joram.

Because Ahab was so evil, the Lord chose a man named Jehu to be king over Israel instead. Jehu killed all of Ahab's family. Because Ahaziah was in Jezreel visiting Joram, he was killed, too. Jezebel also died. Her officials threw her out the window when Jehu came to Jezreel.

Some of her blood splashed on the wall. Some of it splashed on Jehu's chariot horses as they ran over her.

Jehu went inside. He ate and drank. "The LORD put a curse on that woman," he said. "Take proper care of her body. Bury her. After all, she was a king's daughter." So they went out to bury her. But all they found was her head, feet and hands. They went back and reported it to Jehu. He told them, "That's what the LORD said would happen. He announced it through his servant Elijah, who was from Tishbe. He said, 'On a piece of land at Jezreel, dogs will eat up Jezebel's body. Her body will end up as garbage on that piece of land. So no one will be able to say, "Here's where Jezebel is buried." ' "

Jehu destroyed the worship of the god named Baal in Israel. But he didn't turn away from the sins of Jeroboam, the son of Nebat. Jeroboam had caused Israel to commit those same sins. Jehu worshiped the golden calves at Bethel and Dan.

The LORD said to Jehu, "You have done well. You have accomplished what is right in my eyes. You have done to Ahab's royal house everything I wanted you to do. So your sons after you will sit on the throne of Israel. They will rule until the time of your children's grandchildren." But Jehu wasn't careful to obey the law of the LORD. He didn't obey the God of Israel with all his heart. He didn't turn away from the sins of Jeroboam. Jeroboam had caused Israel to commit those same sins.

The other events of Jehu's rule are written down. Everything he did and accomplished is written in the official records of the kings of Israel.

Jehu joined the members of his family who had already died. He was buried in Samaria. His son Jehoahaz became the next king after him. Jehu had ruled over Israel in Samaria for 28 years.

After Ahaziah died, his mother Athaliah tried to kill all the princes of Judah. She wanted to be queen. But Josheba, the sister of Ahaziah, rescued her baby Joash. She hid him in the temple. After six years, a brave priest fought to make Joash the king. Athaliah was killed and Joash became king.

∽✺✺✺◡

Joash was seven years old when he became king.

Joash became king of Judah. It was in the seventh year of Jehu's rule. Joash ruled in Jerusalem for 40 years. His mother's name was Zibiah. She was from Beersheba. Joash did what was right in the eyes of the LORD. Joash lived that way as long as Jehoiada the priest was teaching him. But the high places weren't removed. The people continued to offer sacrifices and burn incense there.

Joash spoke to the priests. He said, "Collect all the money the people bring as sacred offerings to the LORD's temple. That includes the money collected when the men who are able to serve in the army are counted. It includes the money received from people who make a special promise to the LORD. It also includes the money people bring to the temple just because they want to. Let each priest receive the money from one of the people in charge of the temple's treasures. Then use all of that money to repair the temple where it needs it."

It was now the 23rd year of the rule of King Joash. And the priests still hadn't repaired the temple. So the king sent for Jehoiada the priest and the other priests. He asked them, "Why aren't you repairing the temple where it needs it? Don't take any more money from the people in charge of the treasures. Instead, hand it over so the temple can be repaired." The priests agreed that they wouldn't collect any more money from the people. They also agreed that they wouldn't repair the temple themselves.

Jehoiada the priest got a chest. He drilled a hole in its lid. He placed the chest beside the altar for burnt offerings. The chest was on the right side as people enter the Lord's temple. Some priests guarded the entrance. They put into the chest all the money the people brought to the temple. From time to time there was a large amount of money in the chest. When that happened, the royal secretary and the high priest came. They counted the money the people had brought to the temple. Then they put it into bags. After they added it all up, they used it to repair the temple. They gave it to the men who had been put in charge of the work. Those men used it to pay the workers. They paid the builders and those who worked with wood. They paid those who cut stones and those who laid them. They bought lumber and blocks of stone. So they used the money to repair the Lord's temple. They also paid all the other costs to make the temple like new again.

Elisha died and was buried.

Some robbers from Moab used to enter the country of Israel every spring. One day some Israelites were burying a man. Suddenly they saw a group of robbers. So they threw the man's body into Elisha's tomb. The body touched Elisha's bones. When it did, the man came back to life again. He stood up on his feet.

remember what you read

1. What is something you noticed for the first time?

_____

_____

_____

_____

2. What questions did you have?

_____

_____

_____

_____

3. Was there anything that bothered you?

_____

_____

_____

_____

4. What did you learn about loving God?

_____

_____

_____

_____

5. What did you learn about loving others?

_____

_____

_____

_____

SAMUEL-KINGS, PART 12

Several more kings ruled in Israel. They were all evil. Judah continued to have a good king sometimes, but their kings were usually evil also.

〰️

Hoshea became king of Israel in Samaria. It was in the 12th year that Ahaz was king of Judah. Hoshea ruled for nine years. He was the son of Elah. Hoshea did what was evil in the eyes of the LORD. But he wasn't as evil as the kings of Israel who ruled before him.

Shalmaneser came up to attack Hoshea. Shalmaneser was king of Assyria. He had been Hoshea's master. He had forced Hoshea to bring him gifts. But the king of Assyria found out that Hoshea had turned against him. Hoshea had sent messengers to So, the king of Egypt. Hoshea didn't send gifts to the king of Assyria anymore. He had been sending them every year. So Shalmaneser grabbed him and put him in prison. The king of Assyria marched into the whole land of Israel. He marched to Samaria and surrounded it for three years. From time to time he attacked it. Finally, the king of Assyria captured Samaria. It was in the ninth year of Hoshea. The king of Assyria took the Israelites away from their own land. He sent them off to Assyria. He made some of them live in Halah. He made others live in Gozan on the Habor River. And he made others live in the towns of the Medes.

All of this took place because the Israelites had sinned against the LORD their God. He had brought them up out of Egypt. He had brought them out from under the power of Pharaoh, the king of Egypt. But they worshiped other gods. The LORD had driven out other nations to make room for Israel. But they followed the evil practices of those nations. They also followed the practices that the kings of Israel had started. The Israelites did things in secret against the LORD their God. What they did wasn't right. They built high places for worship in all their towns. They built them at lookout towers. They also built them at cities that had high walls around them. They set up sacred stones. And they set up poles used to worship the female god named Asherah. They did that on every high hill and under every green tree. The LORD had driven out nations to make room for Israel. But the Israelites burned incense at every high place, just as those nations had done. The Israelites did evil things that made the LORD very angry. They worshiped statues of gods. They did it even though the LORD had said, "Do not do that." The LORD warned Israel and Judah through all his prophets and seers. He said, "Turn from your evil ways. Keep my commands and rules. Obey every part of my Law. I commanded your people who lived long ago to obey it. And I gave it to you through my servants the prophets."

But the people wouldn't listen. They were as stubborn as their people of long ago had been. Those people didn't trust in the LORD their God. They refused to obey his rules. They broke the covenant he had made with them. They didn't pay any attention to the rules he had warned them to keep. They worshiped worthless statues of gods. Then they themselves became worthless. They followed the example of the nations around them. They did it even though the LORD had ordered them not to. He had said, "Do not do as they do."

They turned away from all the commands of the LORD their God. They made two statues of gods for themselves. The statues were shaped like calves. They made a pole used to worship the female god named Asherah. They bowed down to all the stars. And they worshiped the god named Baal. They sacrificed their sons and daughters in the fire. They practiced all kinds of evil magic. They gave up following God's rules. They did only what was evil in the eyes of the LORD. All these things made him very angry.

So the LORD was very angry with Israel. He removed them from his land. Only the tribe of Judah was left. And even Judah didn't obey the commands of the LORD their God. They followed the practices Israel had started. So the LORD turned his back on all the people of Israel. He made them suffer. He handed them over to people who stole everything they had. And finally he threw them out of his land.

The Lord took control of Israel away from the royal house of David. The Israelites made Jeroboam, the son of Nebat, their king. Jeroboam tried to get Israel to stop following the Lord. He caused them to commit a terrible sin. The Israelites were stubborn. They continued to commit all the sins Jeroboam had committed. They didn't turn away from them. So the Lord removed them from his land. That's what he had warned them he would do. He had given that warning through all his servants the prophets. So the people of Israel were taken away from their country. They were forced to go to Assyria.

Hezekiah began to rule as king over Judah. It was in the third year that Hoshea was king of Israel. He was the son of Elah. Hezekiah was the son of Ahaz. Hezekiah was 25 years old when he became king. He ruled in Jerusalem for 29 years. His mother's name was Abijah. She was the daughter of Zechariah. Hezekiah did what was right in the eyes of the Lord, just as King David had done. Hezekiah removed the high places. He smashed the sacred stones. He cut down the poles used to worship the female god named Asherah. He broke into pieces the bronze snake Moses had made. Up to that time the Israelites had been burning incense to it. They called it Nehushtan.

Hezekiah trusted in the Lord, the God of Israel. There was no one like Hezekiah among all the kings of Judah. There was no king like him either before him or after him. Hezekiah remained faithful to the Lord. He didn't stop serving him. He obeyed the commands the Lord had given Moses. The Lord was with Hezekiah. Because of that, Hezekiah was successful in everything he did. He refused to remain under the control of the king of Assyria.

Sennacherib attacked and captured all the cities of Judah that had high walls around them. It was in the 14th year of the rule of Hezekiah. Sennacherib was king of Assyria.

He sent his highest commander from Lachish to King Hezekiah at Jerusalem. He also sent his chief officer and his field commander along with a large army. All of them came up to Jerusalem. Hezekiah sent his officials to meet them.

The commander spoke out loud in the Hebrew language. He wanted all the people in Jerusalem to hear him. He said, "Pay attention to what the great king of Assyria is telling you. He says, 'Don't let Hezekiah trick you. He can't save you from my power. Don't let Hezekiah talk you into trusting in the Lord. Don't believe him when he says, "You can be sure that the Lord will save us. This city will not be handed over to the king of Assyria."' "

When King Hezekiah heard what the field commander had said, he tore his clothes. He put on the rough clothing people wear when they're sad. Then he went into the Lord's temple. Hezekiah sent Eliakim, who was in charge of the palace, to Isaiah the prophet. Isaiah was the son of Amoz. Hezekiah also sent to Isaiah the leading priests and Shebna the secretary. All of them were wearing the same rough clothing. They told Isaiah, "Hezekiah says, 'Today we're in great trouble. We aren't strong enough to save ourselves. Perhaps the Lord your God will hear everything the field commander has said. His master, the king of Assyria, has sent him to make fun of the living God. Maybe the Lord your God will punish him for what he has heard him say. So pray for the remaining people who are still alive here.' "

Isaiah sent a message to Hezekiah. Isaiah was the son of Amoz. Isaiah said, "The Lord is the God of Israel. The Lord says, 'I have heard your prayer about Sennacherib, the king of Assyria.' Here is the message the Lord has spoken against him. The Lord says,

" 'The king of Assyria will not enter this city.
    He will not even shoot an arrow at it.
He will not come near it with a shield.
    He will not build a ramp in order to climb over its
        walls.
By the same way he came he will go home.
    He will not enter this city,'
    announces the Lord.

"'I will guard this city and save it.
 I will do it for myself. And I will do it for my servant
  David.'"

That night the angel of the LORD went into the camp of the Assyrians. He put to death 185,000 people there. The people of Jerusalem got up the next morning and looked out at the camp. There were all the dead bodies! So Sennacherib, the king of Assyria, took the army tents down. Then he left. He returned to Nineveh and stayed there.

Hezekiah became very sick. Isaiah told him he would die. But Hezekiah prayed, and God sent Isaiah back to Hezekiah to tell him he would be healed. Hezekiah lived 15 more years, and his son Manasseh became king after him.

Manasseh was 12 years old when he became king. He ruled in Jerusalem for 55 years. His mother's name was Hephzibah. Manasseh did what was evil in the eyes of the LORD. He followed the practices of the nations. The LORD hated those practices. He had driven those nations out to make room for the Israelites. Manasseh rebuilt the high places. His father Hezekiah had destroyed them. Manasseh also set up altars to the god named Baal. He made a pole used to worship the female god named Asherah. Ahab, the king of Israel, had done those same things. Manasseh even bowed down to all the stars. And he worshiped them. He built altars in the LORD's temple. The LORD had said about his temple, "I will put my Name there in Jerusalem." In the two courtyards of the LORD's temple Manasseh built altars to honor all the stars. He sacrificed his own son in the fire to another god. He practiced all kinds of evil magic. He got messages from those who had died. He talked to the spirits of the dead. He did many things that were evil in the eyes of the LORD. Manasseh made the LORD very angry.

The LORD spoke through his servants the prophets. He said, "Manasseh, the king of Judah, has committed terrible sins. I hate them. Manasseh has done more evil things than the Amorites who were in the land before him. And he has led Judah to commit sin by worshiping his statues of gods. I am the LORD, the God of Israel. I tell you, 'I am going to bring trouble on Jerusalem and Judah. It will be so horrible that the ears of everyone who hears about it will tingle. That's because my people have done what is evil in my sight. They have made me very angry.' "

Manasseh also spilled the blood of many people who weren't guilty of doing anything wrong. He spilled so much blood that he filled Jerusalem with it from one end of the city to the other. And he caused Judah to commit sin. So they also did what was evil in the eyes of the LORD.

The other events of the rule of Manasseh are written down. That includes the sin he committed. Everything he did is written in the official records of the kings of Judah. Manasseh joined the members of his family who had already died. He was buried in his palace garden. It was called the garden of Uzza. Manasseh's son Amon became the next king after him.

remember what you read

1. What is something you noticed for the first time?

_____

_____

_____

_____

2. What questions did you have?

_____

_____

_____

_____

3. Was there anything that bothered you?

_____

_____

_____

_____

4. What did you learn about loving God?

_____

_____

_____

_____

5. What did you learn about loving others?

_____

_____

_____

_____

Josiah was eight years old when he became king. He ruled in Jerusalem for 31 years. His mother's name was Jedidah. She was the daughter of Adaiah. She was from Bozkath. Josiah did what was right in the eyes of the LORD. He lived the way King David had lived. He didn't turn away from it to the right or the left.

King Josiah sent his secretary Shaphan to the LORD's temple. It was in the 18th year of Josiah's rule. Josiah said, "Go up to Hilkiah the high priest. Have him add up the money that has been brought into the LORD's temple. The men who guard the doors have collected it from the people. Have them put all the money in the care of certain men. These men have been put in charge of the work on the LORD's temple. Have them pay the workers who repair it. Have them pay the builders and those who work with wood. Have them pay those who lay the stones. Also have them buy lumber and blocks of stone to repair the temple. But they don't have to report how they use the money that is given to them. That's because they are completely honest."

Hilkiah the high priest spoke to Shaphan the secretary. Hilkiah said, "I've found the Book of the Law in the LORD's temple." Shaphan read some of it to the king.

The king heard the words of the Book of the Law. When he did, he tore his royal robes. Josiah commanded his officials, "Go. Ask the LORD for advice. Ask him about what is written in this book that has been found. Do it for me. Also do it for the people and the whole nation of Judah. The LORD is very angry with us. That's because our people who have lived before us didn't obey the words of this book. They didn't do everything written there about us."

Then the king called together all the elders of Judah and

Jerusalem. He went up to the Lord's temple. The people of Judah and Jerusalem went with him. So did the priests and prophets. All of them went, from the least important of them to the most important. The king had all the words of the Book of the Covenant read to them. The book had been found in the Lord's temple. The king stood next to his pillar. He agreed to the terms of the covenant in front of the Lord. The king promised to serve the Lord and obey his commands, directions and rules. He promised to obey them with all his heart and with all his soul. So he agreed to the terms of the covenant written down in that book. Then all the people committed themselves to the covenant as well.

Judah's kings did so many terrible things. They put statues of other gods in God's temple. But Josiah got rid of everything that was evil in the temple and in Judah. He even went north to the land of Israel to get rid of evil things there.

There was an altar at Bethel. It was at the high place made by Jeroboam, the son of Nebat. Jeroboam had caused Israel to commit sin. Even that altar and high place were destroyed by Josiah. He burned the high place. He ground it into powder. He also burned the Asherah pole. Then Josiah looked around. He saw the tombs on the side of the hill. He had the bones removed from them. And he burned them on the altar to make it "unclean." That's what the Lord had said would happen. He had spoken that message through a man of God. The man had announced those things long before they took place.

Josiah did in the rest of the northern kingdom the same things he had done at Bethel. He removed all the small temples at the high places. He made them "unclean." The kings of Israel had built them in the towns of the northern kingdom. The people in those towns had made the Lord very angry. Josiah killed all the priests of those high places on the altars. He burned human bones on the altars. Then he went back to Jerusalem.

The king gave an order to all the people. He said, "Celebrate the Passover Feast to honor the Lord your God. Do what is written in this Book of the Covenant." A Passover Feast like that one had not been held for a long time. There hadn't been any like it in the days of the judges who led Israel. And there hadn't been any like it during the whole time the kings of Israel and Judah were ruling. King Josiah celebrated the Passover Feast in Jerusalem to honor the Lord. It was in the 18th year of his rule.

And that's not all. Josiah got rid of those who got messages from people who had died. He got rid of those who talked to the spirits of people who had died. He got rid of the statues of family gods and the statues of other gods. He got rid of everything else the Lord hates that was in Judah and Jerusalem. He did it to carry out what the law required. That law was written in the book that Hilkiah the priest had found in the Lord's temple. There was no king like Josiah either before him or after him. None of them turned to the Lord as he did. He obeyed the Lord with all his heart and all his soul. He obeyed him with all his strength. He did everything the Law of Moses required.

In spite of that, the Lord didn't turn away from his great anger against Judah. That's because of everything Manasseh had done to make him very angry. So the Lord said, "I will remove Judah from my land. I will do to them what I did to Israel. I will turn my back on Jerusalem. It is the city I chose. I will also turn my back on this temple. I spoke about it. I said, 'I will put my Name there.'"

The other events of the rule of Josiah are written down. Everything he did is written in the official records of the kings of Judah.

Pharaoh Necho was king of Egypt. He marched up to the Euphrates River. He went there to help the king of Assyria. It happened while Josiah was king. Josiah marched out to meet Necho in battle. When Necho saw him at Megiddo, he killed him. Josiah's servants brought his body in a chariot from Megiddo to Jerusalem. They buried him in his own tomb. Then the people of the land went and got Jehoahaz. They anointed him as king in place of his father Josiah.

Jehoiachin was 18 years old when he became king. He ruled in Jerusalem for three months. His mother's name was Nehushta.

She was the daughter of Elnathan. She was from Jerusalem. Jehoiachin did what was evil in the eyes of the LORD. He did just as his father Jehoiakim had done.

At that time the officers of Nebuchadnezzar, the king of Babylon, marched to Jerusalem. They surrounded it and got ready to attack it. Nebuchadnezzar himself came up to the city. He arrived while his officers were attacking it. Jehoiachin, the king of Judah, handed himself over to Nebuchadnezzar. Jehoiachin's mother did the same thing. And so did all his attendants, nobles and officials.

Zedekiah was 21 years old when he became king. He ruled in Jerusalem for 11 years. His mother's name was Hamutal. She was the daughter of Jeremiah. She was from Libnah. Zedekiah did what was evil in the eyes of the LORD. He did just as Jehoiakim had done. The enemies of Jerusalem and Judah attacked them because the LORD was angry. In the end the LORD threw them out of his land.

Zedekiah also refused to remain under the control of Nebuchadnezzar.

Nebuchadnezzar was king of Babylon. He marched out against Jerusalem. His whole army went with him. It was in the ninth year of the rule of Zedekiah. It was on the tenth day of the tenth month. Nebuchadnezzar set up camp outside the city. He brought in war machines all around it. It was surrounded until the 11th year of King Zedekiah's rule.

By the ninth day of the fourth month, there wasn't any food left in the city. So the people didn't have anything to eat. Then the Babylonians broke through the city wall. Judah's whole army ran away at night. They went out through the gate between the two walls near the king's garden. They escaped even though the Babylonians surrounded the city. Judah's army ran toward the Arabah Valley. But the Babylonian army chased King Zedekiah. They caught up with him in the plains near Jericho. All his soldiers were separated from him. They had scattered in every direction. The king was captured.

He was taken to the king of Babylon at Riblah. That's where Nebuchadnezzar decided how he would be punished. Nebuchadnezzar's men killed the sons of Zedekiah. They forced him to watch it with his own eyes. Then they poked out his eyes. They put him in bronze chains. And they took him to Babylon.

The Babylonian army destroyed the LORD's temple. They broke the bronze pillars into pieces. They broke up the bronze stands that could be moved around. And they broke up the huge bronze bowl. Then they carried the bronze away to Babylon. They also took away the pots, shovels, wick cutters and dishes. They took away all the bronze objects used for any purpose in the temple. The commander of the royal guard took away the shallow cups for burning incense. He took away the sprinkling bowls. So he took away everything made out of pure gold or silver.

So the people of Judah were taken as prisoners. They were taken far away from their own land.

⟳∿∿⟲

Awel-Marduk set Jehoiachin, the king of Judah, free from prison. It was in the 37th year after Jehoiachin had been taken away to Babylon. It was also the year Awel-Marduk became king of Babylon. It was on the 27th day of the 12th month. Awel-Marduk spoke kindly to Jehoiachin. He gave him a place of honor. Other kings were with Jehoiachin in Babylon. But his place was more important than theirs. So Jehoiachin put his prison clothes away. For the rest of Jehoiachin's life the king provided what he needed. The king did that for Jehoiachin day by day as long as he lived.

remember what you read

1. What is something you noticed for the first time?

_____

_____

_____

_____

2. What questions did you have?

_____

_____

_____

_____

3. Was there anything that bothered you?

_____

_____

_____

_____

4. What did you learn about loving God?

_____

_____

_____

_____

5. What did you learn about loving others?

_____

_____

_____

_____

A Word About
The New International Reader's Version

Have You Ever Heard of the New International Version?

We call it the NIV. Many people read the NIV. In fact, more people read the NIV than any other English Bible. They like it because it's easy to read and understand.

And now we are happy to give you another Bible that's easy to read and understand. It's the New International Reader's Version. We call it the NIrV.

Who Will Enjoy Reading the New International Reader's Version?

People who are just starting to read will understand and enjoy the NIrV. Children will be able to read it and understand it. So will older people who are learning how to read. People who are reading the Bible for the first time will be able to enjoy reading the NIrV. So will people who have a hard time understanding what they read. And so will people who use English as their second language. We hope this Bible will be just right for you.

How Is the NIrV Different From the NIV?

The NIrV is based on the NIV. The NIV Committee on Bible Translation (CBT) didn't produce the NIrV. But a few of us who worked on the NIrV are members of CBT. We worked hard to make the NIrV possible. We used the words of the NIV when we could. When the words of the NIV were too long, we used shorter words. We tried to use words that are easy to understand. We also made the sentences of the NIV much shorter.

Why did we do all these things? Because we wanted to make the NIrV very easy to read and understand.

What Other Helps Does the NIrV Have?

We decided to give you a lot of other help too. For example, sometimes a verse is quoted from another place in the Bible. When it is, we tell you the Bible book, chapter and verse it comes from. We put that information right after the verse that quotes from another place.

We separated each chapter into shorter sections. We gave a title to almost every chapter. Sometimes we even gave a title to a section. We did these things to help you understand what the chapter or section is all about.

Another example of a helpful change has to do with the word "Selah" in the Psalms. What this Hebrew word means is still not clear. So, for now, this word is not helpful for readers. The NIV has moved the word to the bottom of the page. We have followed the NIV and removed this Hebrew word from the NIrV. Perhaps one day we will learn what this word means. But until then, the Psalms are easier to read and understand without it.

Sometimes the writers of the Bible used more than one name for the same person or place. For example, in the New Testament the Sea of Galilee is also called the Sea of Gennesaret. Sometimes it is also called the Sea of Tiberias. But in the NIrV we decided to call it the Sea of Galilee everywhere it appears. We called it that because that is its most familiar name.

We also wanted to help you learn the names of people and places in the Bible. So sometimes we provided names even in verses where those names don't actually appear. For example, sometimes the Bible says "the River" where it means "the Euphrates River." In those places, we used the full name "the Euphrates River." Sometimes the word "Pharaoh" in the Bible means "Pharaoh Hophra." In those places, we used his full name "Pharaoh Hophra." We did all these things in order to make the NIrV as clear as possible.

Does the NIrV Say What the First Writers of the Bible Said?

We wanted the NIrV to say just what the first writers of the Bible said. So we kept checking the Greek New Testament as we did our work. That's because the New Testament's first writers used Greek. We also kept checking the Hebrew Old Testament as we did our work. That's because the Old Testament's first writers used Hebrew.

We used the best copies of the Greek New Testament. We also used the best copies of the Hebrew Old Testament. Older English Bibles couldn't use those copies because they had not yet been found. The oldest copies are best because they are closer in time to the ones the first Bible writers wrote. That's why we kept checking the older copies instead of the newer ones.

Some newer copies of the Greek New Testament added several verses that the older ones don't have. Sometimes it's several verses in a row. This occurs at Mark 16:9 – 20 and John 7:53 — 8:11. We have included these verses in the NIrV. Sometimes the newer copies added only a single verse. An example is Mark 9:44. That verse is not in the oldest Greek New Testaments. So we put the verse number 43/44 right before Mark 9:43. You can look on the list below for Mark 9:44 and locate the verse that was added.

Verses That Were Not Found in Oldest Greek New Testaments

Matthew 17:21	But that kind does not go out except by prayer and fasting.
Matthew 18:11	The Son of Man came to save what was lost.
Matthew 23:14	How terrible for you, teachers of the law and Pharisees! You pretenders! You take over the houses of widows. You say long prayers to show off. So God will punish you much more.
Mark 7:16	Everyone who has ears to hear should listen.
Mark 9:44	In hell, / " 'the worms don't die, / and the fire doesn't go out.'
Mark 9:46	In hell, / " 'the worms don't die, / and the fire doesn't go out.'
Mark 11:26	But if you do not forgive, your Father who is in heaven will not forgive your sins either.
Mark 15:28	Scripture came true. It says, "And he was counted among those who disobey the law."
Luke 17:36	Two men will be in the field. One will be taken and the other left.
Luke 23:17	It was Pilate's duty to let one prisoner go free for them at the Feast.
John 5:4	From time to time an angel of the Lord would come down. The angel would stir up the waters. The first disabled person to go into the pool after it was stirred would be healed.
Acts 8:37	Philip said, "If you believe with all your heart, you can." The official answered, "I believe that Jesus Christ is the Son of God."
Acts 15:34	But Silas decided to remain there.
Acts 24:7	But Lysias, the commander, came. By using a lot of force, he took Paul from our hands.
Acts 28:29	After he said that, the Jews left. They were arguing strongly among themselves.
Romans 16:24	May the grace of our Lord Jesus Christ be with all of you. Amen.

What Is Our Prayer for You?

The Lord has blessed the New International Version in a wonderful way. He has used it to help millions of Bible readers. Many people have put their faith in Jesus after reading it. Many others have become stronger believers because they have read it.

We hope and pray that the New International Reader's Version will help you in the same way. If that happens, we will give God all the glory.

A Word About This Edition

This edition of the New International Reader's Version has been revised to include the changes of the New International Version. Over the years, many helpful changes have been made to the New International Version. Those changes were made because our understanding of the original writings is better. Those changes also include changes that have taken place in the English language. We wanted the New International Reader's Version to include those helpful changes as well. We wanted the New International Reader's Version to be as clear and correct as possible.

We want to thank the people who helped us prepare this new edition. They are Jeannine Brown from Bethel Seminary St. Paul, Yvonne Van Ee from Calvin College, Michael Williams from Calvin Theological Seminary, and Ron Youngblood from Bethel Seminary San Diego. We also want to thank the people at Biblica who encouraged and supported this work.

Kids, Read the Bible in a Whole New Way!

The Books of the Bible is a fresh way for kids to experience Scripture! Perfect for reading together as a family or church group, this 4-part Bible series removes chapter and verse numbers, headings, and special formatting. Now the Bible is easier to read, and reveals the story of God's great love for His people, as one narrative. Features the easy-to-read text of the New International Reader's Version (NIrV). Ages 8-12.

Look for all four books in *The Books of the Bible*:

Covenant History
Discover the Beginnings of God's People   9780310761303

The Prophets
Listen to God's Messengers Tell about Hope and Truth   9780310761358

The Writings
Learn from Stories, Poetry, and Songs   9780310761334

New Testament
Read the Story of Jesus, His Church, and His Return   9780310761310

My Bible Story Coloring Book
The Books of the Bible   9780310761068

The Books of the Bible Children's Curriculum
9780310086161

These engaging lessons are formatted around relatable Scripture references, memory verses, and Bible themes. This curriculum has everything you need for 32 complete lessons for preschool, early elementary, and later elementary classes.

Learn how your church can experience the Bible in community with resources for all ages!

Community
Bible
Experience

CommunityBibleExperience.com